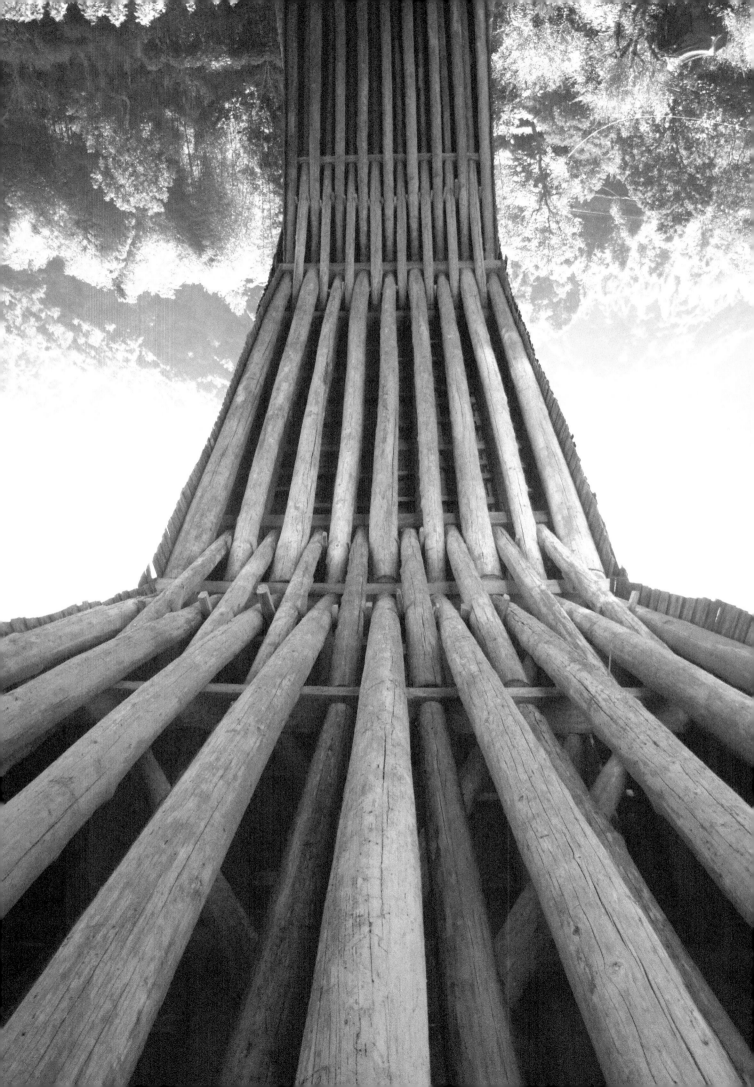

CHINA'S COVERED BRIDGES
Architecture Over Water

Ronald G. Knapp, Terry E. Miller, Liu Jie
Photography by A. Chester Ong, Terry E. Miller, Ronald G. Knapp, and Others

中国廊桥
水上的建筑（英文版）

［美］那仲良 ［美］米泰瑞 刘杰 著
［菲］王行富 ［美］米泰瑞 ［美］那仲良 等 摄影

上海交通大学出版社
SHANGHAI JIAO TONG UNIVERSITY PRESS

First published in 2019 by
Shanghai Jiao Tong University Press
951 Panyu Road, Xuhui District
Shanghai, China
Website: http://www.jiaodapress.com.cn/

British Library Cataloguing-in-Publication Data
A catalogue record for this book is available from the British Library

ISBN:978-1-5262-07

Note to the Reader

Measurements We did not personally measure any of the bridges shown in the book. Length, width, height, etc. were taken from published sources, which are not always consistent. We have chosen what we believe to be the "best" measurements. Metric measurements are rounded to the first digit after the decimal even when the source material goes several digits beyond. Since the international system of metric measurements is not widely accepted in the United States, we have made imperial conversions that appear in the parentheses after the metric unit.

Contemporary Photographs Photographers are identified with the following initials:

ACO	A. Chester Ong	PSCC	Philip S. C. Caston
JDK	Jeffrey D. Knapp	RGK	Ronald G. Knapp
LLK	Larissa L. Knapp	TEM	Terry E. Miller
LY	Liu Yan	XYC	Xue Yichuan

Distributed by:
University of Hawai'i Press

With Gratitude for the Sponsorship of the

Shanghai GuoFeng Charity Foundation
上海国峯慈善基金会

HuaQiao Foundation
华桥基金会

We acknowledge with gratitude the support of Dr. Curtis C. Stone
for the production of this worldwide version
in memory of his late wife, Dr. Margaret Lewis Stone

国家自然科学基金资助项目：
中国古代木构桥梁的发展与演变研究（项目批准号：51478259）
**Project "Research on the Evolution and Development of
China's Traditional Timber Structure Bridges (No. 51478259)"
Supported by the National Natural Science Foundation of China**

国家重点研发计划资助（2017YFC0703500）
National Key R&D Program of China (Grant No. 2017YFC0703500)

金龙桥

彩虹再现凭四境游人悦目赏心

古桥重光接八方过客遮风挡雨

CONTENTS

PREFACE
THE PATH OF DISCOVERY

One of the lessons learned over the decades we have been visiting and researching China's covered bridges is that new evidence continuously emerges, usually unexpectedly and frequently serendipitously. Those of us who carried out field research throughout China's countryside early on, well before the utter transformation of a majority of once traditional landscapes, from time to time encountered covered bridges, usually without any sense that they added up to anything more than the relict old houses, pagodas, ancestral halls, gravesites, and temples that were surviving remnants of once complete villages from China's distant past. Now, at the end of the second decade of the twenty-first century, there is a much better understanding of not only the distribution of covered bridges, as well as other traditional local architectural structures, but also their significance and role in China's traditional economic and social life. The path of discovery has moved along parallel routes, one with evidence collected by Chinese scholars and amateurs and the other collected by foreigners. Today, there is an increasing degree of convergence.

In China, it is estimated that at least 3,000 covered bridges are still standing, a number that far exceeds those elsewhere in the world. However, while no one knows how many were built in total throughout the country over many centuries, the number is certainly significantly greater. In sixteen counties of Fujian and Zhejiang alone, where a tally was done using local records, surviving timber arch covered bridges represent less than 10 percent of those present in the 1800s. Over the centuries, sadly, most of the bridges lost in China were erased quietly because of natural disaster, deterioration, or deliberate replacement. By and large, these losses were only known to the local people who were inconvenienced, and today we have few records of them that would allow us to know how many were actually built over time. As with wooden structures elsewhere in the world, loss came about because of floods, typhoons, fire, neglect, and vandalism, as well as replacement by "modern" structures to meet contemporary needs. In China, moreover, timber bridges were sometimes destroyed or moved in response to judgments of their effectiveness as elements in *fengshui* patterns, a subject that will be discussed later.

Historical documents sometimes mention the destruction of a covered bridge and rebuilding, but this was not common. Unlike some demolished nineteenth-century covered bridges in the United States where old stone abutments and piers still stand, this is rarely the case in China. The ruins of old covered bridges, such as abutments and piers, are not easy to spot in China because stone and timber were usually quickly scavenged for use as building materials for other projects. Still, in some cases there are hints that once there was a bridge at a location along a stream channel because chiseled-out sockets in the surfaces of rock alongside a ravine or midstream can be spotted. In the case of the Santiao Bridge in Taishun County, Zhejiang, records reveal that there was a crossing in the vicinity as early as 1137 and that the bridge was rebuilt numerous times, but it is impossible to know the circumstances that led to variations in the selection of the actual sites.

0.1 Near the current Santiao Bridge in Taishun County, Zhejiang Province, it is still possible to see the sockets of an earlier crossing of the bridge. While there is no record of why the old site was abandoned, it may be that the choice of a new site was considered more auspicious according to *fengshui*. Source: RGK, 2006.

There is evidence that the earliest wooden covered bridge in China dates to the third century BCE during the Western Han Dynasty (206 BCE–CE 220). In 2001, during excavation at the Jinsha archaeological site on the western outskirts of Chengdu, Sichuan, workers uncovered what appeared to be the splayed skeleton of a timber covered bridge (Chengdu, 2008). This discovery subsequently was heralded in the press as the first known timber covered bridge in China, thus also in the world. With a length of 42 meters (138 feet) and variable width of 7–8.8 meters (23–29 feet), the excavated structure not only had visible log abutments and piers but also columns and

scattered roof tiles. Archaeologists surmised that the bridge may have been a prominent part of the thoroughfare leading to Chengdu's West Gate. The remains of a second, perhaps contemporaneous, covered bridge were discovered in 2009 in the Yanshikou area of Chengdu. Unfortunately, there is insufficient tangible or documentary evidence to reconstruct these structures, which likely had rudimentary components below and above the deck that would be recognizable two millennia later. As ancient covered bridges that foreshadowed the structures known today, there is a gap of more than a thousand years from their reputed origin before any other physical timber covered bridge became known.

While it is not possible to determine how many covered bridges were once built and are now lost and forgotten, it is reasonable to ask whether covered bridges seen today are truly representative of those constructed in the past. Fortunately, there is some limited evidence that can be employed to help us understand lost covered bridges even as it is recognized that most lost covered bridges no longer with us are truly forgotten.[1]

Chinese historical records as well as paintings over millennia offer tantalizing, yet fragmentary, confirmation of the existence of covered bridges in the past. The astonishing number of gazetteers or *difangzhi* that specifically chronicle local history provide comprehensive information concerning people and material culture. While lists of bridges, like other landmarks such as city walls and gates, roads, tunnels, canals, granaries, academies, graves, gardens, famous sites, and postal stations, among other common features, are commonly mentioned in *difangzhi*, few include visual depictions of such features, including covered bridges. As will be discussed in Part II.2 concerning folk beliefs, the appearance of a covered bridge in a drawing of a village suggests that it is a *fengshui* feature placed to insure good fortune for the village.

---

[1] In North America, there is an ongoing online database called "Covered Spans of Yesteryear," whose purpose is to assemble visual and other information about past and present covered bridges: http://www.lostbridges.org/ While no such database exists yet in China, there is hope that one will be created.

0.2 Drawing excerpted from an 1877 gazetteer map of Qingyuan County, Zhejiang. Source: *Qingyuan xianzhi*, n.d.

Chinese landscape and general genre paintings sometimes include bridges, some of which are timber covered bridges. However, most of these representations are generic and are not situated in either place or time. Chinese scholars writing about bridges privileged masonry bridges found in imperial precincts and elsewhere, even as they sometimes included depictions of covered bridges.

While old photographs provide evidence of covered bridges once standing, offering a vehicle for comparing locations and forms with those still standing, and, of course, insuring recall of features lost to memory, they are only comparatively recent records. In the late nineteenth century, those who took photographs generally viewed them as merely illustrations to accompany text, but over time such old photographs have come to be seen as primary source artifacts themselves. Even as gathering photographic evidence for China in the nineteenth century is not easy, this has become a compelling activity for some scholars and amateurs. While it is true that cameras began to be used in China during the First Opium War of 1839–42 almost as soon as photography was invented, there were few Chinese or even Western photographers except in the coastal cities where they set up studios principally to do portraits.

For decades, only limited photographs emerged beyond the large metropolitan areas of China, with much of the effort focused on imperial and other structures and landscapes. However, as China increasingly was open to foreigners as a result of Unequal Treaties that granted foreigners

rights to penetrate interior China, the camera often accompanied them. As they uncovered sights that were strikingly different from what was seen in coastal cities, especially as the number of Treaty Ports in interior areas increased, more and more photographs were taken to illustrate observations made in their texts. Many of these photographs reveal types of covered bridges no longer seen today, as will be illustrated by rare historic images throughout this book.

0.3 This covered bridge atop a stone arch along a side gorge in the middle reaches of the Yangzi River at Wanxian was frequently photographed in the late nineteenth and early twentieth centuries. The photograph appeared in many books, often without attribution of origin. Source: Mennie, 1926: Plate XXII.

0.4 The magnificent Anlan Bridge crossed the Nanpan River in Luliang County, Yunnan, early in the twentieth century. At that time, the French were constructing a railroad from Haiphong along the Tonkin Gulf to Kunmingfu, now Kunming. They celebrated this covered bridge with its *pailou*-style portals on a series of postcards, others of which are shown later in Part I.1. The bridge no longer stands and is barely recalled. Source: RGK Collection.

From the late nineteenth century into the first decades of the twentieth century, foreign missionaries, adventurers, botanists, and geologists, among others, traveled into once remote areas of China with their cameras and notebooks. Many books were published with their photographs, which together are textual and visual records that provide important windows into China in the past. More of their materials were stored in their personal archives or simply lost without being preserved in books and periodicals. In recent years, however, as descendants have discovered some of these visual treasures, they have been donated to libraries around the world where the images have been digitized and made available to the public.[2] Undoubtedly, many others remain out of sight and are not yet accessible. Over the past decade in China, a kind of old photograph fever has been sweeping the country. Indeed, there has been a publishing explosion of *lao zhaopian* or old photographs books in China. While some of these photographs surfaced from family collections in China that were not destroyed during war or the Cultural Revolution, many more have been gathered abroad as a result of diligent searching by Chinese bent on recovering images of China's past. Internet sites that sell "antique" postcards and photographs, such as eBay and Delcampe, provide a seemingly bottomless treasure trove of views of old China that will continue to emerge in the coming years.

Accompanying what had been a history of the occasional disconnected surfacing of covered bridges images and information changed as a handful of academics began to build an interest in the subject. In this regard, Liu Jie's 2017 book *Zhongguo mugong langqiao jianzhu yishu* [The Architectural Artistry of China's Timber Arch Covered Bridges] sketches out three periods in the evolutionary sequence of the academic study of timber arched covered bridges in China, with extensive details of the individuals involved in research and publishing. Pioneers in the first period, such as Tang Huancheng, Luo Ying, Mao Yisheng, and Liu Dunzhen, offered tantalizing insights into timber bridges and their structures. Interestingly, Tang Huancheng used the term *qiaowu* or "bridge house" in 1957 to describe China's covered bridges. However, it was not until Liu Dunzhen's article "Zhongguo langqiao" [China's Covered Bridges] appeared in 1979, a decade after he died, that the words *langqiao* (covered bridges) as a type appeared in Chinese. A second period from 1980 to 2004 produced a flurry of academic articles, with Tang Huancheng and Zhao Chen, among a few others, reporting on their fieldwork experiences. These efforts generally abandoned what had been purely technical aspects of structure and began to embrace research approaches that were multidisciplinary and comparative, with detailed architectural and cultural connections recorded.

From 2005 to the present, which represents the third period, the field has expanded significantly, including international comparative components that have been driven by a succession of conferences organized by Liu Jie. Beginning in Zhejiang's Taishun County in 2005, other conferences followed, in Shouning, Fujian in 2007; Pingnan, Fujian in 2009; Qingyuan, Zhejiang in 2011; and jointly in Zhenghe, Fujian and Taishun, Zhejiang in 2013. In 2017, the conference moved beyond Fujian and Zhejiang to Zhuoshui, Qianjiang District, Chongqing Municipality. Throughout this period, research regarding covered bridges reached into other areas of China that had not been intensively studied. International recognition of China's covered bridges was acknowledged in 2005 as a result of a project led by Zhao Chen regarding the restoration of the Houkeng Timber Arched Covered Bridge in Qingyuan, Zhejiang.

---

[2] While there are many specialized archives of old photographs, the major aggregator of rare photographs of China is the "Historical Photographs of China" website at the University of Bristol in the United Kingdom. This program has been especially generous in providing hard to locate images we have sought.

This effort led to a UNESCO Asia-Pacific Award for Cultural Heritage Conservation. Following on from this, of great consequence was the inscription in 2009 on the UNESCO List of Intangible Cultural Heritage in Need of Urgent Safeguarding that put a spotlight on "Traditional Design and Practices for Building Chinese Wooden Arch Bridges."[3]

Seven adjacent counties in Fujian and Zhejiang subsequently joined together in late 2012 in an agreement to move forward an application to authorities in Beijing that would insure the placement of "Fujian-Zhejiang Wooden Arch Bridges" on China's UNESCO World Heritage Tentative List. This organization continues to move the application forward, as well as promote events and meetings in order to maintain public interest in the subject.

China's Covered Bridges in Western Languages

Well before information about China began to appear in European languages such as French, German, Italian, and English, merchants from Persia and elsewhere wrote accounts of their travels. However, none of these produced easily accessible descriptions or drawings that provide any information about bridges in China. It was not until the very end of the thirteenth century with the compilation of a book about the travels of Marco Polo that details about itineraries and the nature of routes became part of the narrative about China. While there remain skeptics as to whether Marco Polo actually saw everything recorded in his accounts or simply assembled his details from the hearsay of others, the many versions—perhaps as many as 150 renderings—of his manuscript references a large number of bridges of all types. There is only one mention of a covered bridge.

Thus, it was Marco Polo in the thirteenth century during the Yuan Dynasty (1279–1368) who first described a covered bridge in China in a Western language. In writing about Chengdu, a "rich and noble city" in Sichuan Province, Marco Polo stated, "Let us now speak of a great Bridge which crosses this River within the city. This bridge is of stone; it is seven paces in width and half a mile in length (the river being that much in width as I told you); and all along its length on either side there are columns of marble to bear the roof, for the bridge is roofed over from end to end with timber, and that all richly painted. And on this bridge there are houses in which a great deal of trade and industry is carried on. But these houses are all of wood merely, and they are put up in the morning and taken down in the evening. Also there stands upon the bridge the Great Kaan's Comercque, that is to say, his custom-house, where his toll and tax are levied" (Yule and Cordier, 1903: Vol. 2, Ch. XLIV).

William John Gill and Henry Yule, as reported in *The River of Golden Sand* (1880), visited the Chengdu area and searched for Polo's bridge, observing that the river "is crossed by a covered bridge with huxters' booths, more or less in the style described by Polo, it necessarily falls far short of his great bridge of half a mile in length," now only "90 yards long." They went on to suggest that the river itself had "been drawn off to irrigate the plain ... has long since ceased, on that scale, to flow" and that the covered bridge had been rebuilt shorter (Vol. 1: 37; Vol. 2: 9). Gill regularly commented on all types of bridges, but especially "roofed bridges, so common in China.... The careful way in which everything is roofed here must strike the eye of any traveler; houses, gateways, bridges, triumphal arches, and indeed, almost wherever it is practicable to put a roof, there one is sure to be; so that the timber-work, being built in the most solid manner, and carefully protected from the weather by an efficient covering,

---

[3] https://ich.unesco.org/en/USL/traditional-design-and-practices-for-building-chinese-wooden-arch-bridges-00303

lasts an incredible time, even in a country where rains and snows are regular in their occurrence" (Vol. 1: 283). Gill did not include photographs of covered bridges in his book but a map of Chengdu appears in Yule's *The Book of Ser Marco Polo* (1875) accompanying a text that assesses the views of others about the covered bridges in Chengdu. The larger covered bridge is depicted between the East and South Gates with the smaller bridge in the north. This replacement covered bridge may be on the site Marco Polo wrote about crossing.

0.5 Published by Henry Yule in the later part of the nineteenth century, this map depicts the covered bridges and other landmarks of Chengdu, Sichuan. Source: Yule, 1875.

Between Marco Polo at the end of the thirteenth century and Gill and Yule at the end of the nineteenth, the most encyclopedic treatment of China's geography and material culture was compiled by Jean-Baptiste Du Halde, a French Jesuit historian who lived between 1674 and 1743. Although Du Halde never visited China, he assembled information from seventeen Jesuit missionaries who wrote between 1711 and 1743. Published first in French in four volumes as *Description Geographique, Historique,* *Chronologique, Politique, et Physique de l'Empire de la Chine et de la Tartarie Chinoise* in 1735 and then in English translation in 1739, the book is replete with references to stone and pontoon bridges throughout China. However, peculiarly, none of the numerous maps of walled cities and towns in the book displays a covered bridge.

The Twenty-first Century

Over the past century, as the pages that follow will make clear, there has been an escalation in our knowledge of China's covered bridges, including many that are structurally extraordinary in addition to countless workaday ones. Indeed, China's "covered bridge culture," *langqiao wenhua*, is today promoted by tourist organizations who advertise widely with images and text via various media. Even if Chinese have not visited a covered bridge, considerable numbers today know of the existence of places such as Taishun in Zhejiang that have branded themselves as repositories of countless historical covered bridges. Boosterism, not unexpectedly, has led to competing hyperbolic statements identifying "the oldest," "the longest," "the highest," and "the most beautiful," among other superlatives, even if not entirely correct.

The ubiquity of cameras on mobile phones, countless *boke* (blogs), as well as "Chats" and "Moments" on WeChat, a multi-purpose social media platform with over one billion monthly active users, have fueled an explosion of information about China's covered bridges. Admittedly, a majority of postings are nothing more than a discovery or an appreciation of a structure not previously known to an individual visitor. Many postings, however, broadcast contemporaneous photographic documentation of a flood or fire event that delivers visual evidence, unlike in previous decades when such events would only have been known locally and not shared broadly. Some postings fortuitously also document events rarely seen by outsiders in the past, such as bridge-building rituals and celebrations accompanying the completion of a restored or a newly constructed covered bridge. Throughout this book, photographic evidence of these from our own fieldwork, as well as from Chinese sources, will be presented.

One recent example of the documentation of a catastrophe that reverberated widely with startling though partially imprecise information was the fire that consumed the Buyue Bridge in Jian'ou, a county-level city in northern Fujian Province. Just minutes after the fire started in the early evening of January 31, 2019, there were breathless online announcements of the conflagration with videos and snapshots by on-the-spot witnesses. News reports stated that what had been destroyed was a 500-year-old timber cantilevered bridge—northern Fujian's longest at 418 feet (127.5 meters) with the greatest clear span. It turns out that, yes, an impressive bridge crossed the Yu River 499 years ago. Indeed, a century earlier, in 1291, Marco Polo on his way from Hangzhou to Quanzhou had written that Jianning-fu, the old name then romanized as Quenlinfu, had "… three very handsome bridges, upwards of a hundred paces in length and eight paces in width." Records do not divulge either the nature of these early bridges, nor whether they were covered or not, nor even what the form of the 1520 bridge was as it was rebuilt/renovated many times over the following centuries.

It is impossible to verify retrospectively the extent of past rebuilding, especially how much of the structure that burned in 2019 was five centuries old. Moreover, contemporary accounts reveal that a near total reconstruction was carried out in 1999–2000, necessitated by damage done during a major flood event. Abutments were extended, the entire floor of the bridge was constructed using cement, and pine wood was employed throughout the timbered gallery.

While the cause of the 2019 fire could not be determined immediately in the aftermath, reports acknowledged the possibility of an accidental fire. This is because villagers had a history of hanging lanterns with candles at both the Mid-Autumn Festival and during the Spring Festival (Chinese New Year), which was just days away from the fire. Nonetheless, whatever the cause of the fire or whatever details specialists provide from yet to be discovered historical records about the nature of earlier incarnations of the bridge, we now have a selection of incontrovertible visual evidence of a momentous blaze unlike any documented in the past.

Already there are calls for the rebuilding of the bridge. It will be interesting to see how its form might evolve in terms of maintaining a sense of historical authenticity or merely providing a nostalgic recreation to meet practical needs.

0.6a, b–d (overleaf) Said to have been Fujian's longest covered bridge, dating to 1520, the Buyue span was reconstructed in 1999–2000. Source: Dai Zhijian, 2004.

0.7 Snapped as the fire was raging in the early evening of January 31, 2019, this image captures the rapid consumption of the timber structure. Source: FM1036 http://www.sohu.com. Accessed February 2, 2019

08a, b Taken the morning after the fire, the utter devastation of the wooden superstructure is apparent. Only the stone piers, the deformed cement floor, and the brick portal survived. Source: Duowei xinwen http://photo.dwnews.com/social/photo/2019-02-02/60116509.html#p=1. Accessed February 2, 2019.

"Exporting" China's Woven Arch-Beam Timber Covered Bridges

Not only is much attention being paid to the conservation and renovation of old covered bridges in China today, increasing numbers of new covered bridges utilizing timber and traditional carpentry are being constructed. Yet, who could anticipate that some day China might "export" woven timber arch-beam covered bridges just as they have "exported" authentic classical Chinese gardens to many countries. "Exporting" bridges indeed has begun with one built in Germany in 2015 and another in China's Taiwan in 2018–19. Whether these are harbingers of projects yet to come or simply fashionable one-offs indicating a trend is uncertain.

Spearheaded by Liu Yan, the covered bridge in Bavaria, Germany, is an authentic, fully functioning structure within the curiously named Nepal Himalaya Pavilion, a complex including a botanical garden, a museum, and a site with structures representing cultural heritage. Assisting Liu Yan was master carpenter Zhang Changzhi from Zhouning County, Fujian, whose family had been constructing covered bridges for over 200 years spanning eight generations. Cypress components were prepared in China in October 2014 before being shipped to Germany in Spring 2015, followed by three carpenters to assemble the timbers. Situated over a narrow gully, the bridge has an open span of 7.5 meters (25 feet). Because of the small size of the bridge in comparison with others the carpenters had built in China, Liu Yan utilized computer-aided design to facilitate construction.

On February 24, 2019, Chinese language news reports heralded a ceremony celebrating a "Zhejiang Taishun Covered Bridge" in Jiji Township, Nantou County, Taiwan, China. This news stirred considerable interest in what was described as a "cultural landmark" and "a bridge fostering cultural exchange and friendship." Referred to as a "sister bridge" to one constructed in Xiyang Township, Taishun, in 2012, this Taiwan replica has a length of 43.5 meters (143 feet), a clear span of 28 meters (92 feet), and a width of 5.5 meters (8 feet).

0.10 Constructed in 2012, the Xiyang Township forerunner of the covered bridge in Nantou, Taiwan, China, was situated in a rural environment. Source: Ji Haibo, 2019.

0.11 This full-size replica of a Taishun *langqiao* was completed in a park in Jiji Township, Nantou County, Taiwan. China, in 2019. Source: Ji Haibo, 2019.

0.9 Nearing completion utilizing prefabricated components, a woven timber arch-beam covered bridge took shape in the Bavarian area of Germany in 2015. Source: LY, 2015.

PART I

CHINA'S COVERED BRIDGES
FROM A WORLDWIDE PERSPECTIVE

PART I

CHINA'S COVERED BRIDGES FROM A WORLDWIDE PERSPECTIVE

Humans worldwide face the same problem when confronted with a river or stream of any size: how to cross efficiently, safely, and affordably. There are only a few choices for the passage of people, animals, and vehicles: ford the stream at low water, ferry across the stream on a raft or boat, or build a bridge. The means varies according to the type of land-based conveyances that must move across the stream. Fords fail the efficiency and safety tests because water levels vary and water can freeze, streambeds can acquire rocks and debris, and during high water one can be swept away, along with one's cargo. Using a raft or boat to ferry across a river has similar drawbacks, especially during high water and swift currents as well as ice in the winter. Low water also prohibits ferries from running. If the vehicle cannot be transported, it takes time to transfer cargo to a boat, take it across, and unload it on the other side onto entirely different transport. While fords, ferries, and bridges of many types are near universal approaches, there are several solutions that are unique to China. Among these are sling ropes and floating bamboo pontoons that are found in western China.

I.2 Carrying horses, carriages, and pedestrians, ferries played critical roles in crossing rivers in North America well into the twentieth century. Dunsbach Ferry Crossing the Mohawk River, New York, c.1895. Source: Clifton-Park Halfmoon Public Library, New York.

Mission du Tche Li Sud-Est — Chi-li south-east Catholic Mission

18. - Passage d'un bras du Fleuve Jaune - The Ferry at a branch of the Yellow River

I.3 Where a caravan route met a branch of the Huang He (Yellow River) in Leshou, Hebei Province, this ferry carried pack camels and pedestrians across, early twentieth century. Source: RGK Collection.

I.1 A rare photograph of a mule-drawn carriage fording a shallow water body with a simple trestle footbridge in the background. Northeast China. Issued by South Manchuria Railway as a postcard in the early twentieth century. Source: RGK Collection.

Previous spread, above Perrine's Bridge between Esopus and Rosendale, New York. Source: RGK, 2019; **below** Old Rhine Bridge between Switzerland and Liechtenstein. Source: TEM, 2015.
Left Ashuelot Bridge, New Hampshire, USA. Source: TEM, 2010.

I.4 Among the most ingenious methods of crossing a stream was a "rope bridge" made of twisted bamboo or rattan, which enabled a person in a sitting position or a strapped-in animal to slide from one side to another. Guanxian, Sichuan, c. 1917–19. Source: Sidney D. Gamble photographs, David M. Rubenstein Rare Book & Manuscript Library, Duke University.

I.5 As this drawing shows, "rope bridges," called here "haul bridges," included two woven bamboo cables with one higher than the other that allowed two-way traffic. Leather straps held the passenger in a sitting position and traveled at high speed from one bank to the other while holding on to a sliding cylinder of bamboo. Replaced by steel cables, scores of these crossings continued into the second decade of the twenty-first century. Maozhou, Ngawa Tibetan and Qiang Autonomous Prefecture, Sichuan. Source: Gill and Yule, 1880: 121.

The best solution worldwide has long been a bridge, for it allows passengers and cargo to pass over the watery obstruction or a deep gorge efficiently, safely, and affordably. However, bridge building solutions across the globe are vastly different, some more successful than others. Most fascinating are the fundamentally distinct concepts that underlie the structural solutions chosen in distinct parts of the world. These tell us much about the cultural thinking of the designers and builders and how society views the function of a bridge.

Bridge builders in the past had little choice in the materials they could use. Those readily at hand depended on the location, but they included rattan, bamboo, wood, and stone. By the late eighteenth century, iron also became a choice, but only in areas where the Industrial Revolution had taken root. Not surprisingly, the natural environment limited builders' choices. Bridges formed of twisted vines, rattan, and bamboo, which had to be renewed every few years, especially in wet climates, could carry pedestrians and sometimes even animals. While these are part of China's bridge history, they were generally more common in tropical areas of Africa, Asia, and South America where these materials were readily available and the situation permitted their use.

I.6 Utilizing bamboo poles lashed together and then floated on the water, this pontoon-like "bridge" includes a section that makes foot traffic easier, comprising a long mat of thin slats of woven bamboo laid across slender floating bamboo poles. Western Sichuan. Source: Unknown.

I.7 Left One of the few remaining rattan bridges, Songshui Bridge in Yunnan Province, is preserved in situ in a roadside park northwest of Dali, Yunnan. The bridge crosses the Bijiang, a tributary of the Lancangjiang (Mekong). Source: TEM, 2016.

I.8 Right Photographed by Sidney Gamble between 1917 and 1919, this woven rattan bridge was being crossed by two men carrying a sedan chair. A tall structure on each end covered the mechanism to which the cables were connected. Maozhou Ngawa Tibetan and Qiang Autonomous Prefecture, Sichuan. Source: Sidney D. Gamble photographs, David M. Rubenstein Rare Book & Manuscript Library, Duke University.

I.9 Burnside Bridge, built in 1836 near Sharpsburg, Maryland, USA, was part of the Battle of Antietam, scene of a bloody battle in September 1862 during the Civil War. At 38 meters (125 feet) long, with three arches and constructed of limestone, the bridge provided a route for farmers to take livestock and produce to market. Source: TEM, 2017.

I.10 At 150 meters (492 feet), the Shiqigong ("Seventeen Arch") Bridge is the longest bridge in Beijing's Yihe Yuan (Summer Palace). Source: ACO, 2006.

Wood was plentiful only where forests were present, and stone was not easy to obtain outside rocky or mountainous areas and was difficult to transport. Logs could be floated downstream and prepared on-site, though bringing materials by road or rail was also possible in urban areas. Each material has limitations. While impressive *covered* bamboo bridges have been recently constructed in China, the Philippines, and Indonesia, there is no evidence of the use of bamboo in *covered* bridge construction in Southeast Asia in the past, and thus bamboo is not discussed further here. Stone, naturally, was both the most permanent as well as the most difficult to handle, the slowest to construct, and the most expensive, yet has proven to be aesthetically beautiful. Stone bridges over wide, fast-flowing rivers were possible but required long periods of time for construction, great numbers of workers, and sustained financial support.

The easiest and most versatile material for bridge building was clearly wood. But wooden beams formed into complex supporting structures were also highly susceptible to moisture, especially in the joints where dry rot could form. For Europeans and Americans, the solution was to protect complex structures with a roof and siding, thereby extending their durability from less than ten years to even hundreds of years. This was because European and American bridge structures consisted of "trusses," the complex timber patterns designed to support a lengthy bridge.

I.11 Greisemer's Mill Bridge in Berks County, Pennsylvania, USA, built in 1868 using a double-arched Burr truss, exemplifies a "through truss" structure. Source: TEM, 2011.

In the vast majority of American and European covered bridges, the roadway passes between these trusses, which form the sides, a type called a "through bridge." In a few cases, the trusses are below the roadway and are thus unable to be covered with a roof, a type called a "deck bridge."

I.12 The König-Ludwig-Brücke in Kempten-St. Mang, Germany, built between 1847 and 1851, is a rare example of a wooden trussed "deck bridge," now preserved for pedestrians. Source: PSCC, 2008.

We do not know if Europeans first built *uncovered* trussed bridges and later learned that covering them prolonged their life, but we do know that Americans did begin with uncovered trussed bridges and only began covering them at least ten years later, at the beginning of the nineteenth century. The extraordinary story of covered bridges in China, which differs from those of both America and Europe, will unfold in the pages that follow.

From the outside, covered bridges appear to be whole buildings perched over waterways. Our eyes focus on the color and shape of the siding, the material of the roof, and the framing of the portals. However, the bridge's essence—the truss in the case of American and European covered bridges—is easily overlooked. In China, the supporting timber structure is completely or partially beneath the deck and usually cannot be seen from above. Perhaps an analogy with the human condition will make the point clearer. Humans in their natural state—nude—could theoretically survive, though not for long, because exposure to the climate would result in disease, hypothermia, and death in most areas of the world. Humans, not having body hair or fur like other animals, must wear clothing for protection. With proper raiment, humans can live a normal lifespan in any climate. The same is true of wooden trussed bridges. Yes, they can survive and function without cover, but not for long. And just as "clothes make the man/woman," a bridge's cover defines much of its apparent "personality." But the essence of a human is not in the clothes he or she wears. The same is true of covered bridges.

While protecting the trusses and other framing structures was the only reason for covering a bridge in the West, China's bridges suggest a different logic. Since few Chinese bridges have structures that resemble trusses, and because bridges are typically supported from below the deck, making them, in fact, deck bridges, the roof and siding serve functions beyond just protecting the timber structure. This will become clear in the sections that follow.

China's Covered Bridges focuses on two bridge types: supporting structures covered with a roof and siding, all made of wood, and masonry arch bridges with a wooden roofed "corridor" on top. This second type is unknown in North America, though some covered bridges over stone

bases were built in Europe, usually enclosing shops and houses within. Drawings and photographs of covered bridges in China began to appear in nineteenth-century Western books as odd artifacts, but few paid much attention to them. It was not

I.13 One of only a handful of nineteenth-century drawings that include a covered bridge in China, this one depicts such a structure crossing the Nine Bend Stream in the Wuyi Mountains of Fujian Province. Source: Fortune, 1852: facing p. 241.

until the late twentieth century that scholars began focusing on the most structurally complex Chinese covered bridges, the woven arch specimens of Fujian and Zhejiang provinces. Western observers, of course, have long known of North American and European covered bridges. Although many of Europe's bridges are much older than those in North America, today they are less well-known than one might imagine, perhaps because to Europeans they are simply part of the broader scenery that already includes countless other historical buildings.

I.14 The Neubrügg or Neubrücke near Bern, Switzerland, though dating to 1507 continues to this day to carry modern traffic over the Aare. Source: TEM, 2014.

China's covered bridges, still not fully inventoried and documented, have remained unfamiliar to most covered bridge enthusiasts, be they Chinese or Western. Indeed, we know for certain that there are more covered bridges still standing in China than anywhere else in the world, and others no doubt remain to be discovered and documented in China.

I.15 The dramatically located Xianju Bridge in Xianren Township, Taishun County, Zhejiang, nearly 43 meters (141 feet) long, was first built in 1453, with numerous rebuildings over the years. This version is probably from 1673. Source: ACO, 2005.

The English term "covered bridge," while familiar to virtually everyone, tends to emphasize the roof and siding over the underlying structure. In the German language, the usual terms are *Gedeckte Holzbrücke* (roofed wooden bridge) and *holzbrücke mit dach* (wooden bridge with roof). In French, Italian, and Spanish, the terms for covered bridge similarly emphasize the covering, as in English: *pont couvert*, *ponte coperto*, and *puente cubierto*. However, the most commonly encountered Chinese term today is *langqiao*, which translates literally as "corridor bridge." In Chinese architecture, a *lang* is a covered passageway, such as might be found connecting buildings at a temple or mansion complex. *Qiao* means "bridge." But the literal translation into English fails to communicate a meaning that would be understood by Western bridge connoisseurs. Since Chinese sometimes prefer to translate Western terms into Chinese terms having a similar sound rather than pronouncing the Western term as best they can (for example, Pizza Hut becomes *bi sheng ke*), some Chinese have done the reverse by translating *langqiao* into English as "lounge bridge," which unfortunately fails to communicate the bridge type to English speakers. Many covered bridges in China, especially in areas populated by minority nationalities, are called *fengyuqiao* or "wind-and-rain bridges," a term that suggests their protective function. Where only a small covered structure is above the deck, we use the term "pavilion bridge," which is a direct translation of the Chinese term *tingqiao*. We, however, prefer to retain the usual English term "covered bridge" for most Chinese wooden and masonry bridges with a roof and siding.

The goal of Part I is to introduce some of the issues pertinent to the study of covered bridges in general and China's covered bridges in particular, placing the latter into a worldwide context. Their uniqueness only becomes apparent when viewed in relation to the covered bridges of Europe and the Americas.

Distribution of Covered Bridges Worldwide

The distribution of covered bridges can be described as "worldwide," but in fact only three major regions come into focus: Central Europe, North America, and China. Although Chinese covered bridges originated and developed simultaneously with those of Europe, they will be best understood in relation to and following a discussion of Western bridges.

The vast majority of European bridges were built in Central Europe, principally the German-speaking areas of what are now Germany, Switzerland, and Austria. Because some Swiss cantons are French or Italian speaking but shared the same bridge building technologies found in German-speaking cantons, covered bridges are not exclusive to German language areas. Indeed, there are small numbers of such bridges in eastern France and northern Italy, as well as in the Czech Republic, Slovakia, Romania, and Bulgaria. Of these areas, however, Switzerland is clearly not just the geographical center but also the epicenter of innovation and experimentation. With some of the most challenging mountain geography on earth and numerous waterways, many located in deep valleys and even on mountainsides, Swiss bridge builders had to rise to superhuman levels to create a road-and-bridge system for that seemingly small country. Covered bridges in Europe are significantly older than those of North America. This is understandable considering that Europeans were already building such bridges when their seafaring peers were just "discovering" the New World in the late fifteenth century. Thus, European builders had hundreds of years in which to develop bridge technology before their descendants who migrated to the American colonies began building bridges in New England. Bridges in China parallel European bridges timewise, but each area had its own separate trajectory, with no known relationships.

Although German-speaking people, including many from Switzerland, migrated to the American colonies and the newly founded United States of America during the seventeenth to twentieth centuries, American bridge building does not appear to be a continuation of European traditions but rather an innovative solution to the same challenges faced in Europe. Wooden bridges, at first uncovered and only covered starting in 1804, first developed in New England, particularly Massachusetts and Connecticut, with English-derived builders, most famously Timothy Palmer (1751–1821). In quick succession, two builders of German extraction, one American-born (Theodore Burr, 1771–1822) and one German-born (Lewis Wernwag, 1769–1843), began building innovative structures in New York, Pennsylvania, and later further afield. Bridge building followed the expansion of the young nation whose population was moving to the west and south, and the necessity of developing a growing road and transportation system, including crossing its numerous waterways, both wide rivers and smaller streams. (For a comprehensive view of this subject, see Miller and Knapp, 2014.)

Because so many cities in New England were founded along the region's many wide rivers, a necessity since these rivers provided the water required for power and transportation, they also included the hazard of flooding. Being able to cross them easily and safely was essential if there was to be economic expansion. Other parts of New England were also settled, including the nearby states of New Hampshire, Vermont, and Maine. As a result, the greatest concentrations of covered bridges were in and close to the newly built cities of New England, then later in the areas of expansion, especially the states of New York, New Jersey, Maryland, Pennsylvania, Ohio, Kentucky, and Virginia. Ironically, though, the first documented covered bridge was built in Pennsylvania, not New England. As wider waterways, such as the Hudson, Delaware, Susquehanna, and Ohio rivers, were encountered, longer and more complex covered bridges had to be constructed.

I.18 The western six spans of Theodore Burr's "Camelback" Bridge over the Susquehanna River in Pennsylvania, USA, totaled 384 meters (1,260 feet) in length and were built between 1812 and 1817. Source: RGK Collection.

I.17 William Russell Birch (1755–1834) painted Philadelphia's "Permanent Bridge" shortly after it was covered in early 1805, this being the first documented covered bridge in the United States. Source: American Philosophical Society.

I.16 Switzerland's graceful Punt da Rueun Bridge, built in 1839 and 44.35 meters (146 feet) long, typifies the European-style covered bridge. Source: TEM, 2015.

I.19 The Cow Run Bridge in Ohio's Washington County, now long gone, was typical of the simple and functional bridges crossing America's streams, both small and great. Source: TEM, 1965.

During the first half of the nineteenth century, bridge building continued to flourish elsewhere as newly opened areas were settled, including Indiana, Michigan, Illinois, West Virginia, Tennessee, Georgia, Alabama, Mississippi, and Missouri. Few covered bridges, however, were ever built in the remaining states east of the Mississippi River, such as the Carolinas, Arkansas, Louisiana, and Florida. Similarly, few covered bridges were built in many Great Plains and Rocky Mountain states between the Mississippi River and California, but all three coastal states along the Pacific Ocean—California, Oregon, and Washington—came to have significant numbers of such bridges, especially Oregon where covered bridge building continued well into the twentieth century.

In addition to the United States, Canada has a significant number of covered bridges, with all but one found in just two provinces, Quebec and New Brunswick, both in the east of the country. Today, there is but one bridge in Ontario, but there are also two partially covered rail bridges in British Columbia in the far west. While a few of Quebec's bridges were built in the later nineteenth century, some in fact by Americans, the vast majority are of a highly unified design developed by the highway department during the early twentieth century working with the Bureau of Colonisation, which oversaw an extensive opening up of areas distant from Quebec's original center around Montreal. Although using a different truss design, most of New Brunswick's bridges were also built to a

standard design by the highway department from 1900 onwards. Although American builders erected the longest covered bridges ever built, including the magnificent Columbia-Wrightsville Bridge over the Susquehanna River, some 1,830 meters (6,000 feet) long, the longest remaining historical covered bridge in the world is at Hartland, New Brunswick, around 390 meters (1,282 feet) long (see Figure I.61 below).

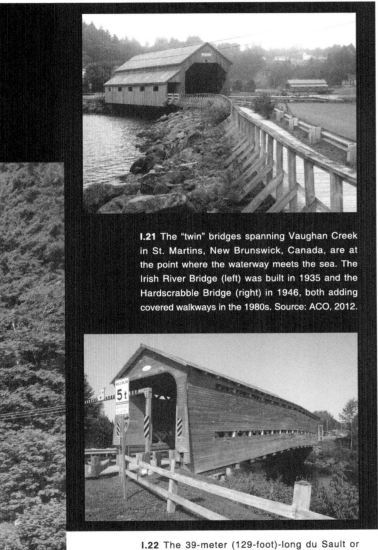

I.21 The "twin" bridges spanning Vaughan Creek in St. Martins, New Brunswick, Canada, are at the point where the waterway meets the sea. The Irish River Bridge (left) was built in 1935 and the Hardscrabble Bridge (right) in 1946, both adding covered walkways in the 1980s. Source: ACO, 2012.

I.22 The 39-meter (129-foot)-long du Sault or Saint-Adalbert Bridge in French-speaking Quebec, Canada, is typical of the standard Town Lattice bridges of that province, this example built in 1943. Source: TEM, 2012.

I.20 Although built in 1938, long after covered bridges had become obsolete in the eastern sections of the United States, Oregon's picturesque Goodpasture Bridge was typical of the west style that continued into the 1960s. Source: TEM, 2012.

China, with an area approximately equal to that of the United States and Europe west of the Urals, a history unrivalled in length, and an ingenious population, has produced an astonishing range of covered bridges. Until recent decades, the best-known covered bridges in China were those with pavilion-like structures on top of them. Yet, over the past several decades, as access to areas once relatively inaccessible because of poor transportation has revealed, there are bridge-building traditions with not only distinctive covers but also ingenious structures beneath the decks that support what are often ostentatious buildings above. Moreover, as seen in photographs from the nineteenth century taken in far-flung drier areas of western China, there were countless workaday timber covered bridges that share bridge-building principles with areas beyond China into the Himalayas.

It is reasonable to ask if Chinese covered bridge technology was also transmitted elsewhere in Asia. The answer appears to be "no." Most of China's existing bridges are found either in obscure mountain counties in eastern China or among minority populations far to the west and southwest, and neither area would have exerted any influence on Korea or Japan. Vietnam, however, still preserves a few covered beam bridges in the central region, but these show no connection to Chinese traditions. Some minority areas in northern Vietnam that share borders with southwest China had, at least in the past, simple trestle-supported covered bridges similar to those in nearby China. Vietnam's now famous "Japanese bridge" in Hoi-an, dating to 1593, is a small wooden structure that includes a temple projected from one side built over a series of brick arches. Such bridges are atypical of those in China, but this lonely survivor suggests such bridges may have been more normal in Japan in the past, if indeed this bridge was built by Japanese.

I.23 One of Hoi-an, Vietnam's most famous landmarks, the UNESCO World Heritage-designated "Japanese Covered Bridge," was built by the Japanese community there in 1719 (some sources say 1590s) to connect it to the Chinese community nearby. Supported on five short stone arches, the wooden structure includes a small temple on the north side (not seen) dedicated to the Taoist God of Weather, Tran Vo Bac De, as earthquakes and flooding are a problem in that area. Source: TEM, 2009.

I.24 This rather fragile trestle bridge in the Sontay District of the Tonkin Delta of Vietnam is covered with thatching. Source: RGK Collection.

I.25–I.27 Located east of Hue, Vietnam, in Thanh Tuan Village, this *cau ngoi* or "tile-roofed bridge," was built in 1776 in imperial style by a member of the royal family, and includes a shrine within the bridge in her honor. Source: TEM, 2009.

Chronology of Covered Bridge Building

Establishing the origin of anything as old as covered bridges is understandably challenging. This is certainly true of covered bridges in the two oldest areas under study, China and Central Europe. Although it is likely true that such bridges were developing simultaneously in both places, there is nothing to suggest builders knew anything about each other. Thus, we treat these as separate histories. Since North America's bridges are more recent, their history is well documented.

The origin of European covered bridges cannot be known precisely, but evidence suggests that such bridges have been built since at least the early fourteenth century. Switzerland's well-known covered walkway bridge in Luzerne, known as the Kapellbrücke, dates to 1333, though it is doubtful anything remains of the original. Luzerne's other bridge, the Spreuerbrücke, dates from 1408, though the present structure more likely dates from 1568.

The oldest bridges still standing in Switzerland today, all located along the Aare River near Bern, date from 1535, 1549, 1555, and 1568 respectively. To put these dates into perspective, Christopher Columbus lived from c. 1451 to 1506, Leonardo da Vinci from 1452 to 1519, and pre-eminent Italian architect Andrea Palladio, who also proposed several wooden bridge designs, from 1508 to 1580. Thus, we can say with some certainty that Swiss builders were already actively building bridges using at least two fundamental trusses when Palladio, possibly unaware of developments to the north, was publishing his otherwise innovative designs.

Covered bridge building has continued with few interruptions since early times to the present in both China and Europe, specifically, Germany, Switzerland, and Austria. In China, relatively young builders in the more remote areas of eastern parts of the country continue to construct new bridges utilizing the same designs

I.28 Luzerne, Switzerland's Spreuerbrücke, first built in 1568 and modified over time, is in two sections. The three spans on the right have queenpost or kingpost trusses while the span on the left is an arch. Source: TEM, 2016.

and practices as those of earlier bridges. In the southwestern provinces, some of the all-wood cantilever and beam bridges are being rebuilt on modern reinforced concrete, which is reasonable considering the scarcity and expense of the giant logs used in the past. As tourism in the minority areas ramps up, more and more otherwise modern bridges are being fitted with wooden "corridors" to mimic the traditional "wind-and-rain bridges." Straying even further from tradition are several large-scale highway bridges fitted with covers constructed of timber that mimic traditional Dong bridges, such as the 368-meter (1,207-foot)-long bridge in Sanjiang City, Guangxi Province. European builders have also continued to build new highway bridges, often with innovative designs, including large-scale laminated arches.

I.29 Completed in late 2010, the 368-meter (1,207-foot)-long New Bridge in Sanjiang, Guangxi Zhuang Autonomous Region, China, was built to resemble Dong minority covered bridges, but the partial wooden cover sits on a massive concrete arch bridge. Source: http://news.sohu.com/20101004/n275419770.shtml. Accessed October 4, 2010.

I.30 The Ruchmülibrücke in Alblingen, BE, Switzerland, was built in 1977 for highway use using a massive glulam laminated arch and steel hangers. Source: TEM, 2016.

North America's history, in contrast, is clearly known but also now fraught with debates about which bridges are "historical" or "authentic," issues to be discussed later. While true that the first documented covered bridge was the "Permanent Bridge" in Philadelphia, Pennsylvania, completed in 1805, in fact its builder, Timothy Palmer, had been building uncovered bridges of similar design in New England since the early 1790s, and the Permanent Bridge itself was first built without a roof or siding in 1804, only to be covered the next year at the suggestion of the bridge's financier, Judge Richard Peters, who saw covering as a way to extend the bridge's life. After that, covering wooden trussed bridges in the United States and later in Canada became standard practice.

But unlike in Europe and China, where such bridges have continued to be built to the present, the American covered wooden trussed bridge was gradually seen as obsolete, first in the eastern, then the midwestern and southern states by the 1920s, in Oregon and Washington only in the 1950s, and in two Canadian provinces, Quebec and New Brunswick, about the same time, though a few were built even after that period. Starting in the second half of the nineteenth century in the United States, iron, and later steel, along with reinforced concrete gradually supplanted wood as the preferred material, thus it was no longer necessary to cover the bridge structure. Although the first major cast-iron bridge had been built over the River Severn at Coalbrookdale, Shropshire, England, in 1781, such bridges were not easily duplicated elsewhere unless the iron was readily available nearby. This was particularly true in the United States where iron was not commonly available, and the few mills capable of producing bridge parts were mostly in the east. In places like the western coastal states, wood was as plentiful as iron was scarce. Therefore, it is logical that covered bridges continued to be built in areas remote from iron factories long after they had become obsolete where such factories existed.

The second matter was design. Where the number of wooden truss designs that were practically used was relatively few—and most developed before the science of engineering had evolved—iron trusses developed after the advent of engineering, gradually from the 1830s and afterwards, thus supplanting timber. During this period, numerous iron bridge companies were founded, some primarily to build this or that innovative patented truss, but many failed or were absorbed through mergers. Designs and patents proliferated, but in the end only a relative handful were widely adopted.

I.31 The Honey Run Grade Bridge in Butte County, California, USA, built in 1896, combines wood and iron in a non-traditional Pratt truss design. The bridge was destroyed on November 8, 2018, in the Camp Fire which also destroyed the nearby city of Paradise. Officials hope to rebuild in the future. Source: TEM, 2012.

Among them were some that combined wood with iron, the so-called "combination" bridges. Builders sometimes covered these bridges, and two remain, both in California.

At the same time, it became possible to treat wood with chemicals, allowing it to resist moisture, and thus most bridges constructed of timber were left uncovered. Covering all-iron bridges was neither known nor necessary because the wooden deck boards were by then treated to be moisture-resistant.

Function of Covered Bridges

Since most remaining covered bridges in Europe and North America are either in rural areas or in semi-retirement within smaller cities, there is a tendency to view them as quaint survivors of a distant past now imagined as simple and pleasant. It is, however, erroneous to characterize that past as uncluttered, pre-modern, clean, idyllic, or even peaceful. Covered bridges on both continents served population centers first, and thus the majority of early bridges were located in urban areas. With the development of industry following the Industrial Revolution, bridges had to serve the ever increasing demands of commerce, expanding economies, growing populations, and new modes of transportation. In North America, especially, covered bridges today continue to be seen as icons of an imaginary romanticized and bucolic past. Thus, remaining covered bridges are featured in nostalgic scenic paintings on tea towels and on Christmas ornaments, cards, and cookie cans, often with horse-drawn sleighs emerging from a red bridge and a white colonial church in the background. In fact, most early bridges sat amidst city buildings, factories, railroad lines, and water-powered mills. It is easy to forget this because those bridges are long gone and forgotten. In North America, surviving covered bridges tend to be on little traveled roads or in small towns or villages. Europe retains more bridges in city centers than does North America, but few of these continue to carry vehicles, having been retired to serve exclusively as pedestrian bridges. Most of them are in rural areas and even on footpaths.

I.32 Pittsburgh, Pennsylvania, in 1902, where a dozen bridges spanned the Alleghany and Monongahela rivers. Only the 1875 Union Bridge (lower left) was covered at that time. Source: Library of Congress LC-DIG-pga-03733.

The great majority of European bridges were originally built for vehicles, though some early bridges certainly were also built for foot traffic, Luzerne's well-known Kapellbrücke being a prime example. Virtually all early covered bridges in North America were intended for animal-drawn vehicles. In contrast, China's covered bridges were built for foot and animal traffic, a limitation often made obvious by the approaching steps or the presence within some of raised plank treads to facilitate secure footing. Many of the historical and contemporary photographs of China's covered bridges shown later will provide substantial evidence of this.

I.35 Typical of rural China even today, a farmer carries a heavy load on a shoulder pole through the Qiancheng Bridge in Pingnan County, Fujian Province, built originally in 1125 and rebuilt in 1820. Source: TEM, 2005.

I.33 The Aare Bruecke in Aarberg, Switzerland, built in 1568, continues to carry modern traffic thanks to its massive timbers originally constructed for heavy wagons and teams of horses. Source: TEM, 2014.

I.34 A buggy emerges from an old and long forgotten bridge over the Yocona River in Lafayette County, Mississippi, in the early 1900s. The Town lattice design was preferred in most parts of the south. This bridge, which no longer stands, would not have been able to support the passage of modern vehicles. Source: Lafayette County, Mississippi Genealogy and History Network.

Many Chinese covered bridges are, nonetheless, as large and robust as vehicular bridges in the West. American writers commonly characterize covered bridges as being inadequate for modern traffic, having come from the "horse and buggy age." Nothing could be further from the truth, except for smaller bridges in rural areas. Even the earliest bridges in both Europe and North America were built to carry heavy wagons laden with industrial and commercial products, such as stone, brick, iron, grain, and timber, pulled by teams of horses or oxen. Indiana's Medora Bridge, considered by many to be the longest surviving historical covered bridge in the United States at 140 meters (459 feet) in three spans, routinely carried heavy loads. The timber sawmills and brick-making industries found throughout North America also depended on sturdy bridges for the heavy loads of raw materials and products that needed to be transported.

In China, we have occasionally seen men pulling carts through bridges, even when this required a difficult passage over the approaching

I.37 In Yunnan's Yunlong County, agricultural goods brought down from mountainside villages on mules cross the Yongzhen Bridge and are transferred to trucks. Source: TEM, 2016.

steps. Motorcycles also today regularly cross such bridges, often having to go up and down steps to enter. Bridges in populated areas connected parts of the town or village separated by a river, but in remote mountain areas there were numerous bridges on a vast network of stone trails that connected villages as well as market towns. Trails running along rivers were intended for humans and animals carrying goods, while those traversing the mountains and hills, even when they were steep, shortened distances for those without heavy burdens, mainly high-value, low-bulk commodities such as medicinal herbs. Thus, bridges were often important junctions on these complex trail systems, many of which remain in existence and continue to be used in remote areas. In southwestern China's Yunnan Province, some bridges served as links as part of an elaborate network called the Tea-Horse Road (*chamadao*), which facilitated the movement principally of tea and salt into Tibet. In Tibet, the tea was exchanged for small horses, medicinal herbs, musk, horn, and other products of the high plateau. These were carried on mules, ponies, and yaks or on the backs of porters over narrow mountain trails that periodically traversed streams via both primitive and well-developed bridges, some of which were covered and will be discussed later.

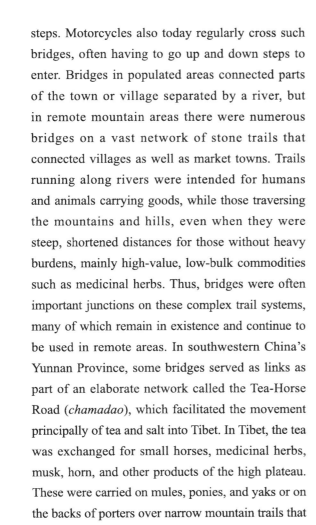

I.36 Porters laden with stacks of brick tea rest along a path in Sichuan Province. One carries about 145 kilos (317 lbs) while the other 135 kilos (298 lbs), 1908. Source: Wilson and Sargent, 1914: facing p. 92.

Some Chinese bridges were built for spiritual reasons more than for practical use. Bridges are encountered in what sometimes seem to be inexplicable places built for the purpose of harnessing positive energy at a point determined by *fengshui*, the Chinese system of manipulating energy forces. To counteract unfortunate circumstances thought to be caused by energy loss, *fengshui* specialists sometimes recommended building one or more *langqiao* at particular sites, either to contain good fortune (*fu*) or to block the loss of a village's energy and to reverse its ill fortune. This subject will be discussed in detail in Part II.2. We have not heard of any spiritual reasons for building bridges in either Europe or North America.

Chinese bridges are also distinctive for the presence of wooden benches running lengthwise on either interior side of most bridges. Where American and European bridges were only intended for the passage of vehicles, albeit with the possibility of a separate covered passageway for pedestrians attached to one or both sides, Chinese bridges carried pedestrians who could then use the bridges for overnight shelter, as a resting place during the day, and in urban areas for socializing. Like countless other covered bridges throughout China, one bridge in Fujian Province's Shouning County now serves as a community center during evenings and weekends, with tables for games, a shop selling snacks, and additional seating for those who come to socialize. In a few cases, bridges also serve as resting spots for wedding parties and even as festival venues. Obviously, then, these bridges had to be stout enough to support large numbers of people.

North American bridges also included categories neither found in Europe nor China, those that carried railroad trains and some that carried water-filled canal troughs, called aqueducts, traversed by canal boats. Because of the extreme weight of steam (and later diesel) locomotives, plus a coal car and rolling stock hauling all manner of goods, both raw and finished, as well as people, rail bridges had to be robustly designed, usually using high trusses that might be doubled in layers, using heavier than normal timbers, and incorporating extra deck bracing.

I.38 Located in an urban area of Shouning County, Fujian Province's largest town, the Xiangong (Yudai) Bridge serves as a community center where people snack, smoke, play games, and socialize. Source: TEM, 2007.

I.40 The only surviving covered canal aqueduct (bridge) in the world is in the village of Metamora in eastern Indiana, USA. Built in 1846, the span carries the Whitewater Canal across Duck Creek but was made obsolete by the parallel rail line. Source: Library of Congress, HAER IN-108-5.

I.39 Though a simply functional beam bridge, the Jiezifang Bridge connects parts of Shijing Village, Yunlong County, Yunnan, and provides a convenient shelter for a lady selling sticks of meatballs. Source: TEM, 2016.

I.41 Until it burned in 1965, this Boston and Maine railroad bridge at Bennington, New Hampshire, built in 1877, was the oldest surviving rail bridge. Source: National Society for the Preservation of Covered Bridges, Richard Sanders Allen Collection.

Though a great number of rail bridges were covered with a roof and siding, a greater number were left open because the live embers from coal- or wood-burning locomotives flying from smokestacks could set the bridge on fire. Uncovered bridges, however, deteriorated rapidly and had to be replaced at least every ten years, if not sooner. Similarly, aqueducts carried a constant load of water and had to be equally robust.

I.42 This uncovered combination wood and iron Post truss rail bridge crossed Clear Creek in Colorado during the Gold Rush era that started in 1859. Source: National Society for the Preservation of Covered Bridges, Richard Sanders Allen Collection.

Where timber was plentiful, doing so was not a problem. Based on current knowledge, we also know that uncovered wooden trussed rail bridges were built in Europe, particularly in Russia, Scandanavia, and Germany during the nineteenth century, all apparently using an American truss, and some were built under the supervision of American engineers. We are unaware of any wooden or covered canal aqueducts in Europe, bearing in mind, of course, that canals were not part of the mountainous Swiss and Austrian landscapes.

Structure of Covered Bridges

Though easily overlooked by casual observers, nothing differentiates covered bridges more than structure, this being the very essence of the type. When viewed superficially, however, a covered bridge appears to be a three-dimensional rectangular building—we could call it a "gestalt"—because the broad surfaces of the roof and siding obscure the inner or underlying framework that must be protected from the elements. In each of the three geographical areas under consideration, builders evolved different ways of joining wooden timbers so as to create a rigid frame capable of carrying the loads required of them. While it comes as no surprise that China's tradition was isolated from both Europe and North America, it is surprising that the latter two were also largely isolated from each other. The European tradition first evolved mostly in Switzerland among German speakers, while the American tradition evolved under English, German, and other non-Swiss descended builders. The broad picture is best understood not by concentrating here on the specifics of structural design but by seeing each tradition as a conceptually different solution. Since the science of structural analysis and engineering schools only developed in the mid-nineteenth century, especially in France where covered bridges were rarely built, the early builders who evolved these separately "discovered" concepts had to have done so intuitively, though likely with a generous portion of experience along with trial and error.

Two matters that have received little attention in the literature but which are absolutely essential are the construction of the foundations, that is, the abutments and piers, be they of stone or other materials, and the erection process of the superstructure. The vast majority of covered bridges in all three areas sit on stone foundations, those on the bank called "abutments" and those in the river called "piers." In Europe, some historical bridges were also built on wooden trestles and a few remain so today. In North America, where many bridges were built in areas with little stone available nearby or where the soil was too unstable to support stone, principally areas of the American Midwest and Quebec, Canada, builders used logs or timbers massed into cribbing, bents similar to those in Europe, or later metal cylinders, perhaps filled with cement, to serve as abutments and piers. Stone masons had to cut the stone from stone quarries and shape the blocks. Transporting them to the site, then placing them in position, particularly in the middle of a river, was both challenging and dangerous. Building the abutments on each shore usually presented fewer problems. But where bridges had to be placed on steep or sheer cliffs, the masons faced the challenge of mixing cut stones with natural outcroppings. When the bridge was high above a river canyon, the building of the abutments required superhuman efforts fraught with danger. Moreover, such foundations were being built long before the age of safety harnesses and sophisticated cranes. Handling blocks of stone weighing hundreds of pounds in these situations required ingenuity, bravery, and strength, even with the assistance of simple derricks.

While abutments presented their own challenges, pier building confronted masons with challenges of an entirely different scale. Normally,

stone foundations were stabilized on wooden pilings driven into the soil. On the riverbank, such work is relatively straightforward. Dig out the soil to expose the site, set up the pile-driving machine, and drive the logs into the ground. This becomes far more difficult in the middle of a river, especially when the water runs deep or swiftly. In the areas of Europe where covered bridges developed, few rivers required bridges longer than around 183 meters (600 feet), though some waterways were indeed deep and swift. The largest river was the Rhine, and numerous covered bridges crossed this river, including Europe's longest remaining bridge between Bad Säckingen, Germany, and Stein, Switzerland, measuring 203 meters (668 feet). And because European bridges built before about 1850 tended to have fairly short spans, a great number of piers would be required. Unfortunately,

I.44 Europe's longest covered bridge crosses the Rhine River between Bad-Säckingem, Germany, and Stein, Switzerland. The earliest of its seven spans were built around 1700 and the last in 1926. Source: TEM, 2014.

I.43 Crossing a deep gorge on unusually high piers, Horton's Mill Bridge in Blount County, Alabama, was built in 1934, but surprisingly no photos of the construction are known to exist. Source: TEM, 2011.

we know little about how early European builders constructed river piers, but in many cases these bridges had piers made of stout wooden beams instead of stone, suggesting that the rivers were not unusually deep. Nonetheless, builders likely built a temporary dam or constructed cofferdams around the spot in the river that allowed workers to descend to the riverbed protected from the flowing river water.

The North American situation was overall far more challenging, however. The Europeans who settled the areas we know as New England and the Middle Atlantic states faced numerous rivers that were commonly 305–1,220 meters (1,000–4,000 feet) wide and, in the case of one river, even 1,828 meters (6,000 feet) wide. New England's road network was forced to cross many such rivers, including the Merrimack and Connecticut, while builders in states to the south, especially New York and Pennsylvania, faced the Delaware, Mohawk, Hudson, and Potomac. Running south through the middle of Pennsylvania, and therefore blocking all traffic running east and west, was the mighty Susquehanna, jokingly described as "a mile wide and an inch deep." Even after American builders learned to build spans routinely 61–91 meters (200–300 feet) long, the world's longest covered bridge over the Susquehanna between Columbia and Wrightsville, Pennsylvania, and nearly 1,828 meters (6,000 feet) long, required 54 piers for the first bridge (1812–14) and 27 for the replacement bridge (1832–4), which lasted until the Civil War in 1863. A third bridge was constructed in 1868 that served until it was demolished by the remnants of a hurricane in 1896. Further west, the city of Pittsburgh was built where two great rivers meet, the Allegheny and Monongahela, to form the mighty Ohio River that flowed from Pittsburgh to Cairo, Illinois. Though numerous bridges were built in and around Pittsburgh, only a few covered bridges ever crossed the Ohio downstream.

The building of America's first fully covered bridge, the "Permanent Bridge" in Philadelphia, completed in 1805, was held up for several years because the Schuylkill River was so deep that stone masons could not construct the piers. It was

I.45 A massive Howe truss rail bridge, the third crossing between Columbia and Wrightsville, Pennsylvania, built in 1868 in 27 spans, only lasted until 1896 when a tornado destroyed it. Source: RGK Collection.

not until 1803 that English stone mason William Weston developed a new caisson technology that allowed builders to reach the dry river bottom for construction of the piers. After that, stone masons across the United States came to excel at building innumerable abutments and piers in the most difficult of circumstances. These brave and strong people, however, remain little known and underappreciated among admirers of covered bridges.

Another group of unsung heroes of bridge building were those who erected the bridges. For Europe's older bridges, we know little of the

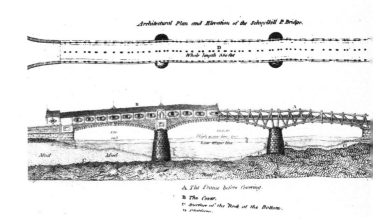

I.46 Timothy Palmer's "Permanent Bridge" over the Schuylkill River in Philadelphia, Pennsylvania, first built uncovered in 1804, had been delayed by unprecedented challenges of building a pier in water too deep for the present technology, but an English engineer solved that in 1803. Source: Peters, 1815: n.p.

process, but by the mid-nineteenth century when photography had become common, we know that European bridges were erected similarly to those in North America. Oddly, few bridge historians in North America wrote about the erection process, and some of the discussions were clearly erroneous. Some speculated that whole trusses were moved onto a temporary base, called "falsework," and raised into position. Others posited that the whole superstructure was built on land and somehow dragged by a team of oxen over the river into position. Neither process has been documented. Written and pictorial evidence both demonstrate that workers first built a falsework/ trestle system across the river to support a platform on which the bridge was to be built. The bridge structure itself was either entirely constructed on land, disassembled, and reassembled on the platform, or the parts were custom-cut as the bridge was erected.

We speak of these workers as unsung heroes because of the challenges and dangers of constructing falsework in deep or fast-moving currents, and then moving all the heavy structural

timbers into place, all without the aid of modern equipment or safety devices. Many old photos of bridges under construction show daredevil workers who have ascended the bridge on exceptionally tall ladders standing unaided on the tops of the trusses. How many workers were injured or killed building bridges is unknown. One shudders to think of the labor involved in moving the structural timbers of the fifteenth span of a 2-kilometer (1-mile)- long bridge over the Susquehanna and hoisting them into place. Old photos also show that bridge building was carried on throughout the harsh northern winters. Workers usually had to live in temporary shelters near the bridge site for months without anything "modern," even by the standards of the 1840s. Women were employed to cook and do laundry for the workers.

Conceptually, the earliest European bridge designs have much in common with roof trusses also being developed at the time, and indeed some bridge builders such as the Grubenmanns

I.47 This multi-span Burr truss bridge with double arches over the White River at White River Junction, Vermont, USA, was built in 1848 in the usual manner—assembled on a "falsework" platform. Source: Fletcher and Snow, 1934: 300.

I.48 Switzerland's Punt Russein Bridge near Disentis in the Grisons was not just the first known use of American William Howe's 1840 patent truss in Switzerland but had to be built on elaborate falsework extending to the bottom of the gorge. Source: https://commons.wikimedia. org/wiki/Category:Punt_ Russein#/media/ File:Russeinerbr%C3%BCcke_ im_Bau_1857.jpg Accessed August 1, 2018.

I.49 With the falsework removed, this gigantic rail bridge is nearly finished. Workers from the Smith Bridge Company of Toledo, Ohio, USA, climb long ladders to work on this unusual combination wood and iron truss that resembles the all-wood Smith truss still seen today. Source: Miriam Wood Collection.

from Teufen, Switzerland, also constructed roof trusses for churches and castles during the later seventeenth century. The most basic concepts are an isosceles triangle with the point above, the horizontal below, and two equal diagonals built to span a defined space, and for longer spans, a trapezoid frame where the longer lower horizontal beam spans the space and the shorter one above fits between the equal diagonals.

The earliest extant covered bridges in Switzerland, those dating from the first half of the sixteenth century, exhibit both plans. English-speaking writers and builders later dubbed these as "kingpost" and "queenpost," respectively, perhaps unintentionally evoking a royal hierarchy. Bridge builders also used another fundamental form—the arch—a pattern commonly seen in stone bridges as well as in some roofs. All three wooden forms work similarly. In bridges, the deck is supported on the lower horizontal from an arch or diagonals above. These are pulled, or stressed, downwards by the load, but they remain rigid because triangles cannot change shape and arches are held firm by being seated into the stone foundations. They remain rigid unless the stress is so great it deforms or breaks the members. Members being stretched, such as the vertical posts and lower horizontal beam, experience "tension," while timbers being squeezed, such as the diagonal beams or an arch, experience "compression." Because all three forms experience similar kinds of compression, some modern engineers, especially those in Europe, prefer to describe "kingpost" and "queenpost" as "polygonal arches," that is, arches consisting of multiple straight segments or having multiple angles, although not continuously curved. Though "polygonal arch" is little known to non-specialists, especially in the United States, and because "kingpost" and "queenpost" have been commonly used in the United States since the nineteenth century, we shall use both to reference those designs and reserve "arch" for continuously curved members.

I.50 The Grubenmann family, Switzerland's most famous bridge builders of the eighteenth century, also built roof trusses. Within the triangular frame is a queenpost truss (lower), quite similar to those in modest bridges. Grubenmann Museum, Teufen, Switzerland. Source: TEM, 2014.

European and North American covered bridges consist of two frames called trusses, parallel to each other. They are separated and made into a rigid square with over- and under-structures connecting them, usually reinforced with angle braces above to keep them square. Normally, the deck sits on the under-structure and between the trusses, called a "through bridge," while some bridges, especially those built for rail lines, sometimes placed the deck on the over-structure, called a "deck bridge." Though the under- and over-structures are important to maintaining the rigid square of the structure, it is the trusses which most interest observers. Three of the most fundamental trusses were discussed above: kingpost, queenpost, and arch. Because the lower horizontal beams, customarily called "lower chords," form the base of the truss, they are connected to it by vertical beams called "posts" or iron rods between the upper and lower chords. Arches can be bolted directly to the vertical posts or support the deck with vertical iron rods connected to the lower chords. Because arches in longer bridges need to be massive, they often consist of layers. Such arches are known as "laminated arches." Normally, the ends of the arches are seated into recesses in the abutments (and piers), but when they are fastened directly to the lower chords they are called "tied arches." A few historical bridges in the United States consist of such arches alone. Engineers in Switzerland continue to design and build wooden highway bridges supported by massive laminated arches. The authors consider arches alone as a kind of truss, but they are aware that some engineers classify arches separately from trusses.

Most European covered bridges built before about 1850 use versions of these three designs, separately or in combination. The simplest are mostly confined to the earliest extant full-sized bridges and to more recent modest highway bridges or to footbridges built from the seventeenth century to the present. Far more interesting are the trusses that combine these fundamental forms,

I.51 The Lincoln Bridge in Windsor County, Vermont, built in 1877, is among the few remaining "tied arch" bridges that use a laminated arch reinforced with wooden verticals but supporting the floor beams with iron rods. Source: TEM, 2017.

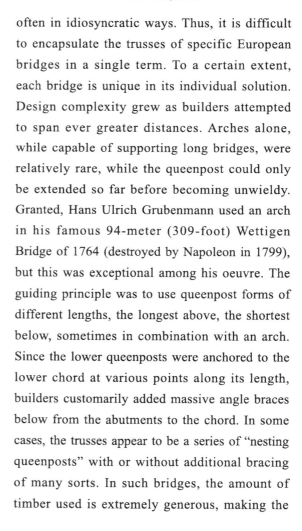

often in idiosyncratic ways. Thus, it is difficult to encapsulate the trusses of specific European bridges in a single term. To a certain extent, each bridge is unique in its individual solution. Design complexity grew as builders attempted to span ever greater distances. Arches alone, while capable of supporting long bridges, were relatively rare, while the queenpost could only be extended so far before becoming unwieldy. Granted, Hans Ulrich Grubenmann used an arch in his famous 94-meter (309-foot) Wettigen Bridge of 1764 (destroyed by Napoleon in 1799), but this was exceptional among his oeuvre. The guiding principle was to use queenpost forms of different lengths, the longest above, the shortest below, sometimes in combination with an arch. Since the lower queenposts were anchored to the lower chord at various points along its length, builders customarily added massive angle braces below from the abutments to the chord. In some cases, the trusses appear to be a series of "nesting queenposts" with or without additional bracing of many sorts. In such bridges, the amount of timber used is extremely generous, making the bridge's deadweight a major factor. Even with these complex designs, spans longer than about 45 meters (150 feet) were uncommon.

American builder Timothy Palmer (1751–1821), who began constructing uncovered trussed bridges in the early 1790s, either knew nothing of the European tradition or chose to ignore it, designing complex trusses combining arch and triangle capable of spanning nearly 65 meters (200 feet). America's earliest, most daring, and creative builders included Palmer, Theodore Burr (1771–1822), and Lewis Wernwag (1769–1843). Palmer preferred his initial designs and simply perfected them over time. Burr, better understood as a visionary, built some bridges that can only be described as experimental or idiosyncratic, though the truss that came to bear his name was among the simplest, combining the arch with a "multiple kingpost" truss for variable length structures. Wernwag was as daring as Burr, constructing numerous bridges over a wide area and extended period, some lasting well into the twentieth century. His most famous bridge, though, was Philadelphia's "Colossus," an arched truss bridge with a 100-meter (330-foot) span, not much shorter than the longest on record, Burr's 110-meter (360-foot) McCall's Ferry Bridge over the Susquehanna in Lancaster County, Pennsylvania, for which there are no images. The latter, however, lasted only three years because of an ice jam, while Wernwag's remarkable bridge lasted until 1843 when it was destroyed by fire.

I.52a–d Four contrasting European truss designs from the old European tradition.
a Neubrügg (Neubrücke) near Bern, Switzerland, 1535, kingpost truss.
b Aarebrücke at Olten, Switzerland, 1805, "nesting" queenpost truss.
c Brunnmattbrücke at Brunnmatt, Switzerland, 1837, arch and queenpost combination.
d Reussbrücke, Sins, Switzerland, c. 1852, complex queenpost combination.
Source: TEM, a–c 2014, d 2016.

I.53 Theodore Burr's bridge over the Mohawk River between Schenectady and Scotia, New York, built soon after 1808, was not just experimental but a failure, requiring extra piers under each span. Source: National Society for the Preservation of Covered Bridges, Richard Sanders Allen Collection.

I.54 Lewis Wernwag's "Colossus," opened in 1813, was a remarkable double-lane bridge with two sidewalks and a span of 104 meters (340 feet). It was set afire by arsonists in 1843 and destroyed in twenty minutes. Source: Yale University Art Gallery.

While it is true that builders of modest bridges used both kingpost and queenpost trusses similar to those of Europe, there is no known direct connection to Europe, these trusses being fundamental designs also universally used in roof building. Over time, American builders created, and usually patented, numerous designs associated with their names. Among them were the Town lattice of Ithiel Town (1784–1844), the Long truss of Stephen H. Long (1784–1864), the Howe truss of William Howe (1803–52), the Paddleford truss of Peter Paddleford (1785–1859), and the Smith truss of Robert W. Smith (1833–98). Where European bridge trusses are difficult to name because they tend to be idiosyncratic, American designs were more standardized, especially the 1846 Howe truss, which came to be used in tens of thousands of bridges, both highway and rail, covered and uncovered. Howe's truss also

became standard in the Canadian province of New Brunswick after 1900, and Town's lattice was the standard truss used by the highway department of another Canadian province, Quebec, from the nineteenth until the mid-twentieth century. Similarly, Howe's truss was standard with bridge builders in the states of Oregon and Washington until the 1950s. In addition to creating patented designs, American builders routinely built spans of 61–76 meters (200–250 feet), even for railroads.

By the mid-nineteenth century, European builders, now more and more trained formally, began studying American designs and saw their efficiency relative to the heavily timbered European designs, as well as their ability to span significantly greater distances. Two American trusses were widely adapted, especially in Switzerland and Austria: Town's lattice and Howe's wood and iron combination. However, the majority of European builders using a Howe design chose his 1840 "double-web" patent over the simpler "single-web" design used almost universally in the United States and Canada. Since Howe's double-web patent was rarely used in American bridges, and probably only on rail lines, students of American bridges have never seen the double-web design in an actual bridge unless they have traveled to Europe. In cases where European engineers borrowed the more common Howe truss, they usually modified it, adding wooden verticals along with iron rods at certain points and using large-scale wooden angle blocks instead of the iron ones used in America.

I.55 William Howe's 1846 patent also included an arch, but the Harpersfield Bridge in Ashtabula County, Ohio, built in 1868, shows the typical Howe truss found all over the United States. Source: TEM, 2015.

I.56 Europeans preferred William Howe's 1840 patent, a "double-web" design, over the simpler form preferred in the United States. The seven-span bridge between Sevelen, Switzerland, and Vaduz, Liechtenstein, was built in 1901 across the Rhine River. Source: TEM, 2014.

Although Europeans continued to build these two American trusses even into the twentieth century, by the end of the nineteenth century they also began designing their own modern-style trusses. Some were as basic as the American multiple kingpost, but others were more sophisticated, even reversing the diagonal braces to a pattern more commonly seen in iron and steel truss bridges. Bridges of this type became standard for many decades, including during World War II when Austria and Germany lost bridges to Allied bombers and replaced them after 1945. In Switzerland, it appears many were built by Swiss army engineers, perhaps as part of an expanded defensive road network. Some were built even later, during the Cold War, when the Swiss were also building concrete gun emplacement bunkers disguised as farm buildings throughout the country, as well as concrete barricades across the lower mountains and hills to foil Soviet tanks.

Covered bridge building has continued in Germany, Switzerland, and Austria to the present, with an increasing number of modern covered bridges of various designs built of "glulam" (glued laminated timbers). Some are trusses but others are massive laminated arches used alone, some serving heavily traveled highways. Since the large dimension timbers used in early bridges are no longer available, engineers now prefer to use glulam beams made up of layers of small timbers glued together. Whether such materials can last as long as full-cut timbers is yet unknown. Luzerne's Spreuerbrücke, with its solid beam laminated arch span, dates from around 1566.

In terms of structure, then, both European and American bridges use the same conceptual model—trusses consisting of timbers and sometimes iron rods, configured into arches and/ or triangles within a rectangular frame to support vehicles, animals, and pedestrians in crossing a body of water. But for the most part, the particulars of these trusses differ markedly between Europe and North America. As mentioned above, there is no known direct historical connection between the two timber bridge traditions.

Knowing this, it becomes easier to recognize what makes Chinese covered bridges distinct. Further, since traditional covered bridge building in China continues to this day, we understand a great deal about Chinese methods. Chinese builders, working independently of any Western influences, have evolved solutions that differ conceptually, though some are nonetheless based on the universal principles of the arch and the triangle. Describing these structures is made more challenging, at least in English, because Chinese bridges rarely use trusses. Thus, we lack ready-made English terms for phenomena that have no Western equivalents.

Among China's covered bridges are timber structures as sophisticated as those found anywhere in the world, but China's bridges also include some which are among the simplest as well—a straight beam placed on two abutments over a stream, with a deck and cover built above. Beyond these elementary structures, which can be found in most places in China, covered or open, generalizations become risky. We have identified at least four more complex patterns which, as far as covered bridges go, are exclusive to China. Some are associated with a particular geographical area and to some extent a culture group. While each will be discussed and illustrated in Part III, an introductory description of each follows.

1. Simple Beam

Beams or logs placed over a stream can be found throughout the world, including China, where they are quite common in rural areas, usually on footpaths through the fields. Only pedestrians can cross most of them, and when there are only a couple of logs, users require a good sense of balance. We have found substantially larger fully covered beam bridges in all the areas explored thus far, including Zhejiang, Fujian, Hunan, Guizhou, and Yunnan provinces. Because unsupported logs over wide waterways will soon sag, these

bridges tend to be relatively short. But in Guizhou, Guangxi, Hunan, and Chongqing we have seen large-scale beam bridges requiring logs of such size that when replacement becomes necessary finding big enough trees has become both difficult and expensive.

I.57a This simple log beam covered bridge crosses a narrow brook in northern Fujian Province. Source: ACO, 2005.

I.57b Located in Anzhou of Mianyang in Sichuan, the Jiemei ("Sisters") Covered Bridges is an inimitably beautiful pair of beam bridges that share a midstream outcrop as a pier. Source: ACO, 2006.

2. Log Cantilever

The cantilever principle involves stacking ever longer logs on each abutment, the shortest being on the bottom, with longer logs placed above in order to reduce the clear span between these extensions. That gap is completed with a straight beam. Log cantilevers are often massive structures of whole tree logs, usually left rounded. Spacers separate each layer to avoid dry rot developing. Such bridges are not common in Fujian and Zhejiang but are the predominate type found in bridges of the Dong, an ethnic minority group who refer to themselves as Kam and who occupy extensive parts of Guizhou, Guangxi, and Hunan provinces. Known as "wind-and-rain bridges" *fengyuqiao*, these massive structures, in addition to being covered with roofs, also have elaborate towers at each end and on each pier in the case of multi-span bridges.

examples. Indeed, the covered cantilevers of Yunnan had remained unknown outside their locality until 2016 when the authors first documented them and began telling their stories in English. While the shortest involves as few as two short cantilever extensions on each end, the longer ones have four or five. Many also have angle braces from below to various points on the underside as reinforcement. In addition, some of those have an independent three-piece polygonal arch/queenpost structure that reinforces the lower horizontal beam with vertical beams usually of wood but sometimes of metal. Thus far, such a combination of polygonal arch with cantilever has only been seen in eight bridges in Yunnan. In a limited way, then, these eight bridges, at least in part, do have a basic truss as understood in the West.

I.59 The Caifeng Bridge in Yunlong County, Yunnan, provides a clear example of an angled cantilever, which is also reinforced with angle braces. Source: TEM, 2016.

I.58 The Batuan Bridge, with log cantilevers atop the piers, was built in 1910 across a narrow section of the Miao Stream in the Sanjiang District of Guangxi. It is 150 meters (492 feet) long and has three pavilions on top. Source: ACO, 2005.

3. Angled Cantilever

The intricate covered interlocking cantilever bridges of Yunnan Province and points further west, as far as Tibet, Nepal, and Bhutan, were little recognized until recently and are also known widely in uncovered

4. Woven Arch

Around a hundred bridges, all in Fujian and Zhejiang provinces, are described as having a "woven arch" design. But the "arches" differ from those of the West in two ways. First, they are in segments (polygonal arches), and second, they are placed beneath the bridge and invisible to travelers passing through the bridge. Some short bridges have a single arch system, but the majority, even many short ones, have two arch systems. Each three-segment arch system consists of parallel lines of logs with intricately framed log sockets at each intersection. The two systems are, however, differentiated into two arches by varying the proportional lengths of the members of each. Thus, the two differentiated but alternating lines can be described as "woven." Such structures require stable foundations, either natural rock faces or heavy stone blocks, because the woven arches only retain their strength by being solidly compressed into the foundations.

If the reason for covering bridges in Europe and North America was to protect the trusses and other structural parts, then why cover Chinese bridges whose supporting structure is nearly always below the deck? Would the deck itself not provide sufficient cover? The *lang* or corridor above comprises merely posts and cross bracing for the sides and roof and is therefore seemingly redundant. It would seem an unnecessary expense if provided only for the comfort of transients. While the corridor's function as shelter for both travelers as well as for community gatherings is not insignificant, one of its functions is to provide

I.60 One of a pair of nearby woven arch covered bridges, the Beijian Bridge, Taishun, Zhejiang, rises more than 11 meters (36 feet) above the water. Source: ACO, 2005.

deadweight on the timber structure beneath. This is because the under-structure, not being a complete and rigid frame, is inherently unstable and vulnerable to both water and wind, which could lift it. Since the under-structure is held together by gravity, were it lifted it would fall into pieces. This is especially true of the log cantilever bridges, since the stack of logs or squared beams is unstable, without significant weight keeping the logs together. The Dong, however, took this necessity and turned it into an architectural distinction, building impressive towers on the abutments and piers that resemble their world-renowned "drum towers."

Bragging Rights: Which Is the "Longest" Bridge?

No one doubts that the first covered bridge over the Susquehanna River between Columbia and Wrightsville, Pennsylvania, built three times, in 1814–32, 1834–63, and 1868–96, and 1,730 meters (5,690 feet) in length, was the "longest covered bridge [ever built] in the world," but this crossing is long gone, leaving the competition to bridges of far more modest dimensions. Hartland, New Brunswick, Canada, has long claimed "the longest in the world," its seven-span bridge being 391 meters (1,282 feet) long. Europe's longest bridge is a six-span crossing between Bad Säckingem, Germany, and Stein, Switzerland, measuring 204 meters (668 feet). Beyond these undisputed claims, however, are three ongoing battles over "longest in the United States," "longest historical in the United States," and "longest in Canada."

The "longest" in the United States is the Smolen-Gulf Bridge, measuring 187 meters (613 feet), in Ashtabula County, Ohio, but it was built in 2008 of modern materials and is therefore not "historical." "Longest historical," however, is in dispute between the bridge over the Connecticut River between Cornish, New Hampshire, and Windsor, Vermont, and another over the White River's East Fork near Medora, Indiana. Most sources list Cornish-Windsor at 137 meters (449 feet) and Medora at 132 meters (434 feet), giving the former a clear edge, but Medora's defenders insist that by measuring only the clear spans gives Medora the trophy. In the Canadian province of Quebec, a debate rages between the Perrault Bridge (151 meters/495 feet) and the Marchand Bridge (152 meters/499 feet). As with the American debate, the dispute centers on what is measured, since the Town lattice truss in the Marchand bridge partially projects past the end of the floor, which is also true of Cornish-Windsor. Those favoring Medora and Perrault refuse to include these overhanging truss extensions.

A new debate has begun over "longest in the world," this new challenge coming from Zhuoshui, China, a small town in the mountainous eastern region of Chongqing Municipality and south of the county town of Qianjiang. Though there are claims regarding an earlier historical bridge, we can only

I.61 Canada's Hartland (New Brunswick) Covered Bridge is today the longest surviving covered bridge in North America. First built as an open bridge in 1901, it was not until 1919 when the trusses were deteriorating that it was covered. Source: ACO, 2012.

document a bridge built in the 1980s consisting of a wooden pedestrian "corridor" on a reinforced concrete base. After the wooden portion burned in 2013 and was rebuilt, officials decided to extend the original part, which is 310 meters (1,017 feet) long, with new construction, adding another 348 meters (1,142 feet) for a total length of 658 meters (2,159 feet), making it the new "longest covered bridge in the world." Considering that North Americans define an "authentic" bridge as being of wood and having a truss, neither of these being true of Zhuoshui's mighty passage, it is doubtful that anyone outside China will accept this new claim.

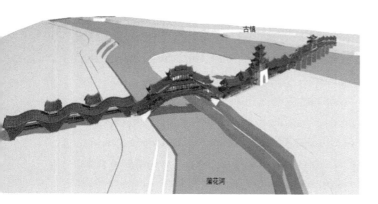

I.62 Schematic model of the Zhuoshui Wind-and-Rain Bridge, which is discussed further as an Exemplary Bridge in Part III. Source: Publicity flyer.

Social Features of Covered Bridges

Even though covered bridges in all areas under study were built both within cities as well as in isolated and desolate areas of the countryside, it is worth noting some of the social and environmental peculiarities of each area. Limiting this discussion to the remaining bridges runs the risk of ignoring important contexts common in the past but no longer observable because of changing demands. Thus, we also take into consideration the evidence seen in historical photographs, paintings, and descriptions.

Earlier, the discrepancy between the modern stereotype of covered bridges signifying the simplicity of rural life and the historical reality was

pointed out. Covered bridges in North America and Europe originated in cities because cities were typically founded in valleys along rivers and commerce was centered within these relatively densely populated areas. Over time, as commercial activity increased and spread, new road networks connecting population centers required bridges to be built in outlying areas. Eventually, this included isolated roads and bridges, some even built into the Swiss, Italian, and Austrian Alps, in the American Appalachians, and in the vast farmlands of America's Midwest. In Europe, a great many bridges located within urban settings were ultimately preserved because new bridges were built nearby to take the strain off the old ones, now seen as part of the architectural heritage. In the United States, however, most bridges in urban and industrial contexts, as well as the great multi-span bridges crossing the major rivers, were lost to floods or tornadoes, or were replaced as they wore out, or became inadequate to increasing demands. As a consequence, most remaining bridges are indeed located in small towns, villages, or rural settings.

In both Europe and North America, bridges were often associated with industrial facilities and commercial centers in urban areas and water-powered grist mills in more rural settings. Most that were built in congested areas of the United States had two lanes separated by a third truss. These are commonly known as "double-barrel" bridges. Double-lane bridges were little known in Europe, however. Both residents and businesses

I.64 "A View of Fairmount and the Water-Works, c. 1837" (watercolor, pencil, and gouache) was painted by John Rubens Smith from the perspective of a hotel veranda looking towards Wernwag's monumental "Colossus." It clearly shows the bridge within the context of human life at the time in a city that was still quite compact. Source: Bridgemen Art Library.

I.63 Baden, Switzerland's Limmatbrücke, built in 1809, sits in the middle of the old city but now carries only pedestrians. Source: TEM, 2014.

benefited because bridges allowed customers from both sides of the river access to homes, mills, stores, taverns, and factories. In the United States, because urban bridges were usually built by private companies for profit, users were required to pay tolls that varied widely for pedestrians, a horse and rider, a light buggy, a heavy wagon pulled by a team, herds of cattle charged "per head," and funeral or wedding processions. These bridges had toll booths at one end, often attached to a home for the toll keeper. In addition, the bridge's entrance could be blocked by a movable turnstile. Because urban bridges carried heavy traffic, including pedestrians, they also became bulletin boards for political and commercial advertising, along with official warnings of load limits or the requirement to "pass no faster than a walk." Violators risked having to pay a fine. Sometimes, bridges were nearly covered with advertisements for stores and products, perhaps the first billboards to appear in the United States.

It was not unusual for prominent urban bridges also to have ostentatious entries framing the

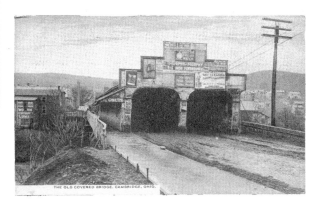

I.65 The portals of this covered bridge over Wills Creek in Cambridge, Ohio, c. 1915, are covered with advertisements for local businesses. Source: TEM Collection.

portals. In the United States, bridges having heavy pedestrian traffic also had covered walkways on one or both sides or, less commonly, between the two lanes. In a few cases, a canal running along one riverbank had to cross to the other using the bridge, requiring the addition of a towpath on the bridge's side for the horses pulling the boats.

As noted earlier under the function of covered bridges, there were numerous covered bridges built on American rail lines, the majority being "through" bridges and a minority "deck" bridges. Most were reserved for trains alone, but in a few cases, such as the second mile-long Columbia-Wrightsville Bridge over Pennsylvania's Susquehanna River, built in 1834 and modified as needs changed, trains, vehicular traffic, a canal towpath, and pedestrians shared the bridge. Covered "through" rail bridges are unknown in Europe, but there were at least a few semi-covered "deck" bridges. One such structure remains preserved in Kempton-St. Mang, Germany. A great many uncovered wooden rail bridges were also built in Europe, particularly in Russia and Scandinavia, often under the supervision of American engineers. Thus, in the United States, covered rail bridges were a normal part of the environment, but being located on rail lines often having no relationship to a road, many would have been difficult to reach. Some of the few remaining covered rail bridges require a substantial hike on the old railbed. Fortunately, many railbeds have been converted into bicycle and walking trails, especially important because walking through such a bridge on the ties/sleepers alone is risky.

Covered bridges in China have entirely different social relationships primarily because,

unlike European and American bridges, they were constructed for foot traffic rather than vehicles. Vehicular bridges prioritize traffic even when pedestrians also use them. Western bridges sometimes have separate walkways attached to the sides, but these are exceptions. Obviously, this is unnecessary in China because covered bridges are covered walkways. Since they have been carrying the same kinds of loads for hundreds of years, the kinds of loads they were designed for, they have not become obsolete. Besides serving foot traffic, they also provide other fortuitous benefits stemming from their location and design. Being covered, bridges in China provide shelter for the people using them. Whether they are on an isolated mountain path a great distance from any village or serve within a town surrounded by buildings, they offer shelter to travelers from rain, snow and, at least on the trails, the vulnerability of night-time danger. The "corridors" consist of evenly spaced bays (*jian*) defined by vertical posts on each side, with overhead cross bracing supporting the roof, often made quite heavy by a ceramic tile covering. Most bridges include either benches or narrow planks within the side structure suitable for anything from resting or eating a picnic lunch, to stretching out for a nap or even for passing the night. In a few unusual situations, we saw evidence of homeless people living in bridges. We have seen bridges located within a large town having been converted into a community center, complete with lighting and tables and chairs, as well as snack and smoke shops, often full of local residents smoking, playing games, eating, or just conversing with friends.

The social feature of Chinese bridges that most sets them apart from European and American

I.66 Erected in 1825, New York State's Hyde Hall Bridge is now the oldest surviving covered bridge in North America. Builder Cyrenus Clark used a modest Burr truss with X panels and a low arch for this private crossing, which is now part of Glimmerglass State Park. Photo is c. 1883. Source: Todd Clark Collection.

I.67 The Qiaozhai Bridge in Pingjia Village, Guizhou Province, first built in 1888 and rebuilt in 1982 following a flood, provides social space for local farmers, members of the Dong minority, to socialize during the growing season. Source: TEM, 2017.

bridges is their association with religion. Though American bridges have no known association with spiritual matters, other than perhaps ghost stories, some European bridges do have small religious shrines mounted inside. These include glass-covered shrines to a particular saint, the most likely being John of Nepomuk, a Bohemian saint who drowned in the Vitava River and is now seen as a patron against drownings, floods, and similar catastrophes, or merely a glass-encased crucifix. Whether these were placed there by individuals or nearby congregations is not known.

Chinese bridges in the eastern and southwestern provinces traditionally had prominent and some-times quite large shrines midpoint in the bridge on one or both sides. Many of these were destroyed, most recently during the Cultural Revolution, but a surprising number are still evident today and in active use, a subject to be discussed Part II.2. Such shrines house statues of various deities and other religious figures, some connected to Buddhism and Daoism, but many honoring local figures deemed to have spiritual powers. While a few shrines retain active incense burners—and we have seen burning incense in some—most bridges now post signs prohibiting the burning of any religious objects, including incense, spirit money, and paper representations of objects, because of the fire hazard. To replace such hazards in the interior of a covered bridge, it is now common to see a separate shrine outside the bridge for this activity.

There is an old saying in China: "Wherever there is a bridge, there is a temple; wherever there is a temple, there is a bridge." Though this is rarely

I.68 The Silvretta Bridge near Gortipohl in western Austria includes a relatively elaborate Roman Catholic shrine despite serving a public road. Source: TEM, 2015.

true for isolated bridges in the mountains, it is often the case for bridges located in or near villages and towns. Some temples are merely nearby, but many are located next to the bridge and are associated with it. When this is so, the shrine inside the bridge is either modest or eliminated entirely in deference to that in the temple. Temples also typically include a stage for the performance of local opera (*xiju*) or narrative singing (*shuochang*). Since the opera is intended to entertain the chief deity of the temple on his/her birthday, it is only incidentally intended for human viewers, and thus there are no provisions for seating an audience. Instead, those watching stand around or go into the balconies usually found on both sides, accessed by steps. If there is no space just offstage for the musicians, they may play from one of these side balconies. The topic of folk religion in relationship to covered bridges is explored further in Part II.2.

Issues Surrounding the Terms "Authentic" and "Historical"

We are unaware of any current debates in Europe or China regarding questions of the "authenticity" or "historical integrity" of covered bridges, but such discussions are increasingly prominent and contentious in the United States. This was not always so, and they have only come to the fore since about 1980. The building and rebuilding of covered bridges have been continuous traditions in Europe and China, but in the United States and Canada there are rough cut-off years for their obsolescence depending on the area. Covered bridges were no longer built routinely after about 1920 in most of the eastern and southern states, after about 1930 in Indiana, after the late 1950s in the northwest, and after about 1965 in Quebec and New Brunswick, Canada. In the eastern, southern, and midwestern states, they came to be viewed increasingly as obsolete and obstacles to progress and modern life after World War II, and their replacement with "modern" bridges was a high priority for most public officials. Government

I.69 Two local women pay respect to the local deities enshrined in the Feiyun Bridge in Houdon Village, Shouning County, Fujian. Source: TEM, 2007.

officials, impatient for a new bridge, allowed old timber bridges to deteriorate by providing no maintenance, even stripping them of siding or roof, and sometimes burning them because of liability issues. Citizens, indeed, sometimes took matters into their own hands by burning the offending covered bridge to force the issue. The recognition that covered bridges have historical value or demonstrate the creativity and accomplishments of past generations did not become part of national thinking until the end of the twentieth century. Before that, only a few isolated individuals championed the preservation of covered bridges. The most important one was Richard Sanders Allen, who founded the National Society for the Preservation of Covered Bridges in 1949. Members, however, faced intense skepticism from both officials and the general public as they sought to keep these "historical landmarks" safe from extermination.

Following the loss of thousands of old bridges in the United States, a new awareness of their value only gradually crept into the public discourse. While this led to the preservation of many bridges, the long-standing problems of flooding, tornadoes, overloaded trucks, and arsonists continued to

plague the covered bridge world. Additionally, most surviving bridges were now more than a hundred years old, and while they had been designed to carry loads equivalent to those of most modern vehicles, the wear and tear of weather, time and use had caused serious deterioration, and many were so compromised as to be unsafe for school buses, ambulances, fire trucks, and modern farm equipment. Government officials and public engineers, now being inclined to "preserving" covered bridges, began to "restore," "refurbish," "rebuild," "overhaul," or "renovate" bridges. But the actions taken under these terms ran the gamut from replacing only a limited number of worn and ephemeral parts such as siding, roofing, and flooring to complete replacement in which the original bridge was destroyed and an entirely new copy, or near copy, was built using modern construction methods. In some cases, signage or historical markers continue to proclaim that the bridge was built in 18xx when, in fact, there is little or no material from that time.

At the present time, there is much tension between "timber framers" at one end of the spectrum and modern "professional engineers" at the other. Timber framers seek to maintain the historical integrity of a bridge, replacing only what is necessary and doing so even using tools, materials, and processes identical to those of the original builder. At the other extreme, university-educated structural engineers are accused of sacrificing historical integrity for modern efficiency and safety. Officials charged with safeguarding both public safety while exercising fiscal restraint, tend to choose the solution that is least expensive, and that is more often than not a modern choice in materials, fasteners, and methods. Professional engineers, having little or no training in historical building methods or structures, do what they were trained to do. When deciding which timbers are no longer serviceable, they apply strict industry standards which err on the side of skepticism: "If in doubt, replace." Today in the United States, we are

faced with an increasing number of "refurbished" bridges retaining only a percentage of original materials, varying from perhaps 70 percent to as little as 20 percent, or even less. And so the debate rages over whether a bridge consisting of, say, only 40 per cent original materials is "historical" or not. The loss of original materials also means the loss of all evidence of how the original builders worked, down to such details as saw and adze markings, builders' marks in the timbers that helped them match parts, and original hardware. As a result, there is general disagreement among bridge historians, aficionados, restorers, and engineers over how to restore a covered bridge and whether to consider it historical or not.

Arguments over which bridges are "authentic" are equally thorny. The issue of authenticity arose because of a trend that started around the middle

I.70 The Thomas Mill Bridge in Indiana County, Pennsylvania, was originally built in 1879, but although still serviceable it was torn down and replaced with a replica in 1998. Source: TEM, 2007.

of the twentieth century of building completely new covered bridges, usually in parks, at private homes, but even on public roads, that superficially resembled the historical types but were either steel and concrete bridges underneath with a wooden cover or sometimes all-wood designs using modern trusses constructed variously of either glulam wood, metal, or a combination. Even the least significant of them, some being little more than small-scale backyard decorations, came to dominate the main covered bridge periodical, *Covered Bridge Topics*, in the 1960s and 1970s, and this sparked an increasingly heated debate over whether these were "authentic" covered bridges and should be given official numbers in the *World Guide to Covered Bridges* that suggested equivalency to genuinely historical structures having an identifiable truss. Various compromises over the years reduced the tension through an agreement to differentiate "authentic bridges," that is, ones that have a working truss, from "romantic shelters," since most were built simply to look like covered bridges and meant to be nostalgic symbols of a supposed simple and bucolic past.

Beyond these otherwise innocuous bridges found over wide areas of the United States, engineers have also constructed modern full-size covered bridges capable of carrying all manner of vehicles, including large trucks. Although a few were built as early as the 1950s, the majority were constructed after 1980. Rather than being reproductions of historical bridges, they are reconceived to use modern engineered trusses and materials, the roof and siding being the only justification for calling them "covered bridges." Most are on public roads and were built with public funds. Milton Graton of New Hampshire, dubbed "the last of the covered bridge builders," and his son Arnold designed and built many such bridges, the most spectacular being the 73-meter (239-foot) oversized Zehnder's Bridge built in 1980 in Frankenmuth, Michigan. Ohio engineer John Smolen is now the leading designer of such bridges, his Smolen-Gulf Bridge near Ashtabula, Ohio, being 187 meters (613 feet) in length and capable of supporting the heaviest transport permitted. It also has the distinction of being the "longest covered bridge in the United States" but

not the "longest historical bridge." Nonetheless, if being supported by a working truss defines "authentic," then Smolen's mighty crossing is indeed authentic, but obviously not "historical."

In many ways, the American conundrum regarding these bridges is confounded by the European attitude, since there has been a nearly

continuous tradition of building such bridges. A surprising percentage of bridges in Germany, Switzerland, and Austria were built from the 1940s on, including to the present day. The newer European bridges are mostly of two types: modest structures, some for vehicles, some for pedestrians only, using an all-wood truss such as kingpost,

queenpost, or multiple kingpost; and large-scale bridges using "modern" truss designs or massive laminated arches. Many observers in the United States, by contrast, distinguish between building covered wooden bridges purely as a practical matter, still normal in Europe and China, from building them self-consciously, often to attract

tourists and invoke notions of that allegedly romantic past. In the case of old bridges, however, Europeans have also been more careful to maintain their historical integrity without resorting to wholesale reproduction. Lacking covered bridge societies and thousands of bridge enthusiasts as is the case in North America, Europe and China have apparently been spared debates like those in the United States.

China has begun treading a path between these extremes. There is general agreement that covered bridge building is a living, continuing tradition. Woven arch bridges continue to be constructed in the traditional manner in several eastern provinces, while the Dong, Miao, and Tujia ethnic minorities in the south and southwest continue building *fengyuqiao* "wind-and-rain bridges" along with other "traditional" structures, such as homes and drum towers. But two factors are having a growing influence on this tradition. First, an increasing number of ethnic minority villages are being developed for tourism, and part of the attraction is having exotic-looking structures. In Dong, Miao, and Tujia villages and towns, bridges are among the most distinctive structures, and there is a trend to turn many otherwise uncovered bridges built for vehicles using modern materials like prestressed concrete into covered ones by adding a traditional wooden corridor above. In late July 2018 in Langgan Village, Tonglu County, Hangzhou City, Zhejiang Province, the corridor gallery of such a combination bridge was blown off its base by winds of up to 88 kilometers (55 miles) per hour killing eight people who had taken shelter within.

This trend also intersects with the second issue, which is the decreasing availability of the large sized logs necessary for both beam and cantilever bridges. Thus, it is far more economical to recreate bridges, whether replacements or new, using reinforced concrete bases. When the great bridge in Zhuoshui Village, Qianjiang County, Chongqing, evidently having been built about 1980, burned in 2013, only the cover was lost because it was built

I.72 A Dong-style corridor under construction on a stone arch road bridge near Liping, Guizhou Province. Source: TEM, 2017.

on a concrete base. Its replacement, which was completed in 2017, extends the original bridge into the distant fields.

In 2009, UNESCO inscribed the traditional design and practices for building Chinese wooden arch bridges as Intangible Cultural Heritage in Need of Urgent Safeguarding. Emphasizing both the carpentry as well as the small number of living carpenters, this inscription brought to the fore the craftsmanship that continues to be passed on orally and through personal demonstration from one generation to another. This successful designation put an international spotlight on covered bridges as important components of China's architectural heritage. Such an inscription also spurred the continuing identification and support of elderly craftsmen, the establishment of apprenticeship programs, investment in preservation and restoration activities, the collection of historical records, the creation of a digital database, the opening of exhibition spaces, and, importantly,

nurturing a continuing series of international covered bridge symposiums open to specialists as well as the public. At the time of writing, an application that focuses on the bridges themselves is competing against a large number of other applications from within China, which already has a list of 61 sites on its Tentative List of worthy applications, some of which have languished since 1996. Still, without a doubt, China's *langqiao* have become widely known now not only in China but even beyond China.

As with other features of the cultural landscape, Chinese covered bridges increasingly have come to be seen, as in the United States and Canada, as having the potential to attract tourists to the regions that have them in significant numbers. In counties where covered bridge tourism has become important, such as Zhejiang's Qingyuan and Taishun counties, new covered bridges supplement the historical ones. Some of these are traditional in design, others are modified, such as the new three-span bridge in the middle of Qingyuan City. Indeed, Qingyuan and Taishun now boast large and elegant museums dedicated to China's tradition of covered bridges. Elsewhere in China, however, as mentioned above, there is a trend to add wooden covers—"corridors"— over otherwise modern concrete and steel bridges. Arguments against seeing these as "authentic" run afoul of the long tradition of building wooden corridors over stone arch bridges. Thus far, there is only limited discussion in China over how to respond to such new and transparently untraditional bridges.

Conclusions

From an outsider's view, the covered bridges of all three regions—Europe, North America, and China—are similar enough to be recognizable as a single genre. There are fundamental distinctions, however, both structurally and functionally. Understanding these differences requires a closer examination of real specimens than photographs alone can provide. Building historians, architects, restoration specialists, and engineers will more likely focus on differences in design and construction. Here there is much to marvel over since the bridges in each region reflect the individual solutions that evolved. All three areas conceptualized the problems and solutions differently, all long before the science of engineering systematized bridge engineering. The early builders depended on intuition, trial and error, and knowledge transferred from similar experiences, such as house and church building, to solve the challenge of crossing streams and rivers safely and efficiently.

Humanists, including historians, folklorists, cultural geographers, and sociologists, will likely emphasize differences in function, context and relationships to the local community. Even if one pays little attention to structural distinctions, there is an array of non-structural matters that make each area unique. These differences will be immediately apparent to people visiting each area. In North America and Europe, unless one is visiting a bridge moved to a park, or bypassed, or a footbridge, one must be careful of vehicle traffic. Wearing dark colored clothes and walking through a darkened interior with cars and trucks passing closely by is clearly dangerous. Visiting Chinese bridges is safer without vehicles, though a few bridges, particularly in southwestern China, have an extremely steep arch made more treacherous by the addition of blocks on the floor that help animals navigate and avoid slipping. The presence of shrines on Chinese bridges introduces an entirely different dimension that might include active worship, festivals, and related customs.

Photographers and casual visitors can take in the whole as well as the details. Many, but not all, bridges may be surrounded by scenery or buildings that may be equally interesting, especially in China and Europe. In North America, a bright red bridge nestled in the green countryside near a white wooden church under a solid blue sky is irresistible to anyone, whether peering through a camera or not. If the bridge is in a safe, quiet place, it might offer an environment for a picnic, shelter from a thunderstorm, a unique site for wedding photographs, or relief from the midday sun. And while some bridges of the past were closely associated with industry, urban environments, and heavy traffic, most that survive do indeed offer connections to the past, however romanticized. They are humanly created objects open to multiple interpretations depending on one's background, interests, and attention.

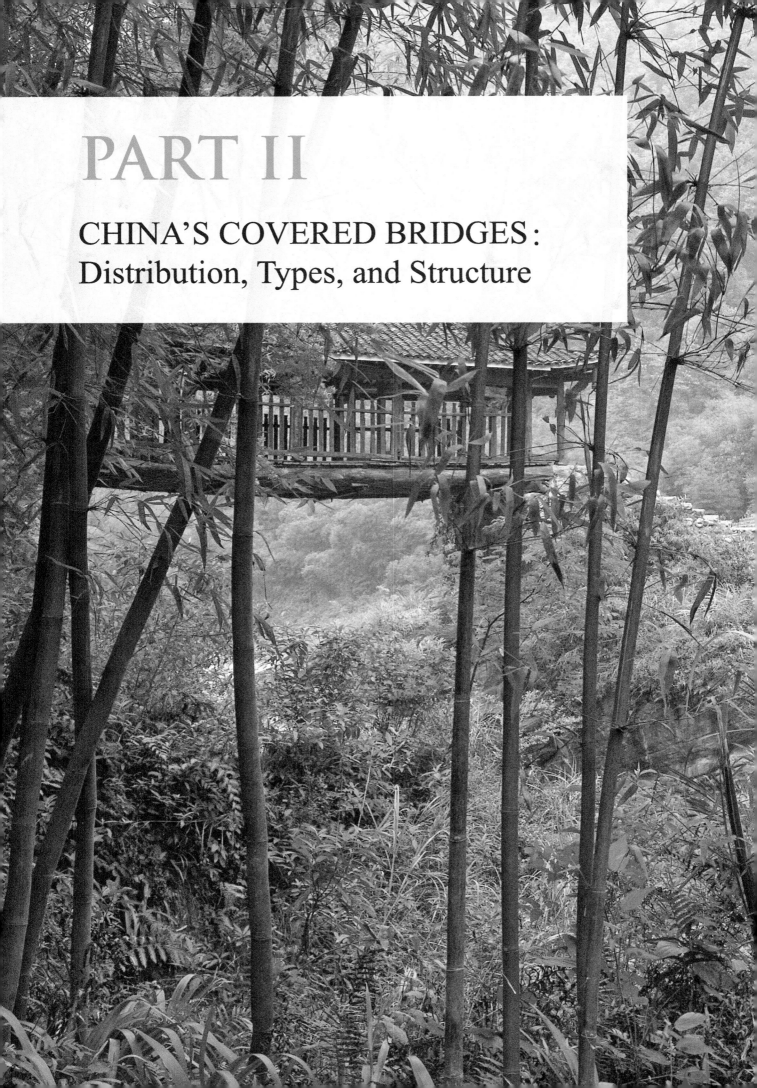

PART II

CHINA'S COVERED BRIDGES:
Distribution, Types, and Structure

Pavilion Bridges and Corridor Bridges

Having glimpsed examples of various types of covered bridges in Part I, we now outline the range of types, their distribution in China, as well as their structural properties. Covered bridges vary in size from very small structures across a narrow stream to extremely long structures that rise high across a deep gorge. Some are made of stone or wood that have a pavilion on top. Others have a long corridor usually constructed of wood atop either a masonry or timber substructure. While some function essentially as a crossing, most are also lined with benches where villagers or transients can rest. Depending on the area, covered bridges often have a religious shrine inside midway across the bridge. Others have a temple or shrine at one end of the bridge. Many are as stunningly beautiful as they are structurally complex.

The most common Chinese term employed for covered bridges is *langqiao*, which can be translated as "corridor bridge." *Lang* itself is a common architectural term to describe a veranda, walkway, gallery, colonnade, and even porch.

While each of these terms applies to a wooden structure that is usually attached to a larger building, they all denote a covered passageway, and it is this notion that is most appropriate in its use to describe a type of bridge. Indeed, for the most part, the "covers" on most *lang* are constructed of wood in much the same manner as *lang* found associated with a temple, house, or garden. While the walls on some *langqiao* are composed of bricks and then capped with a clay tiled roof, the interior framework supporting the roof is always timber construction. In south-central China, in areas dominated by ethnic minority groups, a distinctive type of *langqiao* has the evocative name "wind-and-rain bridges" *fengyuqiao*. In some areas, they are also called "wind-and-rain corridor bridges" *fengyu lang/huaqiao* or "flowery bridges" *huaqiao*, underscoring their comparative elaborateness. In times past, the regional use of these terms was reasonably clear but today, with the construction of countless covered bridges of many styles throughout the country, the descriptive terms are employed rather indiscriminately.

A distinct type of covered bridge, whose purpose is more a place to tarry than to cross, is referred to as a "pavilion bridge" *tingqiao*. *Tingqiao*

II.1.1 Although not a bridge, this "corridor" (Chinese, *lang*) seen at the Prince Gong's Mansion in Beijing and dating from the Qing Dynasty (1644–1911), exemplifies the type of building also placed on bridge structures. Source: TEM, 2005.

Previous spread Jiemei Bridge, Anzhou District, Sichuan. Source: ACO, 2006.
Left The Santiao Bridge spans an impressive gorge on the border between Zhouling and Yangxi townships in Taishun County, Zhejiang. Source: TEM, 2013.

in many ways are the overwater equivalent of *liangting* or simply *tingzi*, free-standing pleasure pavilions commonly found within imperial and literati gardens. Such structures are usually open without walls with seating along the sides or around a central table. Fine examples are found in the literati gardens of Suzhou, as well as along the Su Causeway in historic Hangzhou. In some cases, as with Yangzhou's famed Wuting Bridge, five pavilions are assembled together to form a large *tingqiao* within Slender West Lake. Chinese emperors who made excursions to the Jiangnan region made efforts to recreate in their imperial enclaves in the north architectural elements they encountered in the south. For example, in Beijing's Yihe Yuan, also called the Summer Palace, which is viewed as an ensemble masterpiece of Chinese landscape garden design, five of the six bridges along the Western Embankment are elegant pavilion bridges crafted to resemble those found along West Lake in Hangzhou. Within the imperial Bishushanzhuang Mountain Resort at Chengde, three pavilion bridges are aligned along Shuixinxie ("Pavilions in the Heart of the Waters"). Modeled after wooden ones, *tingqiao* constructed with stone columns and balustrades are called *shiting* and have existed since the Tang Dynasty (618–907). A significant example is the square-shaped commemorative Taiji Pavilion Bridge in Tengchong, Yunnan, which provides a prospect for enjoying a waterfall.

Although less refined, structures similar to pavilion bridges are found along countryside paths where they are called *luting*, offering shelter for villagers as they travel between their homes and fields. In addition, many *fengyuqiao* wind-and-rain bridges, as can be seen throughout this book, incorporate pavilions methodically along their axes. In these cases, the multi-tiered roofs of the pavilions make an architectural statement that goes without amplifying any specific internal use of the pavilion space.

II.1.2 A rural pathside *luting*, sometimes called a *liangting*, for the use of villagers in southern Zhejiang Province. Source: RGK, 1987.

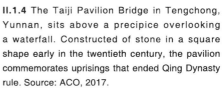

II.1.4 The Taiji Pavilion Bridge in Tengchong, Yunnan, sits above a precipice overlooking a waterfall. Constructed of stone in a square shape early in the twentieth century, the pavilion commemorates uprisings that ended Qing Dynasty rule. Source: ACO, 2017.

II.1.3a, b Although the stone bases differ, these two majestic pavilion bridges with their double-tiered roofline are quite similar. (a) Yudai Bridge along the Su Causeway in Hangzhou's West Lake. (b) Binfeng Bridge, one of six bridges along the causeway in Beijing's Yihe Yuan that separates two sections of Kunming Lake. Source: ACO, 2006; ACO, 2006.

Distribution of China's Covered Bridges

It is likely that covered bridges once were found in many areas of China beyond those known today. Yet, even as a large number have been lost without having been recorded, current fieldwork and textual sources help in identifying seven major regions of concentration. These concentrations, which are based on extensive clusters of similar types, are listed in the table below where it is clear that some regions cross provincial boundaries. Within regions, there is a remarkable similarity in the structural principles of the covered bridges, but in others there is heterogeneity. Some are pavilion-type covered bridges in gardens or parks, some are old and others new, and many are true covered bridges in that a shelter runs their full length. The final portion of this book identifies the environmental, cultural, and economic significance of most of these seven regions. Exemplary covered bridges are spotlighted in Part III.

> **II.1.5** Most of the 3,000 covered bridges still standing in China are concentrated within these seven regions:
>
> 1. Northern Fujian and Southern Zhejiang
> 2. Southern Fujian, Southern Jiangxi, and Northern Guangdong
> 3. Guangxi and Guizhou
> 4. Hunan, Hubei, and the Municipality of Chongqing
> 5. Yunnan and Sichuan
> 6. Hebei and Shanxi
> 7. Gansu, Qinghai, and Eastern Tibet

1. Northern Fujian and Southern Zhejiang

Covered bridges here are found principally in the rugged mountainous counties of the interior, and there are at least a hundred using a design particular to these provinces, the "woven arch" pattern. This distinguishes them from other areas where this pattern is little known. Some bridges are wooden structures on an arched masonry base.

II.1.6 The Qiancheng Bridge in Tangkou Village, Pingnan County, Fujian, some 63 meters (206 feet) long in two spans, exemplifies the "woven arch" designs distinctive to the northern Fujian/ Southern Zhejiang area. Source: TEM, 2005.

II.1.7 Situated on a path well below the newer road above, the Banluting Bridge in Zhongjii Village, Qingyuan County, Zhejiang, is made even more attractive by the small dam below. Source: TEM, 2011.

2. Southern Fujian, Southern Jiangxi, and Northern Guangdong

Although fewer covered bridges are still found today in this region, there were in the past some notably unique structures as well as a large number of fairly simple covered bridges. Most of the old common bridges in the past that served pedestrian traffic across the tributaries of larger rivers were replaced by township and county bridges to carry vehicular traffic.

II.1.8 This structure of brick and stone is the Taiping Bridge in Longnan County, southern Jiangxi, near the border with Guangdong Province. Constructed in the sixteenth century, it served as a customs facility along an important route. Source: http://www.tuniu.com/guide/v-ganzhoutaipingqiao-791002/tupian. Accessed February 19, 2019.

II.1.9 This region of steep hills and narrow valleys traditionally had many short timber beam bridges utilizing logs cut in the nearby forests. Photograph taken by John Preston Maxwell, a medical missionary in the first decade of the twentieth century. Yongchun County, Fujian. Source: Cadbury Research Library, Special Collections, University of Birmingham (DA26) and Historical Photographs of China, University of Bristol.

3. Guangxi and Guizhou

Until the later part of the twentieth century, only a handful of stone arched and simple log beam covered bridges were known in the heavily touristed area along the Li River. Later given prominence are China's most striking, even flamboyant, covered bridges, those of the Dong and Miao ethnic minority groups. With massive log cantilever structures, the bridges also feature elaborate towers over the piers and abutments that call to mind other Dong structures, especially the drum towers for which these minorities are so well-known. Less massive but striking, nonetheless, are many log beam bridges in the same area, as well as many covered stone arched structures that are now known to Chinese and foreign trekkers.

II.1.11 The missionary presence in towns and villages along the rivers of Guangxi left behind many photographs of life along and on the water. Source: Peter Lockhart Smith and Historical Photographs of China, University of Bristol.

II.1.10 This covered bridge, which spans the Li River near Guilin, sits atop a cut-stone base with four arches among the karst landscape in Guangxi Zhuang Autonomous Region, c. 1900–30. Today, it provides an entry into the Seven-Star Park. Source: Peter Lockhart Smith and Historical Photographs of China, University of Bristol.

II.1.13 Located in the remote Dong minority Pingjia Village, Guizhou, the Qiaozhai Wind-and-Rain Bridge was first built in 1885, rebuilt after a flood in 1888, and again for the same reason in 1982. Though the Dong excelled at cantilever structures, this bridge is supported solely by beams. Source: TEM, 2017.

II.1.12 The Batuan Bridge in Dundong township is unique among Dong minority covered bridges in that it has two separate corridors, one for animals and one for pedestrians. Source: ACO, 2005.

4. Hunan, Hubei, and the Municipality of Chongqing

There is very little documentation about covered bridges in this region, except for sporadic mention of small bridges, some of which held temples above them. Until the early 1990s, the older, rather modest covered bridges of the Tujia minority were unknown. Improvements in land and rail transport over the past decade have brought once remote old, yet quite substantial bridges to light and spurred as well the construction of newer, more extravagant structures in many Tujia communities.

II.1.14 Although the exact location of this structure in Hunan is not clear, the wooden structure above the stone arch is likely to have been a temple along a path between villages. Source: Peter Lockhart Smith and Historical Photographs of China, University of Bristol.

II.1.15 Constructed by the Tujia minority, the Kezhai Wind-and-Rain Bridge in Qingxichang Town, Chongqing Municipality, may date back to the Yuan Dynasty (1279–1368), although it was renovated as recently as 1952. Each of the six spans is built on simple beams, now sagging, with a stone path running through the center of the bridge. Source: TEM, 2017.

II.1.16 The Yanzi ("Swallow") Bridge, which crosses the Yi River, is one of the 29 Wind-and-Rain bridges in Anhua County, Hunan Province. Constructed first between 1736 and 1795, then reconstructed in 1822, the bridge has a cantilevered timber understructure with a 38.5-meter (126-foot) corridor above. Source: Liu Jie, 2017: 41.

5. Yunnan and Sichuan

Both Yunnan and Sichuan have a long history of frontier settlement, with extensive construction of bridges of all types as the pioneers pushed from the basins into the hills. While stone arch and suspension bridges were often recorded and sometimes photographed, only a few covered bridges were repeatedly noted. However, in recent years, the extensive distribution of covered bridges has been brought to light. Part III will present the contexts for this. In Yunnan, covered bridges are found primarily in the areas of the Bai minority in the western and northern parts of the province. These bridges are distinctive for their timber structures, which differ significantly from the masonry bases of Sichuan covered bridges. In park-like settings in rural and urban areas, new covered bridges are being constructed in both traditional forms as well as soaring styles that sometimes even include within them restaurants and other leisure time public facilities. Even an overpass across a busy street, as in Sichuan's capital Chengdu, can be transformed from a mere pedestrian crossing into a celebration of multi-tiered roofs mimicking a bridge style that never existed.

II.1.18 An unidentified covered bridge in Luoyan, Yunnan, encountered by Fritz Weiss, German Consul in Yunnan. Source: Weiss and Weiss, 2009: 244.

II.1.17 Crossing a tributary of the Yangzi River in Guanxian, Sichuan, this covered bridge is supported by both a stone and a timber pier. The palisaded siding is unique. Source: Sidney D. Gamble photographs, David M. Rubenstein Rare Book & Manuscript Library, Duke University.

II.1.19 As a component in a park-like setting along a small stream in Jinhua Township, Jianchuan County, Yunnan, the Jinlong Bridge is heavily ornamented with Bai minority nationality ornamentation. Source: ACO, 2016.

II.1.20 Though fragile looking, the Tongji Bridge in Tengchong County, Yunnan, is solidly built on a multi-level cantilever system. Source: TEM, 2016.

II.1.21a Said to have been constructed on the site of a century's old crossing as well as one lost in the 1980s, Chengdu's Anshun Bridge was constructed in 2003. The structure at night has a brilliant display of lighting. It is linked to a promenade along the banks of the Jin River. Some claim this location was the site of the covered bridge Marco Polo wrote about. Source: ACO, 2006.

II.1.21b Mirroring a covered bridge crossing a deep gorge, this pedestrian crossing in Chengdu, Sichuan, imaginatively provides a steep climb to cross a city boulevard. Source: ACO, 2006.

6. Hebei and Shanxi

These northern provinces feature both pavilion-type and generic covered bridges, all on stone bases. Hebei Province surrounds Beijing with its numerous imperial precincts that include both lakeside and bridge-like pavilions over water. Shanxi is noted for its temples and monasteries that also have pavilions atop bridges of many sizes. While small pavilions on bridges are found in monasteries and temples, an exceptional one called Qiaolou Hall is in the mountains near Shijiazhuang. This extraordinary structure is discussed in Part III. We have not been able to locate any timber or masonry-based corridor-type covered bridges in these two provinces.

II.1.22 Appearing suspended on top of the Jingxing (Qiaoloudian) Bridge in the gap between two facing cliffs of the Cangyan Mountains, the Qiaolou Hall is a major Buddhist temple outside Shijiazhuang, Hebei Province. Source: JDK, 2006.

II.1.23 One of the many timber-framed pavilion-style covered bridges with an arch structure beneath it in the Forbidden City in Beijing. Source: ACO, 2006.

7. Gansu, Qinghai, and Eastern Tibet

Historical photographs confirm the presence of many modest covered bridges in Gansu as well as on the eastern portions of the Tibetan plateau in what is today Qinghai Province, but no existing covered bridges are known in Qinghai and Tibet today. Historical photographs of covered bridges in Gansu and Qinghai are found in Part III. The covered bridges in the past employed angled cantilevers for both covered and uncovered bridges. These patterns extend beyond the Tibetan plateau into the Himalayan kingdoms of Nepal and Bhutan. Only one covered bridge completely constructed of timber is known to be still standing in relatively arid Gansu Province in northwest China. This is the Baling Bridge in Weiyuan County in eastern Gansu, which is an Exemplary Bridge discussed in more detail in Part III.

Superstructure: Masonry and Wooden Covers

Langqiao or "corridor bridges" may be differentiated by the nature of the base upon which the corridor is attached, as will be discussed in a later section, as well as by the character of the corridor itself. As even a cursory view of *langqiao* seen in this book reveals, there is great diversity in their outward appearance. This is particularly striking when compared with covered bridges in North America, which are more alike in their exterior form, the cover. The variations of external form within China are especially noticeable when viewed from region to region in terms of size and structural complexity. Indigenous customs and the ingenuity of local carpenters help explain these differences, but are not the only reasons.

II.1.24 This cantilevered covered bridge straddles a gorge between treeless areas in Qinghai and Gansu provinces. The bridge is covered with substantial entryways at each end. Photograph by Carter Holton c. 1933. Source: © President and Fellows of Harvard College.

Interior Framing Systems

The corridors of *langqiao* are appropriately referred to in Chinese as *langwu* or "gallery houses" because their structural form is essentially identical to that of common houses. This should not come as a surprise since the carpenters and the carpentry involved in both are usually the same. In examining *langwu*, it is especially useful to look both at the internal structure supporting the roof as well as the exterior walls and roof that provide the cover. Sturdy load-bearing walls are the exception in Chinese buildings, including covered bridges. Even when the exterior wall is solid, it is a non-load-bearing curtain wall that either completely encircles an interior wooden skeleton or fills the gaps between the columns or pillars that comprise the interior. An example that shows this clearly is Bei'an Bridge in Shexian County, Anhui, an Exemplary Bridge discussed further in Part III. Constructed during the Ming Dynasty (1368–1644), with solid walls of fired brick atop three stone arches with two midstream piers, the interior comprises a timber framework that supports the tiled roof. As most of the images of frameworks reveal, the interior woodwork is usually left to weather without painting. With newly constructed bridges, on the other hand, sometimes the interiors are lavishly ornamented. A good example is the Jinlong Bridge in Jianchuan County, Yunnan. Built on a concrete slab, the corridor is reminiscent of a gallery in an imperial enclave.

II.1.25 The interior of the Bei'an Bridge in Anhui Province comprises a wooden framework of eleven bays. As seen in this image, the substantial columns and beams are assembled in the *tailiang* columns-and-beams form. Source: ACO, 2006.

II.1.26 Reminiscent of a gallery in Beijing's imperial Summer Palace, this new pavilion-style covered bridge is called Jinlong ("Golden Dragon") Bridge. It is the signature structure in a park in Jinhua Town, Jianchuan County, Dali Prefecture, Yunnan. Source: ACO, 2016.

Two basic wood framework systems—columns-and-beams and pillars-and-transverse-tie beams—employed in buildings, including covered bridges, are common throughout China.

While columns-and-beams construction is widespread in northern China, it is found in southern China as well as shown in southern Anhui's Bei'an Bridge above. More common in southern China are frameworks that employ slender pillars-and-transverse-tie beams. Both of these framing systems are illustrated in Qing Dynasty (1644–1911) woodblock prints and can be seen in buildings that are much older. While the term "column" and "pillar" are usually described in Chinese using the same term, *zhu*, they are differentiated here in English in terms of "columns" being thicker and "pillars" more slender. A pair of columns typically can directly support a heavy beam without bowing under the weight. The rigidity of a set of parallel pillars sufficient to support a heavy load is only made possible because of the use of transverse-tie beams mortised-and-tenoned into the pillars. Columns-and-beams construction is referred to in Chinese as the *tailiang* framing system. In some cases, the interior framework is a mixture of *tailiang* and *chuandou* forms, as seen in the Jiezifang Bridge, Yunlong County, Yunnan.

The *chuandou*, which is the usual framing system in covered bridges and houses in southern China, differs from the *tailiang* system in three important ways: the number of vertical components is greater, yet the pillars all have a smaller diameter; each of the slender pillars is notched at the top to directly support a longitudinal roof purlin; and horizontal tie beam members, called *chuanfang*, are mortised directly into or tenoned through the pillars in order to inhibit skewing of what would otherwise be a relatively flexible frame. Smaller diameter *chuandou* pillars,

often only 20–30 centimeters (8–12 inches), are less expensive than the larger timbers required in a *tailiang* frame. Trees as young as five years can be used for purlins, *chuandou* pillars, and tie beams, while it takes at least a generation for columns and beams to mature to sufficient size for use in a *tailiang* structure. In constructing a bridge, each bent—a transverse frame comprising two pillars and a connecting beam—is assembled flat and then lifted where it is connected to an earlier positioned bent.

II.1.27 Employing a piled set of beams that support the ridge beam, this framing system also has beams slotted through the outside pairs of pillars, which is characteristic of *chuandou* structures. Jiezifang Bridge, Yunlong County, Yunnan. Source: TEM, 2016.

II.1.28 Eaves extension as part of a *chuandou* wooden framework, Xidong Bridge, Taishun, Zhejiang. Source: ACO. 2005.

II.1.29 A slender pillar-and-transverse-tie beam *chuandou* framing system in the gallery of the Yongqing Bridge, Sankui Township, Taishun County, Zhejiang. This 3-meter (10-foot)-wide bridge, which rests on a single stone pier, was constructed in 1797. Source: ACO, 2005.

II.1.30 This *chuandou* framing system was relatively new before the Xuezhai Bridge was washed away in 2016. The bridge has now been rebuilt. Taishun County, Zhejiang. Source: ACO, 2005.

II.1.32a In assembling the timber components of a *langwu* corridor, men lift up a bent—a transverse frame comprising two pillars and a connecting beam—which is then connected to the adjacent bent. Badou Township, Sanjiang, Guangxi. Source: RGK, 2007.

II.1.32b Before the ridgepole can be put in place, each of the assembled bents must be raised and secured. Tongle Bridge, Taishun County, Zhejiang. Source: XYC, 2004.

II.1.31 The narrow Yezhujing Bridge in Tengchong, Yunnan, has eleven bays across its full length. Each bent includes four pillars and a curved transverse beam supported by angle braces, which together support the ridgepole. Source: ACO, 2016.

II.1.32c Once the bents are raised, the connecting components must be tapped securely with a mallet. Tongle Bridge, Taishun County, Zhejiang. Source: XYC, 2004.

In lifting the roof of a covered bridge, the multi-tiered *chuandou* pillar-and-beams framing system is effective in controlling the elevation and even the curvature of the roof. The spacing of pillars that support purlins and the height of individual purlins define the slope of the roof. Where the relative position of the purlins remains fixed, there is a constant downward slope to the roofline, without a break. If a curved roofline is desired, the pitch is varied from one purlin to another in a regular mathematical relationship. The *chuandou* frame also provides for the flexible positioning of the eaves overhangs alongside that help shelter the sides of the corridor.

II.1.34 Two brackets beneath the crossbeam provide support for the overhanging eaves. Yuwen Bridge, Zhoubian Village, Zhouling Township, Taishun County, Zhejiang. Source: ACO, 2005.

II.1.33 Using a mallet and a spacer, these carpenters are fitting together the mortise-and-tenon joinery for a new corridor bridge. Sanjiang County, Guangxi Zhuang Autonomous Region. Source: ACO, 2006.

II.1.35 Each of the three pavilions atop this new unnamed covered bridge is multi-tiered, which involves complex carpentry. Sanjiang County, Guangxi. Source: ACO, 2006.

Many covered bridges have external wooden cladding to protect the gallery and/or the underlying timber structure even as it allows cross-ventilation. The gallery of the Wan'an Bridge in Pingnan County, Fujian, is completely open along the sides, with protection only provided by a broad overhang. Beneath the gallery, vertical boards shield the timbers supporting the bridge. The Xuezhai Bridge in Taishun County, Zhejiang, while open just beneath the eaves, as with many other covered bridges, has overlapping wooden cladding on the lower register of each side that helps protect the interior as well as the timber structure beneath. The venerable Rulong Bridge, which is considered the oldest standing covered bridge in China, dating to the end of the seventeenth century, has sides that are essentially completely covered. Only six small circular windows on each side of the board covering allow air and light to enter.

II.1.36 Vertical boards hung from the bridge beams shelter the timbers that form the structure beneath the Wan'an Bridge, Pingnan County, Fujian. Source: ACO, 2007.

Profiles and Portals

As previous photographs reveal, some covered bridges are relatively flat in profile while others soar upwards from their abutments. The entry portals to some are quite plain while others are truly grand. Many of those that are level are modest bridges constructed at grade utilizing straight timber beams from one bank's abutment to another. Others, like the Xiaohuang Bridge in Congjiang County, Guizhou, were constructed on stone arch bases that were extended as stone causeways across broad floodplains, which are farmed when water in the stream channel is low. As the accompanying covered bridge image lays bare, the profiles of covered bridges are sometimes enriched by multi-tiered towers that rise above the roofline. Usually such bridges with conspicuous above the roofline features also have striking entry portals. Some portals are constructed of bricks with only an open entry while others are much more elaborate with tiered sets of brackets utilizing both timber and glazed tiles.

II.1.37 With just an extended eaves overhang to protect those sitting on the benches in the interior, the Wan'an Bridge in Pingnan County, Fujian, only has additional siding that protects the timbers beneath. Source: ACO, 2007.

II.1.38a–c The two portals of the Rulong Bridge, which is highlighted as an Exemplary Bridge in Part III, differ significantly, one with an impressive triple-tiered, pagoda-style portal while the backside porte-cochère has a double tier. Yueshan Village, Ju Township, Qingyuan County, Zhejiang. Source: ACO 2005; Liu Jie, 2016, TEM 2011.

II.1.39 Adjacent to a temple that dates to the Song Dynasty (960–1279), the Yingjie Bridge, Jushui Township, Qingyuan County, Zhejiang, was rebuilt in 1662 and restored in 1850 to its current state. Source: ACO, 2007.

II.1.40 This timber beam bridge is supported by three midstream posts. Sanzhu Bridge, Xiawuyang Village, Sankui Township, Taishun County, Zhejiang. Source: ACO, 2005.

II.1.41 Stretching across a wide river valley, the Xiaohuang Bridge in Congjiang County, Guizhou, includes an elongated stone base as well as a single open arch for the stream to pass through. Source: TEM, 2017.

Others that are horizontal from abutment to abutment do so only because of the addition of stone steps that rise to lift the base of the flat bridge above any possibility of flooding. Historical records, indeed, reveal that the loss of a bridge due to flooding frequently led to rebuilding atop taller piers and higher abutments reachable only by the addition of a flight of stone steps. High steps also avoid the ups and downs on a multi-span bridge. Many of the wind-and-rain bridges constructed in the Dong, Miao, and Tujia areas are elevated above the river channel, with steps for villagers to climb to reach the level corridor.

II.1.42 Steep steps rise from the streamside to the arched Tongjing Bridge, Changxin Township, Yunlong County, Dali Prefecture, Yunnan. Source: ACO, 2016.

II.1.43 The free-standing embankments and piers of the Bajiang Bridge, Sanjiang Dong Nationality Autonomous Count, Guangxi. Source: ACO, 2006.

No profiles are more dramatic than the timber arch structures that rear up rather abruptly from their abutments, sometimes seeming to soar dramatically as they cross over a steep chasm or even a relatively level streambed. These are especially common in the rugged mountains of Fujian, Yunnan, and Zhejiang provinces. Local people in southern Zhejiang and adjacent areas in northern Fujian refer to these dramatically ascending types as "centipede bridges" *wugongqiao* because of their resemblance to the arch-like rise of a long arthropod's body as it crawls. These soaring bridges are all lifted by the "woven arch" framework beneath, which is discussed in detail in a later section. The Santiao Bridge, built in 1843 to straddle a rock-strewn ravine, rises some 10 meters (33 feet) above the streambed. The Beijian Bridge, built in 1674, rises even higher, some 11.22 meters (36.8 feet) above what appears here to be a sluggish watercourse passing under it. Rushing torrents of water can bring seasonal flooding, as in September 2005 when floodwaters submerged the abutments and wreaked considerable damage but failed to sweep away the bridge. In September 2016, three of Taishun counties historic bridges (Xuezhai, Wenxing, and Wenzhong) were swept away during a flash flood connected with Typhoon Meranti. In the rugged terrain of Fujian and Zhejiang, where the narrow valleys are V-shaped, the paths that must reach the optimal location for a woven arch covered bridge must either drop from a higher elevation or climb to the preferred site for the bridge. Rather than human-built abutments, these bridges often spring from rock outcrops into which the timbers are socketed, sometimes aided by piled stones to help support the timbers.

II.1.45 The underside of the soaring Santiao Bridge connecting Zhouling and Yangxi townships, Taishun County, Zhejiang. Source: ACO, 2005.

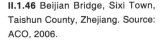

II.1.46 Beijian Bridge, Sixi Town, Taishun County, Zhejiang. Source: ACO, 2006.

Crossing some of the tributaries of the Nu (Irrawaddy) and Lancang (Mekong) rivers in western Yunnan Province are cantilevered bridges that inscribe a majestic upward sweep from bank to bank. An outstanding example is the Yezhujing Bridge, which soars at least 10 meters (33 feet) above the Longchuan River in Tengchong County. Although not as obvious, another cantilevered bridge in Yunlong County, the Tongjing (Chengde) Bridge, rises some 12.5 meters (41 feet) above the Bi River. Of course, these heights vary according to the seasonal flow of the river beneath, which suggests a practical understanding of the need to anticipate periodic flash floods that could be devastating to a critical crossing.

While these two important covered bridges are still standing, there were likely others that were equally dramatic but are no longer present for us to visit. For example, photographs of a bridge that underscores this point was celebrated on French postcards at the beginning of the twentieth century. Though facts relating to its structure and extent are not known, this bridge has been identified as the Anlan Bridge in Luliang County, eastern Yunnan Province. Ironically, its name is emblazoned above the entry with the additional characters *yongqing* "eternally celebrated," but few know that it once existed. Inside the portal, as shown in a later photograph, a signboard states *chang hong fei gua* "a long rainbow flying suspended."

II.1.47 Yezhujing Bridge, also known as the Chengde Bridge, crossing the Longchuan River, a tributary of the Nu River, in Qingqiao Village, Qushi Township, Tengchong County, Yunnan. Source: ACO, 2016.

II.1.48 The Tongjing Bridge rises some 12.5 meters (41 feet) above the Bi River and has a clear span of more than 29 meters (95 feet). Yunlong County, Yunnan. Source: ACO, 2016.

483. YUNNAN - Le Pont de Pou-I - Ensemble

23 — CHEMINS de FER du YUNNAN
Pont couvert de Pouo-Hi

II.1.49a, b The Anlan Bridge in Luliang County in eastern Yunnan had a sweeping arch-like profile and a large entry portico. Source: RGK Collection.

Just as profiles and structures differ, so do the entryways, the portals called *qiaomen* at each end of a covered bridge. Some modest covered bridges lack a formal portal, with the entry being nothing more than the truncated open end of the timber gallery. Others are essentially brick or pounded earth walls, with a gaping entrance in the middle. On the other hand, many *qiaomen* are imposing, even extravagant in their form and coloration, to the degree that they mimic the entries to temples and shrines. This, of course, reflects the fact that a vast majority of covered bridges have within them shrines of various sizes. With assurance one can say that the magnificence of the entryway correlates well with the complexity and scale of the covered bridge corridor and the shrine within. On the other hand, we have encountered a few covered bridges that have an ornate portal that leads to a rather ordinary covered bridge gallery.

Throughout the country, some entry portals are essentially a brick or adobe wall that is attached to the interior wooden framework. With an arched opening as well as a pediment above of various shapes, these openings are serviceable, economical, and without pretense, merely a façade. With fired brick walls on both sides and supported by a stone base with three arched openings, the tunnel-like entry to the Ming Dynasty (1368–1644) Bei'an Bridge is quite plain and unassuming. Only the whitewashed walls, the black tile coping, and the three-character name give it prominence. White walls and black tiles are characteristic of residences and temples throughout the Huizhou region. Solid portals of this type are found even in areas where ornate entryways are dominate.

Not seen today are elaborate *pailou*-style entryways supported by large columns that lift a tiered structure with upturned eaves, reminiscent of ceremonial gateways traditionally found straddling important streets and lanes. Two of these were photographed by Sidney Gamble in Sichuan Province between 1917 and1919. Embraced by the shops on both sides of the stone-lined lane leading to it, the entry to the Red Army Bridge in Sichuan similarly has a double-tiered form, which by comparison with most is rather plain. Connecting a

II.1.50 With contrasting white walls and black tiles, the appearance of the Bei'an Bridge is quite similar to other architectural features in the Huizhou region. Source: ACO, 2007.

II.1.52 Kezhai Bridge, Chongqing Municipality, Qingxichang Town. Source: TEM, 2017.

II.1.53 Surviving photographs from early in the twentieth century reveal that the portals of some covered bridges were much more elaborate than those seen today. Yongji Bridge, Anju Township, today's Chongqing Municipality, c. 1917. Source: Sidney D. Gamble photographs, David M. Rubenstein Rare Book & Manuscript Library, Duke University.

II.1.51 Tiansheng Wind-and-Rain Bridge, Xiushan County, Xikou Town over Rongxi Stream. Source: RGK, 2017.

market town on both sides of a stream, the bridge was traditionally called Heyi ("Combined Benefit") Bridge. Rising above the roofline is a small garret, which at one time served as a shrine with a deity. Today it is empty.

While not as dramatic as *pailou*-style portals, the upturned eaves characteristic of many covered bridges in Zhejiang and Fujian are nonetheless impressive. The 41.7-meter (137-foot)-long Xidong Bridge in Xisi Township, Taishun County, Zhejiang, which dates from 1570, has a set of asymmetric portals. One provides an open to the sides cover for the gently sloping stone steps on one end, while the other offers a covered drive-through for a roadway. The extensive elevated multiple-bay pavilion above the central portion of the bridge rises above an impressively large shrine within the corridor.

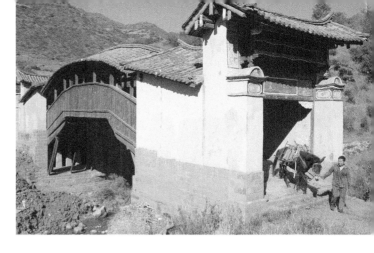

II.1.55 This is clearly a necessary crossing for villagers living in the mountains who must bring their laden mules from upland areas down to market towns in the valleys. The newly restored portal, as ornamental and imposing as it is, may be less grand than the one existing in the past. Source: ACO, 2016.

II.1.54 Although much of Anju Town in Tongliang County, Chongqing Municipality, has been restored and is well-known as one of the region's best preserved old towns, this imposing triple-tiered entry across the Fujiang River is only a memory. Source: Sidney D. Gamble photographs, David M. Rubenstein Rare Book & Manuscript Library, Duke University.

II.1.56 Clutched between the shops at its entry, the portal of the Red Army (Hongjun) Bridge in Qinglinkou Town, Sichuan Province, is completely constructed of timber period. Source: ACO, 2006.

II.1.57a, b As will be shown in Part III, both ends of the Xidong Bridge reveal similar "swallow's tail" upturned eaves even as both serve different purposes to cover those accessing the bridge. One end has a rather rarely seen porte-cochère. Source: ACO, 2005.

Among the most elaborate portals are those on covered bridges associated with ethnic minorities, especially the Dong, Miao, Bai, and Tujia, where even smaller roadside bridges have rather striking entries.

II.1.59 The back end entrance to the Dong minority Xiaohuang Bridge, Guizhou. Source: RGK, 2017.

II.1.58 Resting atop a single stone arch, this short bridge in Zhouchen Township, Binchuan County, Dali Prefecture, Yunnan, has an impressive Bai nationality-type entry with "flying eaves." Source: ACO, 2016.

II.1.60 Dibu, a short covered bridge in Liping County, Guizhou, has an impressive set of three pavilions. Source: TEM, 2017.

As some of these photographs reveal, the sheltered entry portal, whether ornate or plain, extends beyond the gallery of the covered bridge and provides cover for the steps leading to the bridge. Although appearing rather plain from a distance, the entry to the Yezhujing Bridge, also called Chengde Bridge, in Tengchong, Yunnan, has a carved multi-tiered bracket set. Although a covered bridge has been at this site since 1882, it has been rebuilt several times during the twentieth century. Since the brackets appear completely new, it is not clear whether they are true to whatever the originals were like. Similarly, the Tongjing and Yongzhen bridges, two grand bridges in Yunlong County, Yunnan, have rebuilt replacement portals. While the portals are substantial, they may not be as grand as those that once graced the bridges. Having been recognized as historically significant, the Tongjing and Yongzhen bridges, like others in western Yunnan that have been restored in recent years, have rather similar *qiaolou* constructed of adobe bricks that have been whitewashed. While each has some rather distinctive ornamentation—drawings, paintings, and carved wood—none is as spectacular as the few that were photographed early in the twentieth century.

One outstanding example of a lost bridge with two ostentatious portals is the Anlan Bridge that crossed the Nanpan River in Luliang County, east of Kunming. On one end was a double-tiered *pailou*-style portal that led to a deep entryway which ran the full length of the broad abutments, while on the other end a single-tiered elevated roof feature was supported by a stack of wooden brackets. The soaring eaves at both ends, the multiple layers of ornamented brackets, and the etched horizontal boards affirm the significance of this covered bridge. However, today this magnificent covered bridge is only recalled by a handful of images taken during the period 1904–10 that appear on hard to find French postcards in Indo-China. "Le Pont de Posi" or "Pont couvert de Pouo-Hi" is how the bridge was named on the postcards, but evidence of the lost bridge is rarely found in any Chinese publication, thus is a forgotten element of Chinese covered bridge history. This loss makes one curious about what other significant bridges vanished during the past century.

II.1.61a, b The entry portico leading to the gallery of Yezhujing Bridge is a double-sloped mortise-and-tenon structure with an intricate bracket set supporting the overhanging eaves. Source: ACO, 2017.

II.1.62 Crafted of adobe bricks and a simple roof, the portal to the Tongjing Bridge, Yunlong County, Yunnan, while functional, may not be an accurate reproduction of one that once served as the entry. Source: TEM, 2016.

YUNNAN — Entrée du Pont couvert de Pouo-Hi

II.1.64a, b Views of both portals of the Anlan Bridge that crossed the Nanpan River in Luliang County, Yunnan. On one end was a double-tiered *pailou*-style portal that led to a deep entryway running the full length of the broad abutments, while on the other end a single-tiered elevated roof feature was supported by a stack of wooden brackets. Source: RGK Collection.

Understructure:
Masonry and Timber Bases

The understructure of a *langqiao*, which supports the full weight of the corridor above, is either a masonry base or one utilizing timbers in configurations that may be ordinary or, specifically in the case of China, ingenious, utilizing not only cantilevers but also "woven arches." Masonry bridge foundations, as can be seen throughout China, have been fashioned traditionally out of rough-cut stone, river cobblestone, or fired bricks or adobe blocks fitted to fully occupy the spandrel, the space between the deck and one or more arches beneath. Sometimes the arch and spandrel are essentially the same length as the bridge, as can be seen in the small 6-meter (19.5-foot)-long Gankeng Bridge in Yueshan Village, Jushui Township, Qingyuan County, Zhejiang. The cut-stone base has only a small 3-meter (10-foot)-wide

arched opening for the stream draining the adjacent paddy fields. Others, such as is the case with the Buchan Bridge nearby, is a 52-meter (170-foot)-long bridge with a 17-meter (55-foot) semi-circular arched opening. The base of the Long'e Bridge in Guizhou is a series of low arches that run from bank to bank of the streambed, which is farmed when the water is low.

II.1.65 While the exact location in Sichuan is unknown, this photo was taken by Mary Alice Thompson, who served as a missionary of the Church Missionary Society. Source: Cadbury Research Library, University of Birmingham CMS/ACC608 and Historical Photographs of China, University of Bristol.

II.1.66 The Zhang Gong Shenjun Bridge is adjacent to the Daoist Zhang Gong Shenjun Temple, Yunlong County, Dali Prefecture, Yunnan. Source: ACO, 2016.

II.1.63 A close-up of the painted entry to the Yongzhen Bridge, Yunlong County, Yunnan. Source: ACO, 2016.

II.1.67 The full length of the cover of the Gankeng Bridge in Yueshan Village, Jushui Township, Qingyuan County, Zhejiang. matches the stone arch base beneath. Source: RGK, 2006.

II.1.68 Buchan Bridge, Yueshan Village, Jushui Township, Qingyuan County, Zhejiang. Source: TEM, 2007.

Timber Understructure

Anyone who has examined a European or American covered bridge likely noticed the structure that supports it—the trusses—which are visible to all who cross. Trusses create a rigid framework of triangularly connected beams that support the deck, while the function of the roof is to protect the trusses, especially their joints, from moisture. Anyone with this expectation entering a Chinese covered bridge not constructed on a masonry base may be surprised at the apparent absence of a timber truss. Instead, one sees only posts and crossbeams to frame the sides and roof, these being similar to those used in the construction of houses and temples. This is because the supporting structure in wooden Chinese covered bridges is below the deck and is not easily observed, especially if the bridge spans a gorge from rock face to rock face.

With the exception of one type (explained later), Chinese bridges seen today have no timber trusses as understood in the West.[1] The understructures support the deck and covering, but they are not truss-like frameworks of triangles

formed into what engineers call a "beam." Our observations suggest there are regional structural patterns, that is, defined geographical areas in China that favor particular designs. These designs, however, can vary greatly. This is because Chinese builders understand structure conceptually, which allows for a variety of realizations, quite unlike the more uniform structures in the United States stemming from codification in the form of patents. Considering the regional isolation characteristic of China's mountainous terrain, the spread of particular realizations may be limited. Such knowledge was likely transmitted orally rather than in written or drawn form. The descriptions that follow, though proceeding in a simple to complex pattern, do not suggest a developmental chronology, a matter as yet unknown.

Describing Chinese structural patterns in English is especially challenging because, even in Chinese, there is little fixed vocabulary, and equivalent structures in the Western world having English terms hardly exist. Thus, the terms used here reflect an initial attempt to classify and describe Chinese covered bridge structures. We

---

[1] A small number of historical photographs show bridges in Qinghai Province that appear to have truss-like structures above the deck, but we know too little about them to speculate about how they were built and who constructed them. See illustrations III.8.2 and III.8.3 of covered bridges near Xunhua in Qinghai taken early in the twentieth century.

II.1.69 Long'e Bridge, Long'e Township, Liping County, Guizhou. Source: TEM, 2017.

will name, describe, and qualify structures using the terms in the listing below. Though admittedly unscientific, of the 100 all-wood covered bridges surveyed in preparation for this study, we found the percentages as indicated after each term, giving a rough idea of their prevalence. The list with percentages is in the order of the extensive discussion that follows.

The number of "woven arch" or "woven arch-beam" bridges, if all known bridges throughout China are taken into consideration, will dominate to an even greater extent than our percentages below, while the third most dominant type, the "horizontal cantilever," would also expand if all the bridges in the Dong/Miao minority areas of the southwest are considered. There are much higher numbers of "simple beam" bridges scattered throughout China, but these have attracted little attention among Chinese bridge scholars. Many examples of covered bridges with beam structures, including timber as well as stone beams, are seen throughout the book. The number of "arched cantilever," with or without a "polygonal arch," is not likely to expand greatly unless yet unknown pockets of such structures are found.

21% Simple beam bridge

19% Horizontal cantilever bridge

2% Angled cantilever bridge

8% Angled cantilever bridge with "polygonal arch" above

4% Single "polygonal arch" below

45% "Woven arch"/"woven arch-beam" bridge

1% "Polygonal arch" with beam

Chinese bridge scholars and architects are rightly most proud of the "woven arch" ("woven arch-beam") structures found in the mountainous regions of Fujian and Zhejiang in southeastern China because this design originated in that area among rural builders without any known outside influence, and certainly none from the West since structures of this type are unknown outside China. Simple beam and horizontal cantilever structures are found worldwide, but the complex arched cantilever bridges appear to be unique to parts of Yunnan and further west into Tibet, as well as neighboring Nepal and Bhutan, though rarely covered in the latter areas.

While a comprehensive history of Chinese covered bridge design does not yet exist, it is nonetheless clear that all-wood bridges resulted from this amorphous term "tradition," that is, concepts, patterns, procedures, and methods passed informally from generation to generation and among people within areas where there is mutual communication. It is also likely that master builders sometimes considered their knowledge to be secret, kept within a clan, or among apprentices. Such attitudes are common among masters of many of China's arts, including, for example, martial arts and music. But unlike something as secretive as martial arts, where transmission takes place in private, bridge building would have been visible to the entire community, thus limiting secrecy.

1. Simple Beam Bridges

Most anywhere in China, and around the world for that matter, one commonly encounters "simple beam" bridges. Placing a log over a stream was likely the earliest form of bridge anywhere, though perhaps with improvements such as flattening the walking surface or adding a handrail.

II.1.71 Slender logs held together by iron staples and laid across a shallow running stream serve here not only as a temporary bridge but also as a convenient place to wash vegetables. Sanjiang County, Guangxi Zhuang Autonomous Region. Source: ACO, 2006.

II.1.70 Four logs bound together provide a crossing of a narrow stream in Pingjia Village, Guizhou. Source: TEM, 2017.

II.1.72 Double log bridge in Shijing Village, Yunlong County, Dali Prefecture. Source: ACO, 2016.

Since China also has a long history of building bridges utilizing cut-stone beams, it should not be surprising that some covered bridges also are set upon stone beams.

Simple beam wooden *covered* bridges occur across China, from the mountain counties of Zhejiang and Fujian to Guizhou, Guangxi, and Yunnan in the southwest.

II.1.73 The Gao Bridge in Yunnan's Tengchong County, Yunnan, consists of three spans supported by simple beams. Source: ACO, 2016.

II.1.74 The Hulong Bridge in Yangjiazhuang Village in Qingyuan Province, only 27.75 meters (91 feet) long, spans an intermittent stream using a simple beam structure. Source: TEM, 2007.

While the structure is simple—many employ unfinished logs—unprotected wood lasts only a few years at best unless protected from the elements. Even a modest timber beam bridge, such as seen in Shijing Village, Yunlong County, Yunnan, not only carries pedestrians between the two parts of town but provides space for vendors to sell food and people to stop and converse.

Wooden beam bridges are relatively easy to build, but they also present many problems. First, the beams, being of wood, a porous material, sag over time. And as they are compromised, they also lose their ability to support loads. True, one can use ever larger beams that would better resist sag, but besides being inefficient such logs are difficult to find, transport, and place since the larger the beam, the heavier it is. Moreover, there are limitations on how many such trees exist. Because spans are necessarily short, such bridges require an inordinate number of stone piers. This challenge is ameliorated in areas with plentiful rock and shallow waterways.

In stark contrast, American builders strove to construct structures that could span great distances, thereby reducing both labor and materials. Using a variety of truss designs, American builders routinely built single-span bridges of 61 meters (200 feet), and one builder, Lewis Wernwag, up to 100 meters (330 feet) in length. Chinese builders evolved entirely different solutions to crossing streams but were limited to spans of about 40 meters (130 feet). Simple beam spans rarely exceed 25 meters (82 feet).

The Tiansheng Bridge, built in 1849 by Tujia minority carpenters and spanning Rongxi Stream in Xihou Town, Chongqing Municipality, is only 55.65 meters (182 feet) long but requires five spans, each just 11 meters (36 feet) long. With such short spans, typical of simple beam bridges, builders had to construct four 20-meter (65-foot)-high stone piers in addition to the abutments. The mammoth logs required for the Tiansheng Bridge are no longer available in China, and in 2017, when the bridge was renovated, creosoted logs had to be imported from Siberia.

II.1.75 The modest Jiezifang Bridge in Yunlong County's (Yunnan) Shijing Village connects two parts of town on a simple beam structure. Source: ACO, 2016.

II.1.76a, b The six spans of the Tiansheng Bridge in Xikou Town, Chongqing Municipality, are supported on massive beams no longer available in China. For the latest renovation, begun in March 2017, creosoted beams had to be brought from Siberia. Source: TEM, 2017.

Not far away, the Kezhai Bridge, said to date to the Yuan Dynasty (1279–1368), was also built by the Tujia minority. Its six spans cover 58.2 meters (191 feet), with each span only 9.7 meters (32 feet) long. The surprisingly slender logs have developed a noticeable sag over the centuries, understandable when you consider the interior was paved with 93 stone slabs.

The twenty or so remaining covered bridges in the Ningbo area of Zhejiang Province are all simple beam bridges, the shallow streams allowing for the many piers required. The two-span Dong Bridge, only 26.2 meters (86 feet long), is typical of the modest timber beam bridges of eastern China.

II.1.77a, b Dating to the Yuan Dynasty, the Kezhai Bridge in Qingxichang Town, Chongqing Municipality, has five spans supported on slender beams, now sagging and resting precipitously on the piers. Nonetheless, they support a stone slab walkway down the center. Source: TEM, 2017.

II.1.78a, b The Dong Bridge, located within the Yinzhou district of Ningbo, Zhejiang, was simply constructed using parallel beams, the ends of which are visible. Source: TEM, 2016.

The nearby Yinzhou Dong Bridge, with seven spans and a total length of 77.4 meters (254 feet), is Ningbo's longest remaining covered bridge. Also known as the Bailiang ("Hundred Logs") Bridge, that may be an underestimation considering how many logs are required for each span.

Liping county, Guizhou Province, retains six of a reputed eleven stone slab covered bridges, all found in Gaojin Village. The Yinglong Bridge was commemorated on a postage stamp in 1996 without specifically naming it, calling it instead simply "*fengyuqiao* in a field." The builders are presumed to be Dong minority, since the village is Dong. The most visible of them, the Yingcun Bridge, uses stone slabs 5.5 meters (18 feet) long, 1.2 meters (4 feet) wide, and 20 centimeters (8 inches) thick, upon which sixteen wooden columns support the roof, each beam being set on a carved stone base. The longest in the village is 6 meters (20 feet), demonstrating the absolute limitations on length for such unusual bridges.

Reinforcing a beam bridge with angled braces, also called corbels or struts, might obstruct the stream, but this is not so within the modest but

II.1.80 The Yinglong Bridge, said to date from 1765 and rebuilt several times, is located in Gaojin Village in Maogong Township, Guizhou. Source: RGK Collection.

II.1.81 Having multiple stone slab bridges, Gaojin Village in Liping County, Guizhou, inhabited by the Dong minority, is evidently located near a quarry for such stone. Source: TEM, 2017.

often-photographed Baiyun ("White Cloud") Bridge in Qingyuan County, Zhejiang. Built in the 1600s, the structure is only 8.34 meters (27 feet) long but houses a substantial shrine and is paved with small stones laid in intricate patterns. Though the open span is only 5.75 meters (19 feet), the builders reinforced it with angled braces, these seeming to form the Chinese character for "eight," giving rise to the bridge's other name, Baqiao Bridge. Some commentators have called this structure a "propped beam bridge."

Simple beam bridges are limited not only by the length of the materials but by their ability to remain rigid when loaded or to resist sag over time.

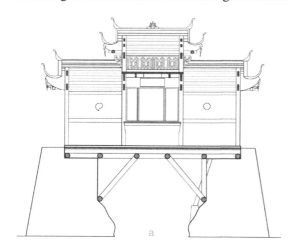

II.1.82a, b Baiyun Bridge in Qingyuan County, Zhejiang, is a rare example of a reinforced beam bridge with poles that prop up the beams. Source: Liu Jie, 2017: 136; TEM, 2007.

Obviously, only wood sags because stone does not flex without breaking. Spanning great distances, therefore, is not possible with the simple beam design. Builders worldwide strove to extend their spans, evolving what was logically the next step, the "cantilever."

2. Cantilevers: Timber and Stone

Cantilevers were a next logical step, but whether the idea proceeded chronologically from beam bridges or occurred simultaneously with them, cantilevers are not evenly distributed throughout China. There are several types of cantilever structures in Chinese covered bridges. The simpler horizontal type, most commonly encountered in Guizhou, Guangxi, and Hunan provinces and typical of the Dong and Miao minorities, could also be described as "reinforced beam bridges" since the staggered projections beneath the beams reinforce them rather than reduce the length of the beam. Angle braces work similarly but are vulnerable to flood and debris since they are seated into the abutment/pier.

In a second type, complex cantilever structures (treated in the following section), builders anchor

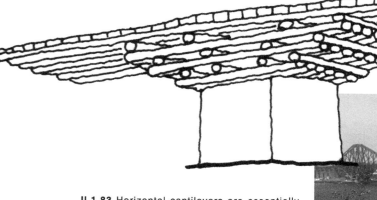

II.1.83 Horizontal cantilevers are essentially reinforcing extensions beneath simple beams to reduce their clear span. Drawing after Mao, 1986. Source: Liu Jie, 2017: 50.

beams at an upward angle into rock, rock piles, or abutments on each bank, with the shortest on the bottom and the longest on top in order to create support. The banks, therefore, provide counter support to the exposed ends over the water, which then support a beam to complete the crossing. In some cases, covered masonry entries create additional weight.

Cantilevers greatly reduce the distance remaining to be spanned by the beam. In the

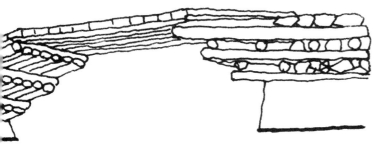

II.1.84 Angled cantilevers extend outwards in order to reduce the remaining gap, which is spanned by a simple beam. Drawing after Mao, 1986. Source: Liu Jie, 2017: 50.

case of Chinese wooden bridges, the cantilever projections never evolved into trusses, as was the case later in Europe where such bridges, having massive metal cantilevered trusses, could span remarkable distances, and their construction did not require falsework. This was true of Scotland's famous Firth of Forth Railway Bridge built between 1882 and 1890, which is 2,467 meters (8,094 feet) long, with each span being 521 meters (1,709 feet).

This method of construction may also have been true for wooden cantilevers in China and nearby countries, since many span roaring rivers

II.1.85 Scotland's famous Firth of Forth Railway Bridge, northwest of Edinburgh, is a massive set of three metal cantilevers. Source: TEM, 1982.

where falsework would be near impossible. Multi-span horizontal cantilevers are common, but none of the complex angled cantilevers known to us are multiple span, since a pier capable of stabilizing two opposing cantilevers would have to be massive.

Covered cantilever bridges are widely distributed in China, but the greatest numbers and design variations occur in the southwestern provinces of Guizhou, Guangxi, Hunan, and Yunnan where they are the dominant design. In eastern China, however, cantilevers seen today tend to be modest and are not numerous.

Among the least known bridges of Taishun County, Zhejiang, the Duoyun Bridge has minimal cantilevering on the pier only. It is, in short, a slightly reinforced beam bridge. Another example in Taishun, the 41.7-meter (138-foot)-long Nanyang Bridge, built in 1871 in Yantou Village, Sixi Township, uses short stone cantilevers on the

II.1.86a, b The easily overlooked Dengyun Bridge in Taishun County, Zhejiang, has a simple horizontal cantilever system only on the center pier. Source: TEM, 2005.

pier. This is also true of the well-known Dongguan Bridge in Fujian.

More complex horizontal cantilevers occur elsewhere in eastern China, especially in Fujian Province's Zhenghe County. In these bridges, the

cantilevers could also be described as log cribbing that projects further and further outwards with each layer. Each layer is separated by smaller "spacer" logs, which provide circulation throughout the cribbing, though they also add a vulnerability in that the integrity of the pile depends on these modest members.

The Shuiwei ("Water Tail") Bridge at the entrance to Jinping Village in an isolated corner of Zhenghe County, Fujian, is an excellent example, now protected as a county-level "cultural relic." Seated on four layers of spaced logs, this 1858 cantilevered structure, 26.20 meters (86 feet) long, still has an especially rugged look. A full-length beam placed atop the cantilever spans the entire length. Even with the added support of the cantilevers, the top (main) beam has sagged noticeably over the years.

II.1.87a, b Both the Nanyang Bridge in Taishun County, Zhejiang (top) and the Dongguan Bridge in Fujian (bottom) have stone cantilevers. Those of the Dongguan Bridge appear to have been added when raising the structure against floods. Source: TEM, 2005; ACO, 2006.

II.1.88 The rugged looking Shuiwei Bridge in Zhenghe County, Zhejiang, built in 1858, uses horizontal cantilevers resembling cribbing to reinforce the simple beam, which is sagging nonetheless. Source: TEM, 2011.

The best-known and most striking horizontal cantilever structures are those of the Dong minority in Guizhou and Guangxi provinces, especially in Sanjiang Dong Autonomous County, Guangxi Province. Because Chengyang Village, with its three striking covered, all-wood, multi-span cantilever *fengyuqiao* wind-and-rain bridges was the first Dong center for tourism, these structures have been widely photographed and posted online, especially the magnificent bridge at the village entry, originally built in 1912. The Dong are famous for their massive multistoried wooden houses and spectacular drum towers as well as their bridges. Although local village drum towers are considerably less ambitious, a memorial tower built in 2002 in Sanjiang City is 42.6 meters (140 feet) high and has 27 levels.

II.1.90a Chengyang, also called Linxi Village, has three massive cantilever bridges, the most famous being the four-span Yongji Wind-and-Rain Bridge at the village entrance. Source: TEM, 2007.

The Dong minority in both Guizhou and Guangxi provinces are renowned for their massive wooden structures, especially their huge horizontal cantilever wind-and-rain bridges.

II.1.90b Helong Bridge, Linxi Village. Source: TEM, 2007.

II.1.89 The horizontal members of Shuiwei's cantilever system are divided by perpendicular members of equal size. Source: TEM, 2011.

II.1.90c Puji Bridge, Linxi Village, Guangxi. Source: TEM, 2007.

The Dong also build modest beam bridges and small-scale cantilevers, not to mention corridors on stone arches or modern concrete arches, especially in Guizhou Province. The most eye-catching characteristic of Dong bridges is not their underlying structure but the tower-like pavilions on the ends and above the piers, some of which resemble the Dong's signature drum towers. These are almost always present regardless of bridge type, which raises questions as to their function. Some towers allow visitors to ascend to the top by way of steps, but most do not. It appears that the towers provide weight on the cantilever systems to keep them stable, but aesthetics and custom apparently also play overriding roles in the case of concrete and masonry arches.

Among the more modest Dong cantilever bridges is the Liuyue Bridge in Liuyue Township, Liping County, Guizhou Province, said to have been built in 1863 to honor the Goddess Sa Sui. Its two spans total 32 meters (105 feet), making each span approximately 16 meters (52.5 feet), considerably longer than the simple beam bridges previously noted. The increased span lengths suggest the benefit of cantilevers. Those on the abutments consist of two layers beneath the full-length beam, the first cantilever extending little, the second much further, while those on the narrow center pier, also two-layered, extend more evenly, suggesting the shape of an inverted pyramid. The outer ends of the cantilever layers are stabilized by a long, slender wooden pin passing through the main logs. Unlike most Dong bridges, the Liuyue Bridge has only one modest tower, on the end near the road, with the rest of the roofline being basically flat. This suggests that the tower's function to stabilize the structure may not actually be necessary.

By the early twenty-first century, after domestic tourism developed in the Chengyang area, modern bridges built on concrete arches or reinforced concrete beams have proliferated, as Dong bridges have become what might be called "objectified culture" designed to attract visitors. Indeed, as more and more Dong villages and towns in southwestern China have opened to both international and

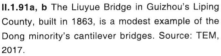

II.1.91a, b The Liuyue Bridge in Guizhou's Liping County, built in 1863, is a modest example of the Dong minority's cantilever bridges. Source: TEM, 2017.

domestic tourism, modern *fengyuqiao* have continued to proliferate.

In our 2007 visits, nine multi-span, all-wood "wind-and-rain bridges" were seen in the region, all having similar structural features, though varying greatly in length, width, and height. In each case, both abutments and piers, all constructed of cut stone, supported robust four-layer racks of cantilevered logs separated by smaller logs at 90 degrees and stabilized at the outer ends by slender beams passing through channels in the entire layer of logs. In each instance, the first layer was the shortest and the second longer. For piers, the projections were symmetrical for balance. The top two layers, however, were beams spanning the complete length of the bridge. This is why we can also speak of such bridges as reinforced beam bridges.

II.1.92a–c Puji Bridge in Linxi Village, Guangxi, is a splendid example of a Dong minority cantilever structure. Note how spacers between layers allow for the free circulation of air. Source: TEM, 2007.

Among these bridges are both massive structures large enough for local people to market their products and house a substantial religious shrine, as well as much narrower functional bridges meant only to get pedestrians across the stream. In one case, the Huaxie Bridge in Guandong Village, Guangxi Province, which is some 67.2 meters (206 feet) long but with an interior width of only 2.4 meters (8 feet), led only to paddy fields.

A number of modern or rebuilt Dong bridges simulate the appearance of log cantilevers. The newly famous Tujia minority Canglang Bridge in Zhuoshui Town in eastern Chongqing Municipality, which is discussed in detail in Part III, was rebuilt in 2014 after a fire in 2013 burned the original from the 1980s, and claims to be "the longest covered bridge in the world" at 658 meters (2,159 feet). The version of the bridge from the

II.1.93a–c Huaxia Bridge connects Guandong Village, Guangxi, to paddy fields. The unusually narrow cantilever rack on the pier reflects the bridge's narrow internal width. Source: TEM, 2007.

1980s, copied in the 2014 rebuilding, was only 310 meters (1,017 feet) in nine spans. While the base is made entirely of reinforced concrete on concrete piers, the builders added light panels of simulated cantilevers at each abutment and pier, suggesting a known pattern seen in Dong and Miao bridges but not in the known Tujia bridges of the area. It may be that this bridge was designed by civil engineers from outside and that they invoked the appearance of the Dong bridges for good effect.

II.1.94 Built to attract tourists to Zhuoshui Town, four hours east of Chongqing City, the Canglang Bridge was rebuilt in 2014 after a 2013 fire destroyed the 1980s structure. Engineers provided simulated cantilevers beneath the reinforced concrete spans to create the appearance of "Dongness." Source: TEM, 2017.

3. Complex Angled Cantilevers

Up to this point, the only complex angled cantilever covered bridges known in China are confined to western and northern Yunnan Province where the Bai minority is concentrated. These were little known outside their immediate area until 2016 when the authors documented all those known to us, only ten. The structures in question could be called "true" cantilevers because the projecting beams are deeply embedded into the abutments and angle upwards. The portions within the abutments must be stabilized both vertically and laterally to counterbalance both the outward beams and the loads carried by the bridge. While all those seen in Yunnan today are covered, historical photographs by travelers and missionaries from Europe and the United States show uncovered cantilevers over a wide area, including in Qinghai, Sichuan, and Tibet. Similar structures, both covered and uncovered, exist or existed in areas further to the west as far as Nepal and Bhutan. Indeed, Bhutan is currently promoting tourism using photos of existing covered cantilever bridges The most remarkable of them is the 2008 rebuilding of the Punakha Dzong [palace] Bazam [bridge] by a German firm sponsored by Pro Bhutan, Germany, with a clear span of 56 meters (184 feet). It replaced the 1637 original destroyed in a flood in

² For additional information, visit http://www.probhutan.com.

1958, but it is not known if that bridge had such a great span. The construction of the bridge, an entirely modern process, is well documented on the Pro Bhutan website and likely provides some insight into the process of building earlier complex cantilevers, including those in China.

II.1.95 This diagram shows the extreme angle customary in Nepalese cantilever bridges in addition to some in Tibet. Drawing after Mao, 1986. Source: Liu Jie, 2017: 50.

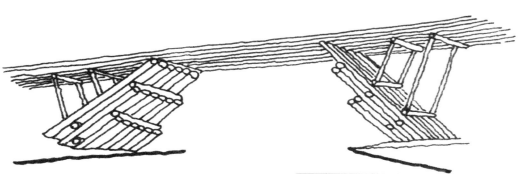

There is great variation among the ten Yunnan cantilevers we documented. They vary from the modest Yongji Bridge in Donglianhua Hui (Han-Muslim) village in Weishan County, Dali Prefecture, approximately 10 meters (33 feet) long, plus masonry entries on both ends, to the magnificent Yezhujing Bridge in Tengchong County, which sweeps high over a wild river with a clear span of 27 meters (88 feet) and a total length of 30 meters (98 feet). Compared to the refined bridges of Bhutan, with their squared and finished beams, those of Yunnan seen today portray a ruggedness that points to reconstruction by local craftsmen using barely worked timbers often straight out of the forest though stripped of bark. In addition, eight bridges also have a polygonal arch support system that will be described after the discussion of cantilever systems.

While there are noticeable variations among these ten bridges, certain factors appear to hold true for all. First, each system is built deeply into abutments on each bank. Most have entries, some wood, some masonry, that add weight to the stone. The cantilever system on each bank must be independently stabilized, built as a rigid framework that will maintain shape in both vertical and horizontal directions. Based on the little we know for sure, along with common sense, the cantilevers are built out from the abutments without falsework, but we can envision craftsmen easily working in some of the placid streambeds,

building the cantilevers above them. In other cases, it is hard to see how workers could build the cantilevers from below on such steep banks above dangerous, roaring rivers. Even though some of these bridges were built or rebuilt during the mid-twentieth century, there were no known local photographers recording the process, which, in any case, would likely have been seen as too routine to merit documentation. Virtually all historical photos of Chinese bridges were made by the rare traveler or missionary, and they would not likely have been in the right place at the right time.

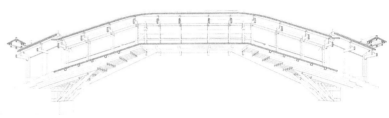

II.1.97 Among Yunnan's covered bridges, the Tongjing Bridge in Yunlong County is probably the most complete and elegant of the cantilever structures. Source: Liu Jie, 2017: 84.

Since the outward tips of these cantilevers must support substantial weight from horizontal beam, cover structure, and live load, the counterbalancing portion is necessarily embedded deeply into the abutments, but this cannot be seen. Thus, we presume that these cantilevers are somewhat like icebergs in that the majority of them are beneath the surface. Even with thousands of words, these systems will best be understood by close examination of actual specimens or photographs. Certain characteristics are common to all of them.

Upward angle. In all cases, the cantilevers project upwards at anything from a slight to a steep angle. As a result, most such bridges have arched decks. Two bridges in Tengchong County (Tongji and Yongshun), however, are nearly flat, and these have nearly flat walkways. Yezhujing, on the other hand, has the steepest rise of all the bridges.

II.1.96a, b Tengchong County, Yunnan, has three fine examples of angled cantilevers. The Tongji Bridge, not having siding, provides a particularly clear view of the structure. Source: TEM, 2016; ACO, 2016.

II.1.98 Yunlong County, Yunnan, retains the best examples of angled cantilevers in China. The Caifeng Bridge's structure is clearly seen here. Source: TEM, 2016.

Arch characteristics. Each cantilever layer is a set of parallel logs, varying from four to six. From bottom to top, each layer extends further than the one beneath. Combined with the upward angle, these graduated layers form at least part of a rough arch and may work similarly since they are put into compression when loaded.

Horizontal stabilizer beams. The outer ends of the parallel logs that make up each cantilever are stabilized horizontally by a crossbar that either runs through the logs near their tip or through a channel cut into the ends. In some cases, for example the Caifeng Bridge, there are two parallel crossbeam stabilizers. These keep each layer from getting out of square.

Vertical stabilizer pins. The systems of vertical wooden dowels with sharp points on the lower ends are visually eye-catching. Some sets penetrate the shorter layer near the ends by penetrating also the longer layer above. In cases where the shorter layer's crossbeam is embedded in *channels*, the pins penetrate the logs of the upper layer and pass in front of the lower layer's channels, blocking its ends.

Horizontal crossbeam. A horizontal beam spans the gap between the two projecting cantilevers. When the cantilevers are only slightly angled, the beam can, and in some cases does, span the entire length, but when the cantilevers are angled upwards, the beam is only slightly longer

than the gap, and its ends sit rather precariously on the tips of the cantilevers' furthest extension, bolstered by some logs to fill in the gaps.

Among Yunnan's cantilever bridges, one stands above the others in terms of its sophisticated construction and daring location high over a wild river, the Yezhujing Bridge in Tengchong County. The clear span of 27 meters (88 feet) consists of four extended cantilever systems with the gap completed by long horizontal beams. Even with a deck that begins well above the lowest cantilevers, the bridge's arch shape is striking, and users encounter an unusually steep arc. Just how the builders accomplished this feat, and likely without falsework, is unknown even though its most recent reconstruction was 1947–8. Local photography would have been unlikely in such a remote location.

With these principles in mind, further verbal description must necessarily give way to pictorial

II.1.100 The Yezhujing Bridge, built high over a wild river in remote Tengchong County, Yunnan, has seven layers of cantilevers to support the remaining gap. Source: ACO, 2016.

experience. In the following photos, readers will be able to see for themselves how beautifully these cantilevers are joined together to create a rigid but visually appealing three-dimensional frame, counterbalanced from within the abutment and able to maintain form under the weight of timbers and human or animal traffic.

II.1.102a, b Two examples of cantilever structures with a polygonal arch in Yunnan Province: Tongjing Bridge, Yunlong Count, and Yongji Bridge, Weishan County. Source: TEM, 2016.

II.1.103a, b The cantilever systems of the Wenming Bridge, Yunlong County, Yunnan, are connected to a polygonal arch within the corridor above. Source: TEM, 2016.

II.1.101 The Caifeng Bridge's cantilever system is reinforced with three angle braces. Source: ACO, 2016.

4. Polygonal Arch Structures

Until our encounters with the ten all-wood bridges of Yunnan in 2016, historians of Chinese covered bridges had not written of any structures in China that could be called trusses. The presence of a truss—a configuration of timbers into rectangles and triangles to form a rigid frame—is the essential defining characteristic of covered bridges in both Europe and North America. Chinese bridges use non-truss support systems in all known cases except for eight we documented in Yunnan. We will describe these as "polygonal arches," a term widely known in Europe but less so in North America. A typical arch has an arc shape and works in compression, as loads supported by the arch pull downwards, compressing the arc into its ends which must be securely anchored in order not to move or buckle and cause failure. A polygonal arch, that is, an arch with multiple angles, consists of straight segments joined into a continuous but segmented arch-like beam. The polygonal arches in Yunnan's eight bridges are all in three segments: diagonal beams on each end and a horizontal beam between them.

In both Europe and North America, many modest bridges have what became known, at least in the United States, as a "queenpost" truss. It is essentially a trapezoidal-shaped frame, with verticals between the lower "chord" and the point where the diagonal meets the horizontal above Superficially, the Chinese polygonal arches

II.1.104 Diagram showing a structure combining angled cantilevers, angle braces, and a polygonal arch with attachment to a floor beam. Source: Liu Jie, 2017: 415.

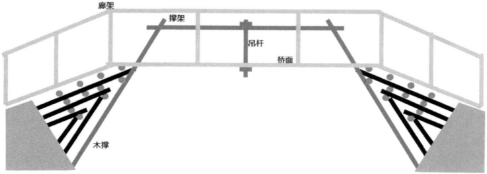

resemble a queenpost, but they are not because there is no complete framework, only three timbers. Therefore, in spite of the outer form, we prefer to call these structures "polygonal arches."

In each case, the Yunnan arches work independently of the cantilevers, which are the primary means of support. The lower ends are

II.1.105 A typical American queenpost truss in Columbia County, Pennsylvania. A true queenpost has a complete trapezoidal frame and, as seen here, internal bracing. Source: TEM, 2007.

II.1.106a–c Yunnan's "polygonal arch" bridges have only three members, comprising two diagonal braces and a horizontal support beam. Wuli Bridge in Yunlong County has a polygonal arch system with two diagonals that pierce and support the horizontal. Two vertical beams from the latter support the floor beams. Source: ACO, 2016.

typically embedded in the abutments or a solid surface slightly away from them and angle between other timbers at least halfway up the inside, ending with a narrow pin carved into their ends. These pins penetrate a horizontal beam running between them. There is, however, considerable variation among these specimens.

The next question is, how does this arch reinforce the rest of the bridge? Since it is independent of the rest of the structure, the arch needs to be joined to some parts of the rest of the bridge if it is to offer additional support. The weakest part of a cantilever structure is the horizontal beam between the cantilevers, since it can potentially sag. Were it overly robust to resist sagging, its weight would then compromise the cantilever system. By being connected to that beam, the arch works, as it were, as the bridge's suspenders/braces, taking some of the pressure off the horizontal beam.

In American covered bridges, the arch may be both dapped into the truss members and support iron rods attached to the lower chord. Since

II.1.108a, b Supported by the three-piece polygonal arch, a rounded vertical post extends below the main beams to support a floor crossbeam. Yongji Bridge, Weishan County, Yunnan. Source: TEM, 2016.

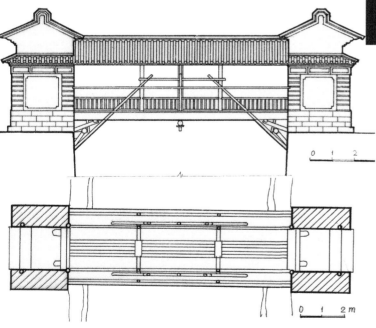

II.1.107 As seen in the diagram, Yongji Bridge in Weishan County, Yunnan, has a sturdy polygonal arch reinforcing a minimal cantilever system. Source: Liu Jie, 2017: 74.

there are no truss members in a Chinese bridge, the connection must necessarily be with the horizontal beam of the cantilever system, but in most bridges we have observed these connections were surprisingly light. In one case, however, the Caifeng Bridge, there are iron rods connected to the lower beam, but in others the connections are slender wooden members.

II.1.110 Similar in principle to the support system of the American Burr truss (see below left), Yunnan's Caifeng Bridge uses a polygonal arch and metal rods to support the floor beams. Source: TEM, 2016.

The system found in the Yezhujing Bridge is made of timbers so modest one barely notices them, and one wonders why they are even there. Again, photos will show the variety of structures found in even so few bridges.

Unique among all of Yunnan's wooden bridges known to us is the three-span Yanjian Bridge in Binchuan County, Dali Bai Autonomous Prefecture. We have seen evidence of at least one other bridge

II.1.109 A typical American Burr truss, the Academia Bridge in Juniata County, Pennsylvania, uses iron rods suspended from wooden blocks on the arch to support the deck beams. Source: TEM, 2015.

II.1.111a–c The polygonal support systems for three Yunnan bridges in Yunlong County: a. Tongjing Bridge; b. Wuli Bridge; c. Jiancao Bridge. Source: ACO, 2016; TEM, 2016; TEM, 2016.

of similar structure in the area, suggesting that it is a local structural plan. At first sight the bridge appears to have two kingpost spans flanking a center queenpost span. Kingpost refers to a two-panel truss with two diagonals inclined to the center vertical, called a kingpost. The queenpost was described in the previous discussion. On closer examination, however, Yanjian Bridge is neither. Beneath, it clearly has no cantilever systems and appears otherwise to be a simple beam bridge.

Each span, however, has a polygonal arch similar to those found in other Yunnan bridges, except that the two outer spans have extremely short horizontals while the middle span has a longer one. The arches are seated on top of the abutments and piers and not into their faces and pass independently of the structure, only supporting the stout crossbeams of the roof system. In short, these arches support only the roof, which then takes much of the weight off the lower beams. There appear to be lightweight wooden connectors between the roof and deck beams but not directly from the arch. With only two known examples, it is difficult to know if this is a significant local pattern.

II.1.112 The Yanjian Bridge in Binchuan County, Yunnan, appears to have two kingpost truss spans flanking a queenpost truss center span, but these are simple beam spans with polygonal arches supporting the roof structure. Source: ACO, 2016.

II.1.113a, b The central span of Yanjian Bridge supports the roof beams but the vertical posts are not connected to it. Source: TEM, 2016.

5. Woven Arch Bridges

The most thoroughly studied Chinese covered bridges are those found in the mountainous border counties of northern Fujian and southern Zhejiang provinces in southeastern China, bridges whose structure is described in English as "woven arch beam" *bianmu gongliang*. In 1953, one of China's greatest paintings, *Qingming Shanghe Tu* ("Along the River During the Qingming Festival"), painted during the Northern Song Dynasty by Zhang Zeduan (1085–1145), was first shown to the public. A young bridge engineer, Tang Huancheng (1926–2014), examined the painting and concluded that the bridge depicted spanning the Bian River at Bianliang (now Kaifeng, Henan Province) revealed a long lost bridge building method. He described these structures as "rainbow bridges." Tang spent

his professional career studying this type of bridge, his views changing over time as new discoveries occurred. At first, he thought the tradition had arisen in the North China Plain from the original fount of Chinese culture and was subsequently lost. When, in 1980, Tang discovered that there were surviving bridges in Zhejiang Province, he assumed that these represented a survival of the rainbow bridge tradition that had diffused from the Southern Song, with its capital in Hangzhou, into Zhejiang Province's remotest areas.

In 1998, Tang, along with other Chinese bridge engineers and American timber framers, attempted to replicate a modest version of a "rainbow bridge" in Jinze, one of the watertowns near Shanghai. This effort was documented by Boston television station WGBH and broadcast on February 29, 2000 as "China Bridge" in their Nova series *Secrets of Lost Empires*. Neither Tang nor his compatriots knew they could have consulted living masters of the bridge-building tradition, because it was not until 2001 that doctoral candidate Liu Jie at Shanghai's Tongji University discovered, with local help, a living builder, Zheng Duojin, in Shouning County, Fujian. His work documenting both the methods and designs found there has continued to the present. An older contemporary of Liu, Swiss-trained architect Zhao Chen, did extensive research as well and first advanced the view that the Fujian-Zhejiang bridges represented a local tradition independent of the historical rainbow bridge, thereby challenging the long-held assumptions claiming that all Chinese culture originated in northern China and diffused to the south and southwest. More recently, German-trained building historian Liu Yan has gone beyond simply describing bridge specimens towards formulating new theories of their construction based on her participation in building an actual bridge with a traditional master carpenter. We are indebted to the work of all four scholars (Tang Huancheng, Liu Jie, Liu Yan, and Zhao Chen) in bringing us to this point of understanding.

The scholars above have all examined numerous bridges in the region, and they have affirmed that "woven arch" is more an idea than a specific plan. Each building family, working within a limited area, evolved over time conclusions about what works best, but there is considerable variation among surviving bridges. Based on modern stress analysis, it seems clear that a number of the variations worked better than others, and the conclusion is that what is called the 3/5 design is the best. What this means is better understood following an introduction to the concept.

As seen in the previous segment relative to Yunnan's cantilevers combined with polygonal arch reinforcements, the arches in woven arch are also polygonal, having from three to five sections. Among all of China's wooden bridge types, the woven arch is capable of the greatest spans. While the longest cantilever clear span, Yunnan's Yezhujing Bridge, is 27 meters (88 feet), there is at least one surviving woven arch bridge, Luanfeng Bridge in Shouning County, Fujian, which has a span of 37.2 meters (122 feet). Nonetheless, woven arches are also used in

surprisingly modest spans as short as 12.4 meters (41 feet), for example, the Shuochun or Wengkeng Bridge in Xixi township, Shouning County, Fujian, built in 1870.

II.1.114 The Shouchun or Wengkeng Bridge in Shouning County, Fujian, built in 1870, is only 12.4 meters (41 feet) long, yet has a woven arch structure. Source: TEM, 2007.

II.1.115a, b As seen in the central span of Yanjian Bridge, the polygonal arch supports the roof beams but the vertical posts are not connected to it. Source: TEM, 2016.

b

Some local builders have used designs that are related to the woven arch but simpler, a single arch. The polygonal arches associated with Yunnan's cantilever bridges rise from below at least to midway within the bridge, and whatever support they offer is *suspended* from them to the lower beams. A few bridges in the Fujian-Zhejiang area also use a single three-section polygonal arch, but it is entirely below the deck. The simplest, and most precarious, is an unnamed bridge in Gutian County, Fujian Province. The polygonal arch consists of seven lines of logs angled from ledges on the abutments to horizontals between, evidently held in place by gravity unless there are pins on the ends of the diagonals fitted into holes in the horizontals. This supports a beam the full length of the bridge.

The Shengxian Bridge in Xianfeng Village, Xixi Township, Shouning County, Fujian, built in 1839, with a span of 14.5 meters (48 feet), is slightly more sophisticated in that the nine lines of logs forming the "arch" rest on reinforcing crossbeams at the joints. Nonetheless, these structures are inherently unstable and require substantial weight from above to hold them in place. Clearly, these arches are in compression.

II.1.117a, b The Shengxian Bridge in Shouning County, Fujian, only 14.5 meters (48 feet) long, is a rarely seen single polygonal arch. Source: TEM, 2005.

II.1.116a, b This modest bridge in Gutian County, Fujian, possibly called the Shuyin Bridge, uses a single polygonal arch beneath the simple beams, all held together by gravity. Source: TEM, 2005.

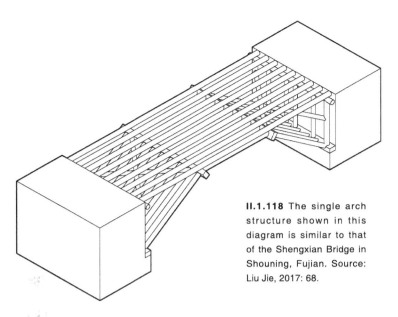

II.1.118 The single arch structure shown in this diagram is similar to that of the Shengxian Bridge in Shouning, Fujian. Source: Liu Jie, 2017: 68.

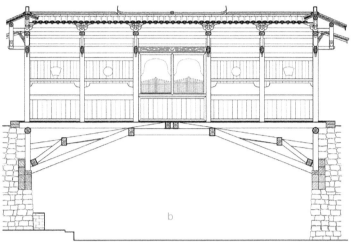

Based on the surviving bridges, some builders have tried various plans to create longer, stronger spans. The basic principle that evolved uses two polygonal arch systems interwoven together, somewhat like cloth, thus giving rise to the term "woven arch." The primary arch is in three sections. The second system, interwoven between the members of the primary arch, however, is variously in three, four, or five sections. The logs of each system alternate, thus giving rise to the visual fascination in seeing two interwoven systems, each with different angles.

II.1.119a–c Though only 11.15 meters (37 feet) long, the Shuangmen Bridge in Qingyuan County, Zhejiang, has two interwoven polygonal arches, also seen in the diagram. Source: TEM, 2011; Liu Jie, 2017: 135; TEM, 2007.

II.1.120 The Putian Bridge in Adji Village, Qingyuan County, Fujian, only 15.5 meters (51 feet) long, nonetheless has a complex woven arch system. Source: TEM, 2007.

II.1.121 Woven arches of the Wan'an Bridge, Pingnan County, Fujian. Source: TEM, 2005.

II.1.122 The complexity of the design is clear in the Yanghou Bridge in Zhenghe County, Fujian. Source: TEM, 2013.

Builders of woven arch bridges have also solved the problem of instability where the arch sections join. At these points they place a heavy squared crossbeam with pre-cut holes to receive the narrow pins on the ends of the horizontal or diagonal timbers, the latter remaining as rounded logs. These crossbeams must be pounded tightly into position with large mallets, a process called *choudu* "knocking the crossbeam," a critical working step documented by Liu Yan during her fieldwork (2017: 116–25). By using these crossbeams to tighten the entire arch into a rigid frame, the bridge is more likely to maintain

stability. But to increase lateral stability, builders often place large X-frames between the diagonals and the abutments/piers.

II.1.123 A scale model of the woven arch understructure made by living covered bridge builder Wu Fuyong of Qingyuan County, Zhejiang. Source: TEM, 2011.

II.1.124 Arches with X framing of the Xianju Bridge in Taishun County, Zhejiang. Source: TEM, 2005.

II.1.125 X-bracing in the single polygonal arch Huaisheng Bridge, Jingning County, Zhejiang. Source: TEM, 2013.

II.1.126 Two diagonals form a triangle to stiffen the woven arches of the Shuangmen Bridge, Qingyuan County, Zhejiang. Source: TEM 2007.

Woven arch covered bridges have long been built in the Fujian and Zhejiang area, but knowing when they began is likely impossible. The oldest documented surviving bridge is the Rulong Bridge in Yueshan Village, Jushi Township, Qingyuan County, Zhejiang, dated to 1626 during the late Ming Dynasty (1368–1644).

II.1.127 The Rulong Bridge in Qingyuan County, Zhejiang, is China's oldest surviving woven arch structure, dating to 1626 during the Ming Dynasty. Source: TEM, 2007.

According to the histories of various bridges, usually carved into stone stele placed at the bridge site, some bridges allegedly date back much further, even to the fifteenth century, but there is little likelihood that these bridges contain any original material or even the original design. Although the Rulong Bridge seems not to have been refurbished

over time, thus making it the oldest, most other bridges dated back centuries have been rebuilt numerous times. Some were destroyed in floods and rebuilt from new or salvaged timbers. Others were dismantled, had deteriorated timbers replaced, and were reassembled sometimes at a different location. This renewal process is normal in China, making it difficult to say in most cases which parts date to earlier centuries and which were added during reconstructions. Since woven arch bridges are highly modular, these procedures are relatively easy to perform.

Because the building of woven arch bridges remains a living tradition performed almost entirely in the manner of the past, but nowadays mostly using modern power tools and metal scaffolding, we can know the process of erection. But when Tang and his colleagues were trying to rebuild a small-scale rainbow bridge in Jinze Town in 1998, they were only able to reimagine the process. Their solution was later seen as mistaken. Tang postulated that carpenters built the diagonal racks on land in a complete frame, then lowered the frame into place using a traditional crane and ropes system, holding it in place until they could complete the crossbeams and horizontal members. Tang and his team moored two small boats in the stream and built a crane on shore with which to assemble the bridge that had been previously built and assembled on land. The crane lowered a limited number of diagonals into place, pounded the crossbeams into place, then filled the gap with the horizontal members. With this stable beginning, they could continue adding additional lines of timbers. While they, in fact, achieved success with this method, they also had plenty of room on each end. Many bridges, including some with the greatest spans, sit against rocks and cliffs, some even

II.1.129 Builders faced nearly insurmountable challenges in building daring bridges in remote locations without modern derricks or safety equipment. This is particularly so in the case of Shouning County, Fujian's famous Yangmeizhou Bridge. Source: TEM, 2007.

II.1.128a–c Workers constructing the Ganzhushan Bridge in Qingyuan County, Zhejiang, in 2013. The first photo shows the use of architectural plans, the second a collection of pre-cut and carved members, and the third workers preparing the beams under cover for the bridge being built nearby. Source: TEM, 2013.

II.1.130a, b The Tongle Bridge in Taishun, Zhejiang, was constructed over a 26-month period between 2004 and 2006, a lengthy period because of the need to adhere to auspicious dates. Here are two of the in-progress images relating to its structure: "setting the arch" and falsework and then after the removal of the falsework a view of the "arch in winter." Other images related to the sequence are found in Part II.2 below. Source: XYC, 2004.

entering from the side because the bridge's end faces a cliff. There is simply no place to assemble frames and lower them into place.

Builders from the living tradition, however, pre-cut some of the members in a separate location, but at the site they build scaffolding (falsework) on which to erect the bridge. Many timbers must be cut in situ, since variations in length may be necessary to build a tight arch. When the arch is self-supporting, the falsework is removed. This method, however, still raises the question of how workers could build falsework in deep, rapidly moving rivers far below the bridge, as is seen in Shouning county's famous Yangmeizhou Bridge, which is 42.5 meters (139 feet) long with a clear span of 35.7 meters (117 feet). The same question arises with American and European bridges, some built similarly over high or rapid rivers, but in those cases we have enough historical photos to show that, indeed, workers could build amazing falsework in seemingly impossible places.

When researchers discovered the woven arch bridges of Fujian and Zhejiang in 1980, they learned that none had been built since the 1970s. But Liu Jie's discovery in 2001 of living builders, mostly members of multi-generational families specializing in bridge construction, has led to a revival of both bridge building in the area as well as the restoration of many bridges. Between 2003 and 2016, of the 23 *langqiao* constructed in Taishun County, Zhejiang, 18 were "woven arch."[3]

Conclusions

Over a remarkably short time, just since the 1990s, China's covered bridges have gone from near total obscurity to international notice. People from a variety of disciplines and interests, from architects and building historians to tourism promoters and party officials, have found the bridges to be fascinating both for their overall aesthetics as well as their structures. While there are no known formations of bridge enthusiasts into organizations comparable to those found in the United States, such as the National Society for the Preservation of Covered Bridges, China's covered bridges are now seen as essential tourist attractions, especially in the minority areas now undergoing rapid development into tourism destinations. If China's application to UNESCO to make the bridges of Fujian and Zhejiang provinces world heritage

[3] https://zh.wikipedia.org/wiki/%E6%B3%B0%E9%A1%BA%E5%BB%8A%E6%A1%A5

sites is accepted, the bridges will instantly attract international attention.

Among Chinese architects and building historians, simple beam and horizontal cantilever bridges have attracted less interest. The angled cantilever structures of Yunnan and immediately west of China have only recently become known. Since their discovery, Chinese scholars have focused most of their attention on the woven arch bridges in the southeast. This is easy to understand since woven arch bridges are unique to China, are structurally fascinating and complex, and were devised by local rural craftsmen families. In addition, they appear to have historical legitimacy stemming from their similarity to the bridge depicted in the famous twelfth-century *Qingming Shanghe Tu* painting discussed earlier. It is also understandable from an engineering perspective, but to lay people the bridges offer numerous other attractive features.

European and American covered bridges are considered utilitarian. They are covered with plain siding boards and simple roof designs to achieve only one goal: protecting the wooden superstructure. Chinese bridges are also utilitarian but their covering serves multiple purposes, most quite different from Western bridges. Since the structural members of Chinese bridge are in nearly all cases below the deck, their protection is less essential than in the West. Because the bridges serve only foot travelers, carts, and animals, not large wheeled vehicles, as is the case in the West, in both remote and urbanized locations, their coverings—corridors and pavilions—offer both shelter for travelers and a covered public space where local people can relax, socialize, and even participate in recreational activities. In the past, perhaps most bridges included religious shrines within the covered bridge or in an adjacent temple, both of great significance to local communities. As will be seen in Part II.2, both itinerant peddlers and local vendors sell food within *langqiao* on a daily basis or on market days.

Besides offering shelter, the "corridors" also allow builders an opportunity to exhibit structural beauty. This can be seen both within and from without. Within, visitors may find carvings of mythological animals, flowers, fish, and other motifs on structural members, the ability to carve such features being a basic skill required of bridge builders. Some bridges also offer painted murals depicting mythological figures or local life. Even the windows may be cut in a variety of non-utilitarian shapes. The more obvious and spectacular features, however, are seen on the exteriors, especially the roofs. These include upward curves in the roof corners, towers, and even temple rooms above, as well as carvings or ironwork along the peak. Many such decorations have deep cultural meaning. Some bridges, particularly those of cantilever design, have elaborate wooden or stone entries, and some woven arch bridges in the southeast have impressive stone facades at each end.

For observers of Western covered bridges, where the "truss" is the essential element to be protected by the cover, Chinese bridges offer challenges in terms of concepts and definitions. Although Chinese bridges superficially resemble those of the West, at least in outward shape and appearance, discounting the "exotic" rooflines, Chinese bridges are conceptually different— as different from Western bridges as Chinese ideographs ("characters") are different from Western alphabets. These fundamental differences include structure, function, and aesthetics. They are one more example of local human ingenuity. They are exceptional expressions of Chinese thinking and the Chinese world view.

Covered Bridges and Folk Culture

China's temples, palaces, ancestral halls, pagodas, tombs, and shrines, even houses, all with obvious tales to tell, easily attract the attention of scholars in many fields who read the "meaning" of their location, layouts, and iconography. In the past, bridges rarely were analyzed in any way that went beyond the mechanics of their construction, which emphasized lines and materials, and highlighted their delightful aesthetics. However, as was revealed in Knapp's 2008 book, *Chinese Bridges: Living Architecture from China's Past*, bridges, especially covered bridges, must be examined like any other Chinese building. Many were traditionally built with careful attention to ritual *yishi* as well as the common elements of *fengshui* in order to influence, even insure, the fate of both the bridge as well as the community within for whom it was an important crossing. While decorative elements are not common on simple wood or stone beam bridges, ornamentation multiplies as structural components rise above the deck. Where the bridge is topped with a structure to become a covered bridge, the *langwu* corridor even may become a "temple" with a similar range of iconographic elements found in other temples. While much of the meaningful trimming found on bridges shares motifs with other architectural forms, some are distinctive to bridges because they relate to the calming of waters and protection against floods.

Fengshui

The staggering number of covered bridges in China makes it impossible to know what attention was actually paid to ritual and *fengshui* for each one. However, just as in the quest for an auspicious location for a house, grave, garden, and temple, it is likely that no bridge of any significance was positioned without attention to *fengshui* and ritual generally. *Fengshui* is rooted in the conscious selection of not only a "site"—the actual space occupied by the bridge—but also its "situation"—the location of the site in relation to its broader surroundings. The search for a suitable, even ideal and optimal spatial setting for a bridge traditionally took considerable time, as did the selection of actual building materials, such as stone and wood. In addition to determining the optimal spatial positioning of a bridge, attention customarily was also paid to the temporal dimension, the propitious timing, of all building activities. Both location and timing involved associated ritual. Traditional almanacs and the *Lu Ban jing* carpenter's manual include notations about auspicious dates for beginning the construction of buildings of many types, including bridges. When the bridge is a covered bridge, with building members like those of a house or temple, even the selection of auspicious dates and hours to fell timbers for ridgepoles and columns traditionally warranted careful consideration. When coupled with bridge-building rituals as well as protective amulets, which are discussed below, *fengshui* contributed

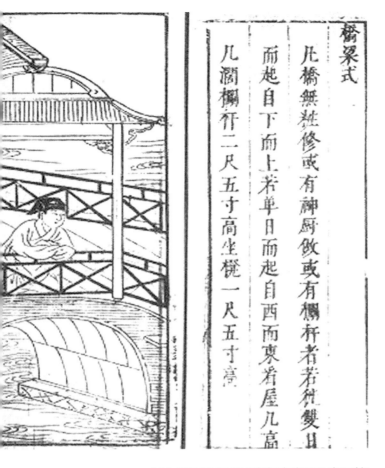

画面右側の縦書きテキスト（橋梁式）:

橋梁式

凡橋無拄修或有神廚敬或有欄杆者若衹雙日

而起自下而上若單日而起自西而東省屋几高

几澗欄杆二尺五寸高坐檻一尺五寸高

II.2.1 Although the prescription in the text alongside this woodcut in the *Lu Ban jing* or carpenter's manual only relates to a modest pavilion atop a masonry arched bridge, there are several admonitions relating to timing and proportions: "If one starts on an even day, one moves from bottom to top; if one starts on an odd day, one moves from east to west. One has to consider the height and the width of the pavilion. The balustrade is 2 *chi* 5 *cun* high, the sitting bench is 1 *chi* 5 *cun* high." Source: Facsimile of *Luban jing* reproduced in Ruitenbeek, 1993: II3.

substantially to assuring villagers and townspeople of a secure and happy life in its environs.

Recent research has provided knowledge and insights into the application of ritual and *fengshui* practices in the construction of covered bridges not only in the past but also in the construction of new covered bridges today. This is especially true in southern China where meandering streams and undulating hills offer myriad elements for thoughtful consideration by *fengshui* masters, the "interpreters of wind and water" of the Configurations School. While we have no photographic depictions of the application of *fengshui* principles in the past, there is physical evidence of decisions derived from *fengshui* considerations. And, of course, with the repair, rebuilding, and building anew of covered bridges over the past decade in Fujian, Guangxi, Guizhou, Yunnan, and Zhejiang, among other provinces, there have been many opportunities to observe and document the rituals involved.

A great many covered bridges are located in remote locations across narrow ravines in the rugged mountains that predominate in southeastern and southwestern China. As far as we have been able to determine, there are no specific records about whether any isolated covered bridge sites were chosen utilizing a geomancer. While it may be that practical considerations related to topographical features dominated, common knowledge of *fengshui* by the carpenters who built such bridges would have undoubtedly helped guide decision-making. Moreover, when a covered bridge was washed away or suffered some other destructive force, the choice of a different site was recognition of the failure, indeed inappropriateness, of the original site. *Fengshui* principles, if applied properly to a bridge, not only would insure an auspicious site but also one that was well-drained, where flooding and erosion were minimized.

Within a village or town, a decision to construct a covered bridge, indeed any type of bridge, would have been viewed as a component of a *fengshui* planned landscape. Bridges, like *fengshui* pagodas, *fengshui* woods (also called *shuikou* woods), and shrines, as well as other minor features were frequently employed in village landscapes to rebalance a site by making modifications that would counter unsatisfactory or ominous terrain characteristics (Coggins, 2012: 52–67). These modifications were assumed to improve the propitious elements of a village's overall geomantic character, a kind of layered "spatial defense" necessary to avoid misfortune. These involved features within and on the periphery of a village. In addition to *fengshui* pagodas and woods, these could include gates, *tudi gong* shrines, and *Taishan shi gandang* stones. Periodic temporal defense required the placement of protective amulets. These traditionally were complemented by the elements that forthrightly pursued good fortune, manifestations of which will be discussed further below.

Sinuous mountains are often metaphorically described as a "dragon" or *long* whose body is an undulating yet interconnected organism that may be extensive and complex or rather simple. In understanding the specific location of some of the soaring covered "rainbow bridges" of southern Zhejiang and northern Fujian, villagers describe the line of the bridge as materially completing a segment of a dragon's body draped across the hillslopes. Undulating ridges and hills to the rear, along with a meandering stream at the front, have traditionally been viewed as necessary components of a favorable village site. This notion is encapsulated in the well-known maxim *fu yang bao yang, bei shan mian shui* "*yin* at one's back, embraced by *yang*, with hills to the back and facing water." Assuming the hills indeed envelop and protect the back of a village site, it is the dynamic aspect of the stream or water that courses across the front that is of prime importance. Typically, along such a stream in a village it is possible to identify the *shuikou*, literally "mouth of the water/stream," as well as the *shuiwei* "tail of the water/stream." In some villages these are called *cunkou* "mouth of the village" and *cunwei* "tail of the village" or *chushuikou* "exit mouth of water/stream." Although these terms are sometimes used interchangeably, we can think of the *shuikou/cunkou* as at an upstream location while the *shuiwei/cunwei/chushuikou* is downstream. Covered or uncovered bridges are often found at both locations and may be referred to as a *fengshuiqiao* "*fengshui* bridge."

It is not always possible to locate a village where historical drawings, textual information, and visible material evidence are all present to outline

and affirm these *fengshui* principles. One such place is Yueshan Village, Jushui Township, Lishui City, Qingyuan County in southwestern Zhejiang Province on the border with Fujian Province. At the end of the Qing Dynasty (1644–1911), it is recorded that there were 230 covered bridges of many types in the county, but today only 97 survive, including 16 wooden arch covered bridges and an extraordinary assemblage of several in one village. Yueshan Village was established during the Song Dynasty (960–1279) by migrant members of a family named Wu, who still dominate today. As the drawing and photograph below reveal, the village is situated between a series of half-moon shaped hills behind named Yue Shan "moon hill," with flourishing stands of bamboo along its slopes, and is embraced by a crescent-shaped bend in Juxi Creek. At one time, there were ten covered bridges along less than a kilometer length of the stream. While today only five covered bridges remain, this is a remarkable number for a small village. Upstream, there are two covered bridges that serve to mark the *shuikou*, the stone arch Laifeng Bridge, and on a tributary, Baiyun Bridge. Downstream, marking the *shuiwei* where Juxi Creek exits the village, are the Rulong Bridge, which dates to 1625 during the Ming Dynasty (1368–1644) and is the oldest surviving timber bridge in China, and the Buchan Bridge. These last two are supplemented with a temple and pagoda downstream that are said to lock in the wealth of the village, thereby preserving its prosperity.

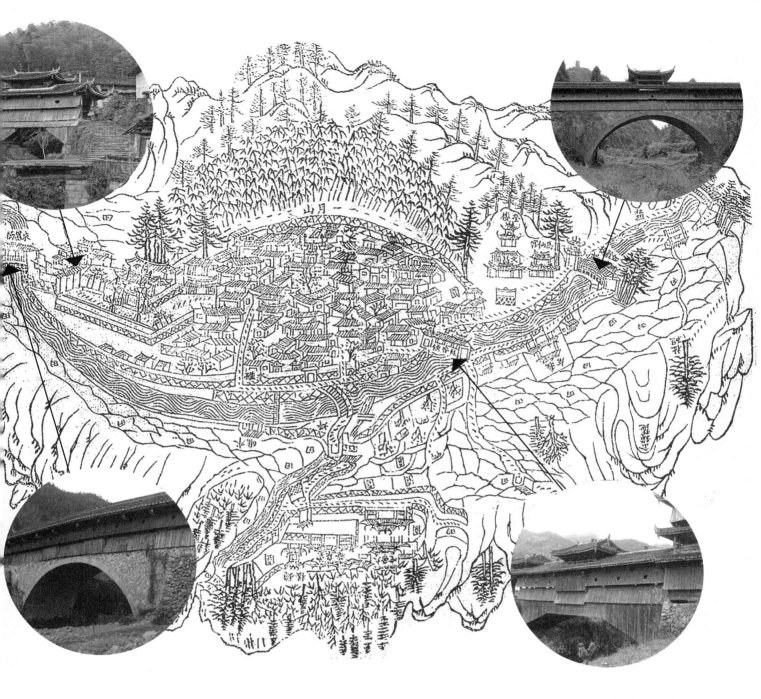

II.2.2 An undated traditional drawing of the Yueshan environs, with contemporary photos showing the location of the four strategically placed covered bridges. Source: Liu and Hu, eds, 2011: 52.

II.2.3 Cradled between a series of mountain ranges and a crescent-shaped stream, Yueshan Village in Qingyuan County, Zhejiang, embodies an ideal *fengshui* landscape. The series of strategically situated bridges enhances the model. Source: https://baike.baidu.com/item/%E6%9C%88%E5%B1%B1%E6%9D%91/8179507. Accessed February 21, 2019.

II.2.4a Laifeng Bridge.
Source: ACO, 2005.

II.2.4b Baiyun Bridge.
Source: ACO, 2005.

II.2.4c Rulong Bridge.
Source: RGK, 2005.

II.2.4d Buchan Bridge. Source: ACO, 2007.

d

Since it is believed that a covered bridge at the *shuiwei/cunwei* location where the stream exits a settlement is said to be able to hold back wealth in a village so that it does not flow away, villagers have been known to move or refashion a terminal bridge to maintain positive village *fengshui*. Indeed, if a settlement grows beyond the location of a *fengshui* bridge, the bridge may be dismantled and moved further downstream where it can serve a similar blocking purpose. A good example is the Bajiang Bridge in Bajiang Township, Sanjiang Dong Autonomous County, Guangxi, which was taken to pieces and then rebuilt some 400 meters (130 feet) downstream. Moreover, a bridge as a *fengshui* object whose presence itself was said to insure good fortune for villagers, especially the prominent families who supported its construction, had to be maintained in good shape. If a bridge were to weaken, even fall into disrepair, villagers would see this as a sign of the coming decline of the village and its inhabitants. It is no wonder then that genealogies give prominence to the charitable works of leading families who built and repaired covered bridges, tracing as it were the interdependence of fortune and landscape features.

It is not unusual to find the presence of an ancient cypress or banyan tree, with gnarled roots and rugged bark, or a *fengshui* woods made up of evergreen trees, all symbols of longevity, in the environs of a covered bridge in a village or town. A nearby shrine to the Earth God or some other spirit alongside a bridgehead further added a common spiritual element. When found together, these underscored the mutual positive complementarity in the scripting of sublime landscapes with the bridge as the unifying focus. On the other hand, the stark presence of modern roads, buildings, and even bridges today, all comparatively crudely inserted into the landscape, stand in contrast to the coordinated and sensitive decision-making often characteristic of *fengshui*.

II.2.5 The Bajiang Bridge, Guangxi, which was taken to pieces and then rebuilt some 400 meters (130 feet) downstream. This view shows the old piers in the foreground and in the distance the reconstructed bridge at a new *shuiwei* location where it serves the blocking purpose. Source: ACO, 2006.

II.2.6 An Earth God (*tudi gong*) shrine adjacent to the Yinglong Bridge, Gaojin Village, Liping County, Qiandongnan Miao and Dong Autonomous Prefecture, Guizhou. Source: TEM, 2017.

Ritual

The first effort to photographically document ceremonies associated with the building of a new *langqiao* was for the Tongle Bridge in Taishun, Zhejiang, which took place over a 26-month period between 2004 and 2006. The lengthy period was a result of the requirement to adhere to auspicious dates, and thus the project could not be hurried to completion. Hundreds of photographs were taken by Xue Yichuan, a young photographer who documented each of the steps carried out by carpenters and ritual specialists, from selecting and felling trees in the forest, carrying the logs, shaping all the timber components, adding auspicious symbols while logs rested in a trestle frame, constructing the timber understructure, fashioning the corridor, offering sacrifices before and then raising the ridgepole, setting off firecrackers, preparing a feast of a whole hog for the carpenters, among many others. A Daoist priest conducted a completion ceremony that was governed by auspicious dates and times. As with houses and temples, the rituals involved the chanting of rhymed "luck bringing" verses and the offering of a basket containing the five grains, incense, steamed buns, food and wine, and a chicken, called *ji* in Chinese and homophonous with "good luck." Each step was governed by calendrical decision-making, with the high point being *shangliang*, the raising of the ridgepole. Others have taken photographs of some of the activities associated with the renovation or construction of covered bridges, but no one has so diligently recorded the full sequence as did Xue Yichuan between 2004 and 2006.

II.2.7a–l Ritual accompanies the selection, cutting, and transporting of what will become the ridgepole for the new covered bridge. The ritual climax attends the positioning, called "raising the ridgepole" or *shangliang*. Source: XYC, 2006.

In November 2006, we witnessed the celebration accompanying the extension of the bays of the wooden framework of a new covered bridge atop a concrete base in the Sanjiang region of northern Guangxi Zhuang Autonomous Region. Replete with costumed elders, a whole roasted pig, fighting water buffalo, and endlessly noisy firecrackers, the activity in preparation for the raising of the ridgepole *shangliang* ritual was truly a community event.

II.2.8a–e Celebrating the stages in extending the framework of a new bridge.

a. Preparing to raise the ridgepole on a new covered bridge being constructed in the Sanjiang region of northern Guangxi. Source: ACO, 2007.

b. This pig, to be shared at a community feast, is paraded through the village. Source: LLK, 2007.

c. Water buffalo fighting as part of the community celebration for the raising of the ridgepole. Source: ACO, 2007.

d. Village elders preparing for the completion of the bridge ceremony. Source: LLK, 2007.

黄牛鬥角

II.2.9a, b Among the paintings that celebrate Dong minority village customs within the Diping Bridge is this depiction of a pair of hornless buffalo battling, which is a mirror that was seen in Guangxi a decade earlier. Diping County, Guizhou. Source: RGK, 2017; RGK, 2007.

II.2.8e Women and men eat in separate venues to celebrate the raising of the ridgepole of the nearby bridge. Source: ACO, 2007.

More recently, Liu Yan, who has completed the most systematic onsite examination of woven arch timber bridges, has videotaped building rituals throughout Zhejiang Province. Her images here focus on preparations for raising the ridgepole of a new covered bridge in Shengshuitang Village, Qingyuan County, Zhejiang Province.

II.2.10a–e This sequence of photos emphasizes the ritual involved in preparing and raising the ridgepole for the new Guanyin Bridge in Shengshuitang Village, Longgong Xiang, Qingyuan County, Zhejiang. Master Wu Fuyong from Daji Village in Qingyuan County presides over the ritual. Source: LY, 2012.

If one glances up at the ridgepole or pays careful attention to some of the columns within any old covered bridge, it is possible to see the residuum of past ritual, arcane characters inscribed directly on the timbers or hung from paper attached to them. These usually include combined *taiji* and *l* symbols as anti-spectral charms, just as traditionally has been the case for the ridgepole of a traditional dwelling. Today, moreover, one sometimes stumbles across an incomplete new covered bridge, seemingly abandoned, but actually only temporarily in a state of suspension until the next appropriate "lucky day" arrives to move on to the next step in the building process. When the bridge is finally completed, a concluding auspicious day must be determined to hold a ceremony of completion, including an expansive banquet, for all of the workers as well as those in the community who contributed to the bridge's construction. Some ornamentation endures because it was carved in stone or wood, while others are only periodically obvious as they appear and reappear as the seasons change. In some cases, the meaning of the imagery is lost because the conditions that made them evident are forgotten or lay latent because they are overlain with newer elements.

II.2.11 A *taiji* symbol visible beneath the ridgepole of a covered bridge in the Sanjiang area, Guangxi. Source: ACO, 2007.

II.2.12 Protective Daoist spirit writing on the Liuzhai Bridge, Sankui Township, Taishun County, Zhejiang. Source: ACO, 2005.

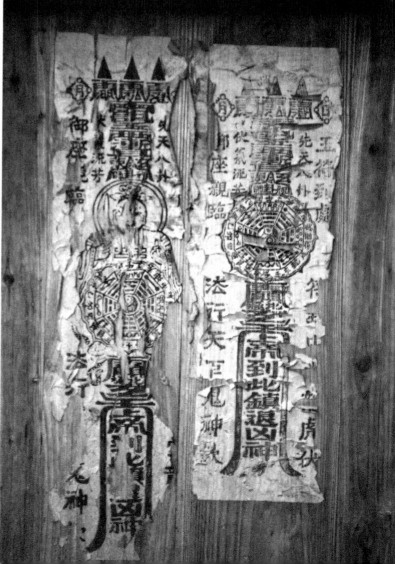

II.2.13 *Taiji* and *bagua* symbols on the ridgepole of the newly rebuilt Shuanglong Bridge, Baishuiyang Shuangxi Township, Pingnan County, Fujian. Source: RGK, 2009.

II.2.14 On the underside of this ridgepole is recorded the July 19, 2000 date when the ritual took place. Reconstructed Wenfeng Bridge, Mappingguan, a trading town on the Tea-Horse Road in southwestern Yunnan. Source: RGK, 2016.

II.2.15 Auspicious banners attached to columns on an uncompleted covered bridge during a respite period while carpenters wait for a "lucky day" to finish the project. Sanjiang Dong Autonomous County, Guangxi. Source: ACO, 2006.

Protective Amulets and Auspicious Charms

There is no documented evidence that carpenters or masons involved in the construction of covered bridges in the past employed the kind of "building magic" common with house building (Knapp, 2005: 109–31). It is nonetheless possible that those responsible for building a bridge sometimes had to counter whatever sorcery was employed by carpenters or masons who had been unhappy with their payment or treatment, in order to "protect" the bridge and those who used it from such malicious efforts. Prophylactic amulets and actions have always been an important preventative measure taken in building in China and it should not be surprising that some are found around and about covered bridges even as most covered bridges are unadorned and rather plain.

A veritable menagerie of both mythological and actual animal forms are common features associated with important old stone bridges throughout China as both protective amulets and auspicious emblems (Knapp, 2008b: 82–5, 119).[4] [For a comprehensive illustrated discussion of animal forms, see Tang Huancheng, 2011: 289–304.] While far fewer have been observed around covered bridges today, old photographs of covered bridges no longer standing reveal the presence of some protecting entry animals not seen today.

Animals as protective amulets whose purpose is the "calming of the waters," essentially protection against floodwaters that too often rise quickly, date back at least 2,000 years. Mythological dragons and *taotie* especially have been seen as having an efficacy against dangers inherent with running water because of their mere presence. Dragons, of course, represent but one manifestation of a creature the Chinese have held to be truly magical and that exists in many configurations. Indeed, the mythological connotations of Chinese dragons are manifold as is their size, shape, and how they are portrayed. Besides being common symbols of good luck and symbolic of imperial power, some of the nine types of dragons traditionally were believed to have utilitarian functions in regard to water. While the spirit dragon *shenlong* lived in the sky and had the capacity to bring needed rain, the water dragon *jiaolong*, sometimes called the "flood dragon," ruled over underground springs and surface water, inhabiting as it did deep pools of water. Here and there in China, such as in Dajitou Village, Lingtou Township, Qingyuan County, Zhejiang, one can encounter a covered or uncovered bridge whose name is Jiaolong Bridge.

According to popular legend, Emperor Yu, while engaged in curbing the great flood that scourged the country in about 2205 BCE, had the assistance of a dragon to map out waterways with its writhing tail. Endowed with the ability to summon clouds and bring forth rain, as well as control floods that cause destruction and death, the dynamic dragon represented a beneficent power. In averting drought, providing needed water, and thus insuring a good harvest, a dragon contributed to the stability of the empire. The dragon, it was said, usually appeared with the spring equinox, the time of planting, and descended into its chasm to rest at the autumn equinox, the end of the flood season. Dragons are carved on brackets and placed above stone piers that point upstream, as in the Jinlong Bridge in Jianchuan County, Yunnan. The Yinglong Bridge, Maogong Township, Liping County, Guizhou, has the evocative name "Welcome the Dragon Bridge," that is accompanied by carved stone dragons at the base of the entry columns. Both of these bridges are further described and illustrated in Part III.

Throughout southern China especially, three-dimensional writhing dragons are positioned as totems above the ridgepole as well as on paintings

---

[4] For a comprehensive illustrated discussion of animal forms, see Tang Huancheng, 2011: 289–304.

within the galleries of covered bridges. A motif that is commonly found on textiles and porcelain is that of a pair of writhing dragons pursuing a mystical and somewhat elusive flaming pearl. The seventeenth-century Liuzhai Bridge and the late twentieth-century Tongle Bridge in Taishun County, Zhejiang, both have this as an exterior motif above the roofline. When coupled together on a bridge, the dragon and phoenix represent a powerfully positive *fengshui* amulet representing balanced *yang* and *yin*, in addition to auspiciousness. The *fenghuang*, a mythological bird that also symbolizes the union of *yin* and *yang*, is sometimes paired with a dragon. Both are poised somewhat precariously and dramatically above the entry to the Beijian Bridge in Taishun, Zhejiang.

c Jinlong Bridge, Jianchuan County, Yunnan. Source: TEM, 2016.

d A dragon at the base of the columns, Yinglong Bridge, Gaojin Village, Maogong Township, Liping County, Guizhou. Source: TEM, 2016.

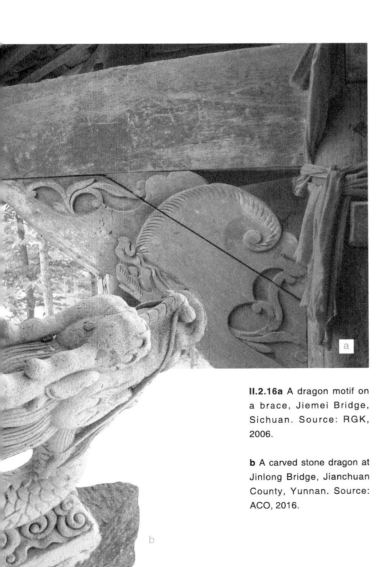

II.2.16a A dragon motif on a brace, Jiemei Bridge, Sichuan. Source: RGK, 2006.

b A carved stone dragon at Jinlong Bridge, Jianchuan County, Yunnan. Source: ACO, 2016.

II.2.17 Here, atop the ridgepole, is a pair of mythical dragons chasing a flaming pearl, a motif suggesting strength and good fortune. Liuzhai Bridge, Taishun. Source: ACO, 2006.

II.2.18a, b Two dragons facing one another in the air and apparently rushing toward a floating pearl. Tongle Bridge, Taishun County, Zhejiang. Source: XYC, 2006.

II.2.19 Auspicious *fenghuang* on the Beijian Bridge, Taishun County, Zhejiang. Source: RGK, 2006.

The supernatural *taotie*, a mythical, ferocious looking beast with a head but no body, said to be the benign offspring of the dragon, is found on many uncovered stone bridges. According to a Song poem, the grimacing and gluttonous *taotie*-like bridge stands ready "to kill the anger of the flood" by devouring the gushing water, much as the use of the Chinese character *tun*, meaning "devour," is sometimes seen written on a mirror above a door to a house. The only *taotie* we have encountered on a covered bridge is on the keystone of the Jingxing (Qiaoloudian) Bridge that has above it the Fuqing Temple, which together span a narrow gorge in the Cangyan Mountains of Hebei Province.

II.2.20 *Taotie*, a ferocious looking beast, is said "to kill the anger of the flood." Jingxing (Qiaoloudian) Bridge in the Fuqing ("Fortune Celebration") Temple, Cangyan Mountains, Hebei Province. Source: ACO, 2006.

Found on the keystone of some stone bridges on the north China plain is a stylized carved animal mask in the shape of a *chiwen*, another spawn of the dragon, which also is carved on the roof ridges of buildings as a defense against fire. Associated with covered bridges, this feature has been observed on the roof of the Wuting Pavilion in Yangzhou, Jiangsu. On the beams of bridges, their appearance reflects their fondness for water. As powerful representative forms, the dragon and the many guises of its offspring clearly serve as protective amulets.

II.2.21 *Chiwen* and *shou* "longevity" ornamentation at the Wuting ("Five Pavilions") Bridge, Yangzhou, Jiangsu. Source: RGK, 2006.

Although elephants are rarely thought of as animals associated with China, they appeared as a motif in traditional Chinese arts and, indeed, several hundred still roam the fragmented seasonal rainforests of southern Yunnan Province bordering Laos and Myanmar. The best-known pair of elephants appear on the west end of the Lugou Bridge, positioned to buttress its structure. While no elephants have been encountered on present-day covered bridges, an early photograph of the portal of a covered bridge near Kunming, Yunnan, depicts two elephants. Likewise, a pair of sturdy cast-iron oxen were positioned as amulets to protect

the Guangji (Xiangzi) Bridge across the Hanjiang River in Chaozhou, Guangdong, in 1724. One was placed in a pavilion on the east end, with the other in a pavilion on the west end. However, in 1842, as a result of a flood, the one on the east side was washed from the abutment and fell into the river. A mismatched pair of weighty stone animals, which may have served a more central function, today rest with a holder for incense at the entry to the Caifeng Bridge in Yunlong County, Yunnan

II.2.24 Although mismatched and likely each was once part of a pair, these chimera-like animals are outside the portal of Caifeng Bridge in Yunlong County, Yunnan. Source: TEM, 2016.

II.2.22 Elephants at the portal of the Anlan Bridge, Kunming, Yunnan. Source: RGK Collection.

II.2.23 The iron ox on the east side of the Hanjiang River at the bridgehead of the Guangji Bridge. Source: Unknown.

II.2.25 A prominent fish, representing abundance, rises here from the gable end of the Xuezhai Bridge, Taishun County, Zhejiang. Source: ACO, 2006.

II.2.26a This protective water amulet above the portal is accompanied by a pair of hanging fish symbolizing prosperity. Xiaguang bridge, Hengkeng Township, Taishun County. Source: TEM, 2005

II.2.26b A water amulet combined with a fish, representing abundance, and a lotus, Xianju Bridge, Taishun, Zhejiang. Source: ACO, 2006.

a

b

Just as they are in homes and temples, pictorial representations of bats are found on and about some bridges. Unlike in the West where bats are generally avoided and sometimes seen as inauspicious, in China they are regarded as graceful flying animals because of the homophonic relationship between the Chinese character *fu*, meaning "good fortune," "blessing," or "luck," and the word for bat *bianfu*. Bats are sometimes shown upside down, as observed in the wooden ceiling structures of covered bridges, with the meaning that "*fu* has arrived," in the belief that stating something will make it happen. Because bats are often portrayed ornately and gracefully, they can be mistaken for butterflies, and the first syllable of the word for butterfly *hudie* is itself a near homonym for *fu*. Throughout southern Fujian, where local dialects pronounce "tiger" as *fu* (*hu* in standard Chinese), the tiger is commonly used as an emblem for good fortune as well. Bats, butterflies, and tigers are occasionally shown in groups of five to represent the five essential components of good fortune or happiness: longevity, wealth, health, love of virtue, and to die a natural death in old age.

II.2.27 A bat, representing good fortune, positioned in the ceiling of Xidong Bridge, Taishun County, Zhejiang. Source: ACO, 2006.

II.2.28 Supplementing this kingpost structure is an ornamental transverse wooden brace in the shape of a stylized bat. Xuezhai Bridge, Sankui Township, Taishun County, Zhejiang. Source: ACO, 2006.

Carpenters and painters sometimes traditionally added ornate decorative panels within the arcades of covered bridges. While some are auspicious emblems incorporated in ornamented patterns employing a pictorial vocabulary that is dense with symbolic meaning, others tell tales of community celebrations, thus are documents regarding local life. Vignettes illustrating themes from opera performances and folktales generally are recognizable in these pictorial compositions. While the motifs incorporating animals and plants are sometimes relatively simple, others are part of narrative scenes that express allegorical morality tales. As places to sit or walk through, China's bridges, like other buildings, provided rich imagery containing easily retrievable and universal messages. During the Cultural Revolution, covered bridges, like other structures, provided blank, yet public, spaces for political exhortations. Even after nearly a half century, faded slogans are still visible. Today, with an emphasis on acclaiming covered bridges as part of a village's cultural heritage, bulbous red lanterns and celebratory *duilian* are often hung inside the bridge corridor, as can be seen in many photographs in this book. Throughout the Dong minority areas of Guizhou and Guangxi, many covered bridges have paintings of local folk practices on the upper registers inside.

Some of the inscriptions seen on and about the shrines invite supplication to the deities represented within the niche. The four characters 有求必应, meaning "one will be granted whatever is requested," are found within some bridges as well on exterior shrines dedicated to that same all-purpose sentiment.

II.2.29 Merely a small roadside covered bridge the Tongde Bridge in Liping County, Guizhou, has many paintings that celebrate local folk customs including instrumental music played by men and spinning carried out by women. Source: TEM 2017.

II.2.30a–c Colorful paintings of local folk practices including music performances during festivals, are found within some covered bridges. a, b Diping Bridge, Liping County, Guizhou; c unnamed bridge Liping County, Guizhou. Source: TEM, 2017.

II.2.31 Placed within the octagonal inset in the ceiling of this bridge are the four beseeching characters 有求必应, meaning "to grant whatever is asked for." Yanghoucuo Bridge, Zhenghe County, Fujian. Source: RGK, 2007.

Some auspicious elements seen within and about *langqiao* are inserted by local villagers and townspeople who believe in their efficacy. Rather than employed by craftspeople during construction, they are placed at irregular times to meet personal needs. One example, occasionally found hanging from the ridgepoles of old and even new covered bridges in southern China, is a wrapped pair of chopsticks because of the homophonous association linking the word for chopsticks *kuaizi* with "sons coming quickly." Sometimes a hollowed-out bamboo tube containing red chopsticks, invoking hopes for fertility and prosperity, is hung at the entrance to the corridor of some bridges These are seen also in rural temples and shrines.

II.2.32 Red chopsticks hanging from the eves of the Jialong Bridge, Dalixi Village, Shuangxi Township, Zhenghe County, Fujian. Source: RGK, 2013.

Although rarely observed in village covered bridges but seen more often in temples are small red cloth packets affixed to columns. A collection of these was spotted at the entrance to the Jiaolong Bridge in Zhenghe County, Fujian. We suspected these packets contained "the five grains," [五谷] an auspicious figure of speech that embraces all grains that are part of the phrase *wu gu fengdeng* [五谷丰登] calling for "an abundant harvest of all food crops." While the names of the five grains have varied over time and differ from region to region, the list usually includes most of the following: rice, wheat, corn, millet, sesame, barley, and soybean. Since it was noted that the contents of one packet had split and spilled its contents, close examination, as seen in the photograph, revealed more than five different types of staple crops, some of which we could not identify.

Buddhism, Public Support, and Bridge Building

During dynastic China, local magistrates had the responsibility for constructing and maintaining bridges of all types. "If the footbridges are built by the eleventh month and the carriage bridges by the twelfth month every year, the people will not suffer the hardship of fording," according to the philosopher Mencius, who said magistrates should show concern for the welfare of the local population (Lau, 1984: 128). Later, it was reported that a Qing magistrate "could be punished with a year's loss of salary if an important bridge in his jurisdiction collapsed, and lashed thirty strokes if he failed to repair a dilapidated bridge" (Kieschnick, 2003: 209). Magistrates, aware of their responsibility, however, still required a trustworthy individual or organization to facilitate the effort involved.

II.2.33a–c Red packets of assorted grain are attached to a bridge column as an invocation for "an abundant harvest of all food crops." Source: RGK, 2013.

Local magistrates in some areas of the country called upon local Buddhist monks not only to accumulate the funds but also to arrange for materials and labor, sometimes even to carry out the design and actual construction. But why monks? Kieschnick outlines five reasons spelled out by a Song Dynasty(960–1279) author: "… monks are devoted to helping others and hence willing to work tirelessly; monks have developed powerful capacities of concentration (through meditation) and hence do not abandon a project before it is completed; a monk is not burdened by wife or children and hence does not keep money for his family; monks believe in the principle of karmic retribution and hence are not corrupt; because the monk is devoted to the task, great men support him and lesser men follow him" (2003: 206).

Extensive records reveal how monks served as linking connections between local government and individuals and families who had the capacity to be actual donors. Community elites often were the object of solicitations of financial support for public works like bridges and roads in addition to community facilities such as temples and academies. Major donors were assured of the importance of their compassionate philanthropy. A necessary task would be accomplished that would benefit the public at large and, sometimes more importantly, as an act of piety, "the good would be rewarded through the Buddhist mechanism of merit of which bridge-building was a part" (Kieschnick, 2003: 213). Of course, with charitable acts, there no doubt was an assortment of motives and a panoply of incentives, some altruistic and benevolent, others selfish and self-serving.

Be this as it may, bridges of incalculable number got built and maintained throughout China because of the mutual interdependence of a triangle of individuals: magistrates-monks-donors. As can still be seen today at the portals of many covered bridges, stone stelae were sometimes carved to memorialize the narrative of giving and accomplishment, often alongside subsidiary stelae with a detailed accounting of each and every contribution made from near and far. The repetition of surnames and association of given names sometimes reveal the power of a local lineage, where each of the specific amounts of the individual contributions by patrons is listed clearly. Many of these stelae include Buddhist imagery and stock phrases relating to gaining merit. Set up at one of the bridgeheads, such stelae over time came to provide a narrative of a community's role in the maintenance of a bridge as a public resource. Although dedicatory stelae still can be seen at the entrance of many covered bridges in China, we have not yet been able to examine the relationships between local officials, monks, and donors.

Yet, even today, the renovation of an old bridge or the building of a new one reflects a level of organization, record keeping, and public display that is remarkable. Throughout rural China,

one can still witness the solicitation of funds in support of a covered bridge. Wooden tablets, paper banners, and stone stelae register the names and specific amounts contributed by donors on a "Public Virtue Roster" *gongde bang*, sometimes ranked in decreasing order according to the amount given and sometimes listed according to when the contributions were made. *Gongde bang* seen today range from handwritten characters on rough boards to inscribed slabs of stone. Today, in addition, corporate and government sponsors play important roles in funding some of the key covered bridges undergoing reconstruction and are acknowledged on the *gongde bang*. Although rare, it is sometimes possible to encounter a monk or a village elder on an out of the way bridge sitting on a bench and soliciting passersby for small donations for the maintenance or rebuilding of the bridge.

Beyond the role of financial managers, there are records that reveal that monks actually designed bridges and were actively involved in arranging materials and labor as well as participating in construction work as carpenters and masons. Some of the best and most accessible documentation of this concerns the building of the megalithic stone bridges in Fujian where a number of well-known monks gained substantial experience as "engineers." Needham (1971: 154–5) highlights the work of the monk Dao Xun, who during the thirteenth century is said to have built more than 200 bridges of many types, calling him and others "monastic technologists." However, having said this, we have not yet uncovered any evidence that a specific covered bridge anywhere in China was either designed or constructed by local monks. The association with adjacent temples and inside shrines suggests that this is a subject worth exploring further.

II.2.34a The names of donors to the Yuwen Bridge are inscribed on wooden and stone plaques. Zhouling Township, Taishun County, Zhejiang. Source: ACO, 2006.

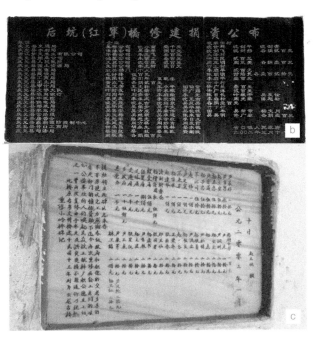

b The restoration of the Houkeng Bridge, also called the Red Army Bridge, benefitted from the contributions of local governmental bureaus, corporations, and local citizens. Zhukou Township, Qingyuan County, Zhejiang. Source: ACO, 2007.

c A plaque commemorating the 2003 renovation of Wenming Bridge, Mapingguan Village, Yunlong County, Yunnan. Source: RGK, 2016.

Bridges and Worship

The commonly heard phrase "where there is a temple, there is a bridge; where there is a bridge, there is a temple" ["庙庙有桥，桥桥有庙" and "有庙有桥，有桥有庙"] points to the centrality of devotion associated with a structure that might at first blush only seem to be a route of passage across water. Yet, historically there was an association of bridges with temples and shrines that was deeply rooted in Chinese culture, even going beyond their construction being supervised by monks and the resources making them possible arising from a quest for merit by the faithful. One of the outstanding pairings is in Pingnan County, Fujian, at the Song Dynasty (960–1279) Wan'an Bridge, which does not have a shrine within. Adjacent to the east end of the bridge is the expansive Shengwang dian (also called Dasheng miao), a temple dedicated to Sun Wukong, the Monkey King. Temples like this are scattered throughout northern Fujian, although this is the only one at the head of a covered bridge. Clad in armor and wielding a cudgel, the Monkey God is said to be benevolent. This temple has a large opera stage with a spacious forecourt to accommodate large crowds of villagers on festival days.

Because of the tumult of the past century and a half in China, countless temples and shrines that were once common were obliterated because of political campaigns and disinterested decay, leaving behind bare traces of an earlier religious building tradition. Sometimes, it is only a local place name that echoes an earlier existence of a bridge. Moreover, throughout China many covered bridges have been stripped of all their religious elements, preserving simply a shell with the empty wooden case or small brick shrine called *shenkan* inside that once held gods and the accouterments of worship but is now empty. In some cases, once vivid religious iconography has been chiseled off, leaving mere scarred suggestions of past practices. In newly reconstructed bridges, empty niches are quite common. Some restored covered bridges lack shrines because they are no longer used as passageways for local villagers and are currently frequented only by Chinese tourists who arrive merely to take photographs. Some covered bridges that have been bypassed no longer are on routes that require villagers to pass through them, thus their role as places to rest or to offer prayers stand rather desolate. Some *langqiao*, nonetheless, have makeshift shrines that serve to meet the needs of an occasional passerby.

II.2.35 As the focus of the Monkey cult, Qitian dasheng and his two attendants each wear a headband and wield a cudgel. Changqiao Township, Pingnan County, Fujian. Source: ACO, 2006.

II.2.36 The successful restoration of the Houkeng Bridge, which received a UNESCO Asia-Pacific Conservation Award in 2005, included an extensive niche that once would have held statues and other ritual paraphernalia. Source: ACO, 2007.

II.2.37 This makeshift shrine in the Guangli Bridge comprises a mixture of salvaged tables, with the high altar table made of common bricks and a wooden top. Lingxia Township, Pingnan County, Fujian. Source: RGK, 2009.

II.2.38 Although the 38-meter (125-foot)-long Qiaozhai Wind-and-Rain Bridge is a popular meeting place for village men, there is no formal shrine. Just two stacks of bricks provide a platform near the bridge with receptacles to hold burning incense. Hongzhou Township, Liping County, Guizhou. Source: TEM, 2017.

II.2.39 This improvised altar sits within a niche that once likely had images of gods, which are all gone and are now replaced by an assortment of cans and bottles and a vessel for incense. He'an Wind-and-Rain Bridge, Liangkou Township, Sanjiang County, Guangxi. Source: TEM, 2017.

II.2.40 Rather remote, the Luoling Bridge is regularly visited by local villagers as they traverse the mountainside paths. Yangyuan Township, Zhenghe County, Fujian. Source: RGK, 2013.

II.2.41 The Guanyin Bridge was restored in 2012 with a solid masonry altar complex that receives heavy visitation, as seen in the residue from the burning of candles and incense. Sheng Shui Tang Village, Longgong Township, Qingyuan County, Zhejiang. Source: RGK, 2009.

Still, in the countryside it is quite common to see active shrines and altars on, within, and adjacent to old covered bridges and even some new bridges, the variety of which resonates the rich diversity of religious traditions in China. Not only were temples sometimes built adjacent to covered bridges as a *fengshui* element related to *shuikou* or *shuiwei*, shrines were frequently built inside the corridor along a wall. In a few cases, as will be seen below, some covered bridges have a full-fledged temple on top. Sometimes the names of a bridge and a nearby temple or shrine are the same, a fact that reinforces their interdependence. Some temples are merely nearby, but many are located next to the bridge and are associated with

it. When this is so, the shrine inside the bridge is either modest or eliminated entirely in deference to that in the temple. Nearby temples typically include a stage for the performance of local opera *xiju* or narrative singing *shuochang*. Since opera is intended to entertain the chief deity of the temple on his/her birthday and is only incidentally intended for human viewers, there are no provisions for seating an audience. Instead, those watching stand around or go into the balconies usually found on both sides of the bridge, which are accessed by steps. If there is no space just offstage for the musicians, they may play from one of these side balconies.

II.2.42a–c This modest single-arch bridge constructed of red lateritic adobe bricks is adjacent to the Guan Gong Shenzhun Temple. Both structures share the same name. Yunlong County, Dali Prefecture, Yunnan. Source: RGK, 2016.

Perhaps nowhere are temples and shrines associated with covered bridges still found in such numbers as in the mountains of Fujian, Jiangxi, and Zhejiang provinces where folk religion is especially syncretistic. In the central portion of most covered bridges in these provinces, altars to major gods in the Daoist or Buddhist pantheon, as well as lesser local or regional gods, are common. Within the Bailiang Bridge in Yin County, Zhejiang, the cases with deities run the full length of the corridor instead of simply in the middle bay. Others, such as the Jinzao Bridge in Pingnan County, Fujian, though not as extensive, occupy at least the middle bay with some behind glass, others open, and still others essentially empty of images but showing evidence of at least occasional use. Chinese characters that once were bold are often barely visible, with their message faded. Wax drippings, ash residue, darkened beams, and burnt incense suggest in many cases continuing use. Some gods can be implored when a villager is facing illness or misfortune. Some exist merely as intermediaries that can be prayed to when assistance is needed from a higher god. The images of deities are found in various forms: printed on paper, molded of clay, or carved out of wood.

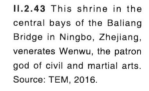

II.2.43 This shrine in the central bays of the Baliang Bridge in Ningbo, Zhejiang, venerates Wenwu, the patron god of civil and martial arts. Source: TEM, 2016.

II.2.44 Located in the central bay of the refurbished Jinzao Bridge, this niche and tables for the accouterments of ritual reveal active use. Jinzao Village, Tangkou Township, Pingnan Country, Fujian. Source: RGK, 2009.

II.2.45 Located along a path that crosses a narrow mountain gully within Yueshan Village, the short Baiyun Bridge has within it a popular shrine. Source: RGK, 2006.

At one time, a stove for burning spirit money was beside every altar, but today, because of the fear of fire and as a precaution, many are placed outside the wooden structure. Some altars are attended, but most are not. Visitors can purchase candles or incense and deposit money into a box. There usually are cushions to kneel on. On the altar of some bridges, as in any temple, is a wooden container holding numbered bamboo sticks, each one with a number and writing that represents an idea, action, or suggestion. The one seeking advice shakes the container until one stick jumps out. This one, which is said to be capable of indicating the future, has a number on it that corresponds with a poetic passage written on a sheet of paper hanging on the wall. While many of these gods and goddesses can be approached at any time, most receive special attention on the birthday of the god or goddess. On these special days, the image is removed from the shrine and set into a wooden palanquin, usually stored in the rafters above the altar, and then carried in a noisy procession before the doors of all families in a village. The cycle of the agricultural calendar in Fujian, Jiangxi, and Zhejiang once was replete with dates to celebrate the gods and goddesses. Today, for the most part, these practices no longer recur with the frequency of past times. Indeed, that most of these storage lofts are empty today indicates the likely absence of periodic parading of deities.

II.2.46a, b An older fired brick and stone furnace inside and a new safer one outside are used for burning paper offerings. Qiancheng Bridge, Tangkou Village, Tangkou Township, Pingnan County, Fujian. Source: RGK, 2009.

II.2.47a–c The incense censer and altar that were once within the Santiao Bridge were moved outside during renovation. Subsequently, the shrine was enlarged. Santiao Bridge, Taishun County, Zhejiang. Source: RGK, 2006.

II.2.48a–e At an active shrine within the Donguan Bridge, spirit money is for sale for burning in the furnace adjacent to the altar. DongmeiVillage, Dongguan Township between Yongchun and Xianyou counties, Fujian. Source: ACO, 2006.

II.2.49 After the reconstruction of the Jinlong Bridge in Jianchuan County, Yunnan, a stone censor was placed outside the wooden structure. Source: TEM, 2016.

While most altars are inserted in a bay at the middle of a covered bridge or in a shrine at the end of the bridge, there are some bridges with a separate space for worship on a second level at the heart of the bridge. Yuwen Bridge in Zhoubian Village, Zhouling Township in Taishun, Zhejiang, is an exquisite open wooden structure built atop a stone base with a single arch. Shaded by a pair of old trees, a gnarled camphor and a pine, and framed by the large boulders of a narrow ravine at the *shuiwei* downstream position for Zhoubian Village, the site is indeed magical. Midway across the span, a wooden ladder leads to a loft on the second story, with a double-tiered flying eaves form similar to that found on top of country temples. The extensive religious space on this second level, called the Wenchang Pavilion, enshrines the Daoist deity Imperial Sovereign Wenchang Di, who is said to be the "Promoter of Benevolence and Controller of Wealth Who Serves the Origin and Initiates Salvation." A compound deity, Wenchang is revered as a model of filial piety and benevolence, especially because of loyalty towards his mother, and as the regulator of appointments of officials. Popularly known to Westerners as the God of Literature, he is usually depicted wearing the robe of an official and holding a scepter. A pair of faithful boy attendants, one named Tianlong, meaning "born deaf," and the other Diya, meaning "born mute," accompanies him. It is said that he intentionally employs two handicapped boys since the one who can hear cannot speak, while

II.2.50 Although the Yuwen Bridge is not large, the second-level space focuses on an important shrine to the Daoist deity Wenchang Di, known as a model of benevolence and filial piety. ZhoulingTownship, Taishun County, Zhejiang. Source: ACO, 2005.

II.2.51 Where a shrine is not incorporated within an old bridge, it is likely to be somewhere nearby. Often created by villagers, these shrines are sometimes crude yet are regularly attended. Caifeng Bridge, Yunlong County, Yunnan. Source: TEM, 2016.

the other can speak but cannot hear, thus insuring confidence.

Another covered bridge with a second-story temple is the Liuzhai Bridge. Dating to the early fifteenth century, the upstairs temple is said to hold artifacts that are over five centuries old.

Constructed at the constricted *shuiwei* location for the village, the bridge not only served as an important link in a rural route network but functioned as a significant ritual site for the community.

Social Spaces

More than a crossing, more than a shrine, more than a *fengshui* element, China's covered bridges are also important social spaces. In a village or town, covered bridges frequently serve as the site of a morning market and as a location for nearby residents to congregate and pass the time with others or to be alone. Today, many are veritable community centers, with tables for games and low stools for socializing. The wooden benches ranged lengthwise on the interior sides provide places to sit and are often wide enough to stretch out for a nap. As will be made clearer when individual bridges are discussed in Part III, what appear to be mere out of the way crossings serve as shelter for itinerant porters to rest or spend the night whether the weather is fine or inclement. In some cases, covered bridges are venues for local festivals. China's covered bridges, unlike those in North America and Europe that were constructed as vehicular crossings, traditionally served only for the passage of pedestrians, animals, and carts, but today increasingly comingle with motorbikes as they provide shortcuts between villages.

The overhang at the entry of a covered bridge, as can be seen in Badou Bridge in the Sanjiang Dong Nationality Autonomous County in Guangxi, provides shelter for local farmers to sell fresh vegetables and meat to local villagers. As will be discussed later as a featured bridge, the reconstructed Longjin Wind-and-Rain Bridge in Zhijiang Town, Hunan Province, is an enormous marketplace with both fixed stalls and itinerant traders that cater to the needs of a continuous stream of townsfolk. Set among the retail and service stalls are spaces for folk to play cards, smoke, and chat. Some covered bridges, however, come to life only during periodic market days when villagers from a distance stream into town to both sell their surplus and to purchase needed supplies. While only a very short covered structure over a gully, the Jiezifang Bridge in Yunnan links paths and a public road to a marketplace. On the bridge,

II.2.52a–c Spanning a narrow stream with only a timber beam structure, the 38.4-meter (126-foot)-long Liuzhai Bridge extends substantially over the embankments. With its low profile and somber colored corridor, it is a surprise that there is a second-level temple accessed by wooden steps. Here, in a brightly lit area are altars on both ends with abundant hangings that indicate active use. Sankui Township, Taishun County, Zhejiang. Source: ACO, 2009.

an entrepreneurial woman regularly sets up on market days a charcoal barbeque with roasted meat for sale. Within many of the new urban covered bridges, components of extensive interconnected riverside parks open only to pedestrians and not vehicular traffic, the open areas are employed for group exercises and dancing.

II.2.53 A morning market at the foot of Badou Bridge in Bajiang Township, Sanjiang County, Guangxi. Source: ACO, 2006.

II.2.55a, b Men are more likely to hang out and pass their time at midday on a covered bridge. Qiaozhai Wind-and-Rain Bridge, Pingjia Village, HongzhouTownship, Liping County, Guizhou. Source: TEM, 2017.

II.2.54 On a periodic market day, the short Jiezifang Bridge provides a critical link between a road and a village marketplace. Here, an enterprising woman sells roasted meat on sticks. Yunlong County, Yunnan. Source: TEM, 2016.

II.2.56a, b Dating from the middle of the Ming Dynasty (1368–1644), the Longjin Wind-and-Rain Bridge provides space for a comprehensive marketplace for goods and services.In addition to a multiplicity of stalls, there are extensive open spaces for sitting, playing games, and chatting with friends. Itinerants are able to sell goods as well. The bridge, which crosses the Wushui River, is 147 meters (482 feet) long.Zhijiang County, Hunan. Source: TEM, 2016.

II.2.57a, b Mornings often bring woman and young girls to the parks alongside streams in Chinese towns where they exercise and dance to recorded music. In some towns, newly constructed covered bridges provide breezy spaces both inside and out for activity. Qianjiang Bridge, Chongqing Municipality. Source: TEM, 2016.

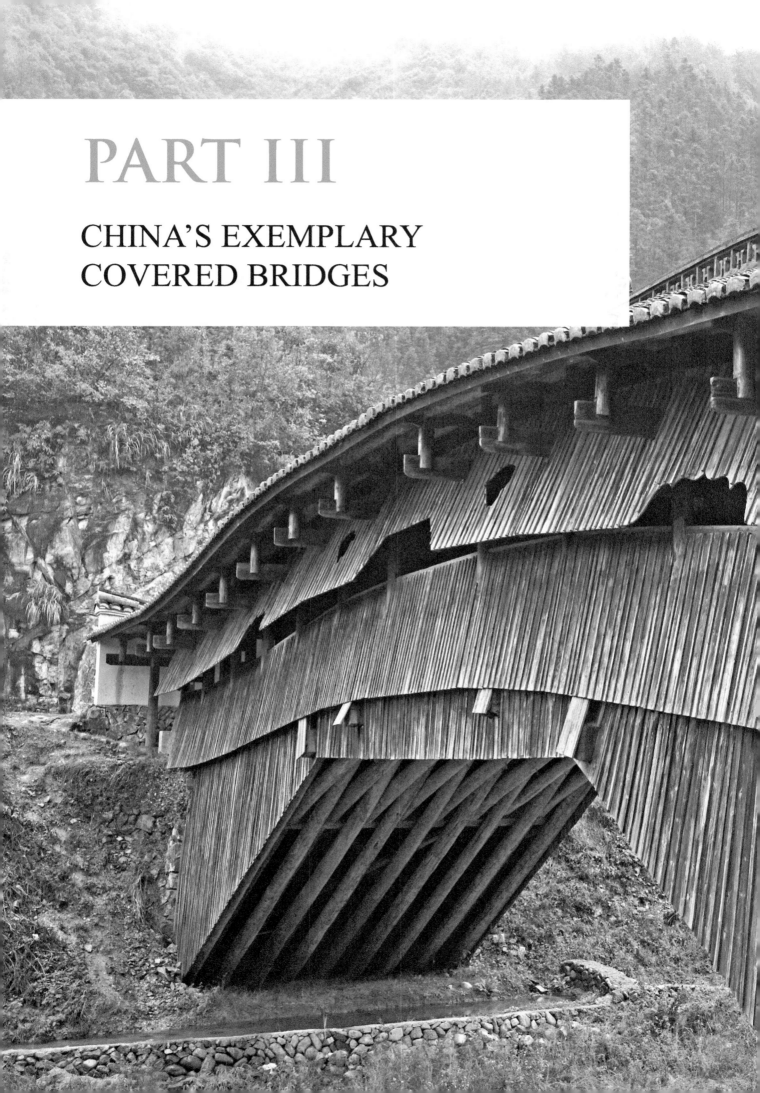

PART III

CHINA'S EXEMPLARY COVERED BRIDGES

Fujian
Covered Bridges

Fujian is the most topographically varied of China's coastal provinces, a tenth more mountainous with a tenth less fields than neighboring Zhejiang, according to a common Chinese phrase. Somewhat surprisingly, the small embayed fertile lowlands, mere coves, along the coastal region, which are created by short streams that drop from the mountain core, are both isolated from each other as well as accessible to the world beyond by virtue of the adjacent sea. Besides the historically significant seaports of Fuzhou, Quanzhou, and Xiamen, countless smaller anchorages were located along the coast. Indeed, these isolating conditions, when linked with numerous waves of in-migration over centuries, led to cultural seclusion that is underscored by an exceptional level of linguistic and cultural diversity. "The fields are few but the sea is vast; so men have made fields from the sea" is how an 1839 gazetteer from Fujian's port city of Xiamen viewed the maritime opportunities afforded its struggling population during thelast century of the Qing Dynasty (1644–1911) (Cushman, 1993: iii). With limited arable land to support a growing population, many Fujianese turned to the neighboring sea, using small boats for fishing and seagoing junks for distant trade to Southeast Asia.

While connections inland were not common, the stone-lined paths that can be seen throughout the lofty and precipitous mountains today attest to a level of interactivity that remains to be documented. Among the important sources for information about areas of Fujian some distance from the coast are the records of foreign missionaries who established outstations where, according to some writings regarding Pingnan County, they found fertile grounds for converting the "teeming unevangelized heathen population" (Barnes,1896: 169). Interestingly, occasional reports in *The Chinese Recorder and Missionary Journal*, which was published from 1867 to 1941, include comments on covered bridges in Fujian that otherwise were not written about until the late twentieth century. One such observation relates to a pair of mid-century covered bridges in Youxi (old spelling Yu-ki) in today's Shouning County, which were encountered after a multi-day trek from Fuzhou. Regarding two wooden covered bridges spanning an arm of the Yu River about a quarter mile apart, Dr R. S. Maclay declared that they were constructed to satisfy "Fung Shui" issues: "The people in certain portions of the district subscribed funds towards the erection of one bridge, and after it was built all the good luck went to them. To counteract this, the people in the other portions of the district then raised a large amount of money towards building a second bridge..." (1872, 4(12): 309–10). Highlighting the covered bridge as a village social space, Maclay continued, "I found one of these bridges an excellent place for out-door preaching."

With their precipitous slopes and chiseled valleys, four mountainous counties of northern Fujian—Pingnan, Shouning, Zhenghe, and Zhouning—account for most of the historically significant "woven arch" covered bridges that soar

Previous spread Houkeng (Hongjun) Bridge, Zhukou Township, Qingyuan County, Zhejiang. Source: ACO, 2007. **Left** Yanghoucuo Bridge, Waitun Township, Zhenghe County, Fujian. Source: TEM, 2013.

above the chasms that characterize them. Peculiarly, none of what we know of the spectacular woven arch bridges in these areas were photographically recorded by missionaries. However, utilizing the ubiquity of stone and timber, countless covered and uncovered bridges of many sizes were constructed across rubble-strewn tributaries in northern Fujian. Together these bridges formed nodes in a network of paths that delineated routes connecting northern Fujian with southern Zhejiang and beyond. The *gudao* "old paths" are well documented beginning in the Ming Dynasty (1368–1644) as radiating out from the gates of Shouning's walled county seat (Liu and Lin, eds, 2007: 113–31). While some of the routes have been succeeded by wider county-level roads, many are still traceable as stone-lined paths that lead to and from still-standing bridges, including imposing covered bridges.

Sadly, while in the 1980s there were 46 "woven arch" timber bridges and more than 10 other timber bridges in Shouning, by the beginning of the twenty-first century only 19 "woven arch" and 9 other timber bridges remained. Although the historical records emphasize the connections between the uplands of Fujian, Guangdong, Jiangxi, and Zhejiang provinces, they provide few specificdetails of what high-value, low-bulk commodities, such as medicinal herbs, were carried along the old mountain paths. Since the Wuyi Mountains have been heralded as a region of extraordinary biodiversity in the designation of the region as a UNESCO World Heritage site, it is certain that a great variety of rare flora was carried beyond its borders in the past. The historic, long-standing appreciation of the quality of tea from the uplands of interior Fujian is highlighted by the fact that it had been sent for centuries as tribute to the imperial court in Beijing. Moroever, from the seventeenth century onward,the specialized black teas from the Wuyi Mountain region were transported great distances farther south by tea peddlers who carried their cargo of tea leaves balanced on shoulder poles along mountain

paths. Along the way, these favored teas were aggregated with teas from other upland areas before reaching Canton (Guangzhou) from where they were shipped to Europe for consumption, an international trade pattern that flourished, especially after the First Opium War (Gardella, 1994; Rawski, 1972; Zhuang, 1998).

III.1.1 To facilitate the passage of porters hauling goods and villagers carrying firewood, crops, and agricultural implements, countless stone bridges were constructed across rubble-strewn gorges in Shouning County and adjacent areas of northern Fujian. Source: RGK, 2006.

III.1.2 Serving even today as a route from the higher woodlands to the lower villages, this stone mountain path drops to the Yanghoucuo Bridge, Zhenghe County, Fujian. Source: RGK, 2013.

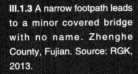

III.1.3 A narrow footpath leads to a minor covered bridge with no name. Zhenghe County, Fujian. Source: RGK, 2013.

Yangmeizhou Bridge

Located in the northern part of Shouning County, the 39.9-meter (131-foot)-long Yangmeizhou Bridge, also called the Feiyun ("Flying Cloud") Bridge, was a critically important link to Taishun in Zhejiang Province from the end of the eighteenth century. Visitors descend from a narrow mountain road down an ancient stone path. When the bridge comes into sight, visitors are struck by its dramatic location high over a rocky gorge filled with blue water, with approaching paths set between the river and high stone mountainsides. Initially built in 1791 and reconstructed in 1841 and 1869 before being totally rebuilt in 1939, the bridge soars with a clear span of 33.8 meters (111 feet) above a boulder-strewn streambed. Unlike most of the covered bridges in the region, the Yangmeizhou corridor utilizes a mix of *tailiang* post-and-beam and *chuandou* pillar-and-tie beam framework for the bents, with each connected via mortise-and-tenon linkages. Wooden arms extend out from the posts to support the overhanging eaves. Two layers of side skirts, constructed using vertical boards, protect the interior even as they allow air to enter the structure. Separate skirts extend below the deck of the bridge to shield the timbers of the arch. During much of the year, the deep valley of the Hou River only has a shallow, languid steam coursing across it, but it is periodically prone to major flooding as evidenced by the massive boulders that have been carried to locations beneath it.

III.1.4 Returning from a day in the fields, this villager crosses the Qiancheng Bridge in Tangkou Village, Tangkou Township, Pingnan County, Fujian. Source: RGK, 2009.

b

III.1.5a, b The Yangmeizhou Bridge seen today was constructed in 1939, but a crossing here dates to 1791. Before a dam was constructed in recent years that raised the level of the water, the river channel was deep, with many large boulders in it. Kengdi Township, Shouning County, Fujian. Source: ACO, 2006; TEM, 2005.

III.1.6 The approach to each portal of the Yangmeizhou Bridge is via a gradually rising stone path. Source: TEM, 2005.

III.1.7 A simple *tailiang* wooden framework constitutes each of the individual bents, each connected with timbers that are mortise-and-tenoned. Source: TEM, 2005.

III.1.8 Curved wooden arms extend out to support the overhanging eaves, which, together with the two layers of side skirts, protect the interior even as air is able to circulate through the structure.Source: TEM, 2005.

Luanfeng Bridge

Among the most outstanding covered bridges in Shouning County is the Luanfeng Bridge in Xiadang Township. Located in the southern portion of the county, the Luanfeng ("Mythical Bird Peak") Bridge, with a length of 45 meters (148 feet) and an open span of 37.1 meters (122 feet), the broadest of any of China's extant "woven arch" timber frame bridges, can only be dated to 1800 although there is some evidence of a bridge existing at this site earlier. The central portion of the timber arch is some 17 meters (55 feet) above the level of the stream. The corridor includes 17 *jian* with 72 pillars supporting the roof. Benches are located along both sides and a shrine to Guan Yin is installed midway across the bridge. The large boulders in the foreground have been carried to this location by floods that may have accompanied a typhoon. Also known as the Xiadang Shuiwei Bridge, the site is also supported with a *fengshui* feature, the eight-sided three-story Wenchang Ge Tower perched on a nearby hill.

III.1.9a, b Both lofty and long, the Luanfeng Bridge rises some 17 meters (55 feet) above the stream beneath and has a length of nearly 45 meters (148 feet). Xiadang Township, Shouning County, Fujian. Source: ACO, 2007.

b

III.1.11 The Luanfeng Bridge today lacks an altar inside even as it has a table with various floral arrangements. The presence of a banner declaring 有求必应 "whatever is asked for will be granted" suggests that prayers also are offered here. Source: RGK, 2009.

III.1.10 As with other covered bridges, an observer sometimes needs to look at its position from a distance in order to better understand the *fengshui* significance of associated structures. Here, the octagonal Wenchang Ge Tower, with its triple-tiered roof, overlooks Xiadang Village. Photograph by Gong Jian. Source: Liu Jie, 2018: 274.

Wan'an Bridge

Unlike the soaring Yangmeizhou and Yuanfeng bridges just discussed, the Wan'an Bridge in Changqiao Village, Changqiao Township, Pingnan County, Fujian, which today has a similar underlying structure, is noted principally for its length. Indeed, crossing the broad Long ("Dragon") River, the bridge today has an overall length of 98.2 meters (322 feet) while being only 8.5 meters (28 feet) above the water. Surprisingly, the level-decked bridge is still often referred to as a "rainbow bridge." Its dimensions have varied over time as the bridge was damaged and then rebuilt more than once. Being this long and with a covered structure running approximately 100 meters (328 feet), it was necessary to have the support of five piers. Between the piers today we can see six woven timber arch-beam structures that vary in their spans, the longest being 15.3 meters (50 feet) and the shortest 10.6 meters (35 feet). Although the bridge inside is level, one must climb 36 steps on the northwest end and 10 steps on the opposite southwest end to reach it. The length of the corridor is impressive, with 156 pillars and finely wrought *chuandou* framework and benches aligned along both sides of the structure.

Incomplete records suggest that the bridge, which was often called the Longjiang Gongji ("Dragon River Public Benefit") Bridge, was destroyed many times over the years, mostly because of local conflicts rather than natural disasters. A bridge was built here first in 1090 during the Song Dynasty (960–1279) as attested to by a chiseled stone inscription found on one of the piers. The structure was destroyed in 1648 during the turmoil of the Ming to Qing dynastic transition, some say by bandits who made off with the wooden components. Although rebuilt in 1742 during the settled early years of the reign of the Qianlong Emperor, a time of great prosperity, it was put out of commission again twenty-five years later. While being rebuilt in 1845, the bridge was consumed by fire in the early Republican period

of the twentieth century. In 1932, when it was rebuilt, the overall structure was lengthened and fundamentally altered.

Side-by-side overlapping photographs taken at the end of the nineteenth century and today reveal a significant change in form. Between 1882 and 1893, Anglican missionary William Banister, who served under the Church Missionary Society in Pingnan County, took photographs of the bridge that reveal it clearly had a cantilevered structure. This has been confirmed by an 81-year-old bridge

builder named Huang Chuncai who examined the old photos and recalled that his father had been involved in altering the underlying structure to a woven arch form after 1933. The photos below reveal this significant transformation, which included lengthening the bridge as well. After 1949, the bridge was renamed the Wan'an ("Eternal Peace") Bridge although it is commonly referred to simply as the Chang ("Long") Bridge because of its length. Flood damage in 1952 subsequently destroyed nearly a third of the wooden structure, which led to reconstruction in 1954 in the form seen today.

Adjacent to the south end of the bridge is a cavernous wooden structure with an impressive opera stage or *xitai*. The 7.2 x 6.8 meter (24 x 22 foot) building is variously referred to as Shengwang *dian* and Shengwang *miao*, the hall or temple for Shengwang. Shengwang, the King of Gods or Sage King, is one of many fabled figures in Fujian Province who are celebrated in stories and, more recently, in videos. Casual visitors to the building today find it empty and generally devoid of a complex set of paraphernalia that would suggest what ritual or other activity might occur within its walls. However, one alcove includes a set of three festooned figures that may baffle even those who have seen deities elsewhere in China. Wrapped in golden armor, these three representations are of the tutelary deity Qitian Dasheng, "Great Sage the Equal of Heaven," which is the self-proclaimed title of the Monkey King Sun Wukong. The Monkey King is especially

III.1.12a–c The late nineteenth-century stitched photograph and the close-up view of the underlying cantilevered timber structure (**a, b**) affirm that the structure seen today (**c**) is relatively new. When the Wan'an Bridge was rebuilt in 1933, the underlying structure was changed from timber cantilevers to a woven arch. Today, it is heralded as the longest example of a woven arch covered bridge. Source: Peter Lockhart Smith and Historical Photographs of China, University of Bristol; ACO, 2009.

venerated in the Fuzhou region. He is viewed as an all-purpose protector and one capable of fulfilling any desire, the notion of which is expressed in wall hangings, calligraphy, and incantations such as *you qiu bi ying* "whatever is asked for will be granted."

III.1.13 The Shengwang Temple is in the background of this view along the inside of the Wan'an Bridge. Source: RGK, 2006.

III.1.14 When rebuilt, essentially all the timbers were new and milled. Source: TEM, 2005.

III.1.15a, b The two entrances to the Wan'an Bridge differ significantly, one with no ornamentation while the other at the top of a long staircase has upturned eaves. Source: TEM, 2005.

III.1.16a, b Throughout the day, the Wan'an Bridge provides a shady and breezy place for villagers to relax, either as groups of chatting men or spread out with more privacy. Source: RGK, 2013; TEM, 2005.

III.1.17a, b At the head of the Wan'an Bridge is a large structure suitable for village events. It is dominated by an opera stage with an impressive eight-sided coffered ceiling as well as various shrines. Source: RGK, 2009; TEM, 2005.

a

III.1.18 Opposite the opera stage is a shrine to the tutelary deity Qitian Dasheng, "Great Sage the Equal of Heaven," which is the self-proclaimed title of the Monkey King Sun Wukong. Source: ACO, 2005.

Encased inside the building is an impressive elevated opera stage elaborately fashioned out of timbers that are embellished with multicolored carvings. Recessed above the opera stage is an octagonal-shaped coffered ceiling. As with many others, this imposing structure likely was repurposed as a storehouse or even a stable during and in the decades after the Cultural Revolution. More than a decade ago, when we first visited the Wan'an Bridge, the building had been cleaned out and tidied, with little evidence of community use except for the Monkey King shrine. Although recent visits do not provide any evidence of regular use, it is certain that the communities on both sides of the bridge come together periodically within it to enjoy traditional opera.

The Wan'an Bridge continues to be an important social space for the village communities on both sides. Whether early in the day when some marketing occurs or in the hours that follow well into the evening, the benches along the interior entice women, men, and children to tarry.

Dongguan (Tongxian) Bridge

The Dongguan ("East Gate") Bridge, also called the Tongxian ("Connecting with Immortals") Bridge, spans the Huyang River in Dongmei Village, Dongguan Township, YongchunCounty. Constructed first in 1145 during the Southern Song Period (1127–1279) and renovated often in succeeding centuries, this cantilevered beam bridge is 85 meters (279 feet) long and 5 meters (16 feet) wide. Each of the four midstream 15-meter (49-foot)-tall stone piers is set upon a base comprised of pine logs pounded into the bottom of the stream. This is a rare combination, which is confirmed and observable each winter when the depth of the river is diminished. Atop each of the bow-shaped stone piers is a stack of cut-stone beams that function as cantilevers supporting 22 massive timber beams that run from pier to pier. Running the length of the exterior are flared skirts that spread gradually outward to protect the corridor from rain that would rot the interior while allowing a breeze to pass across it. When the bridge was photographed during the first decade of the twentieth century, it was entered via steps made of local river stones. At the entryway were several historical stone markers.

III.1.19a, b Photographed a century apart, the four piers and exterior of the bridge show little change.Source: Cadbury Research Library, University of Birmingham Historical Photographs of China, University of Bristol; ACO, 2006.

III.1.20 Recorded in the spelling of the local dialect as the Tang Koan Kio, this photograph in the collection of John Preston Maxwell, an obstetric missionary for the English Presbyterian Church, shows the rough steps and entryway, c. 1900–10. Source: Cadbury Research Library, University of Birmingham and Historical Photographs of China, University of Bristol.

b

Transverse to the timber beams beneath is wooden flooring that runs 5 meters (16 feet) across the interior space with seating on both sides. The corridor itself is completely framed in timber using *chuandou* mortise-and-tenon joinery and capped with fired roof tiles. Evocative paintings relating folk tales have been added between pillars above the piers. Just as with the exterior color, the interior is also painted red. At the center of the Dongguan Bridge is an elaborate shrine to the bodhisattva Guan Yin. As is well-known, folk religion is quite active throughout Fujian. The Dongguan shrine is among the most elaborate and lively found within a wooden covered bridge. At any time during the day, visitors arrive to light incense and burn spirit money.

III.1.21 Six layers of cut stone are employed to form sturdy cantilevers above each of the four piers. Source: ACO, 2006.

III.1.22 Above the stone piers pointing upstream, the overlapping red skirts and roof overhang protect the interior from rain while allowing a breeze to pass through. Source: JDK, 2006.

文王求賢

周文王決心反討.四処
采賢絵访得八十老翁
湘太資士姜子牙.

Ill.1.23 Rectangular stone columns rise above
the piers, with wooden bents utilizing *chuandou*
framing in between. Here also are polygonal
inserts that provide surfaces for paintings of
historical tales. Source: ACO, 2006.

顧瞻佛日菩薩慈子

慈雅生慈海片

稻本之士貞天偌刀伝不墓

东天牌

III.1.24a, b As large as those found in many temples, the shrine and altar tables devoted to Guan Yin occupy the central bay of the bridge. A close-up of the paraphernalia on the altar table. Source: JDK, 2006; ACO, 2006.

a

III.1.25 Incense may be burned on the altar or in a nearby censer. Source: ACO, 2006.

III.1.27 High above the temple is stored the palanquin that is used to parade the goddess Guan Yi through the village on festival days. Source: JDK, 2006.

About 20 meters (66 feet) of the central section, which included the shrine, was swept away. At the beginning of January 2018, news reports heralded the "rebirth" of the Dongguan Bridge.

III.1.28 As the flooding receded, it was quite clear that the middle portion of the bridge, including the shrine, had been swept away. Source: http://qz.fjsen.com/2016-09/15/content_18464015_all.htm. Accessed September 15, 2016.

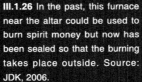
III.1.26 In the past, this furnace near the altar could be used to burn spirit money but now has been sealed so that the burning takes place outside. Source: JDK, 2006.

III.1.29 A close-up of the washed away section of the Dongguan Bridge. Source: http://www.qzcns.com/qznews/2018/0104/511752.html. Accessed January 4, 2018.

In mid-September 2016, the passage of Typhoon Meranti , which is said to have been the most powerful storm ever to impact Fujian and Zhejiang provinces, brought with it heavy rain and damaging winds that led to flash flooding which seriously damaged the Dongguan Bridge. Although many contemporaneous news reports stated the bridge was "destroyed," this was not the case.

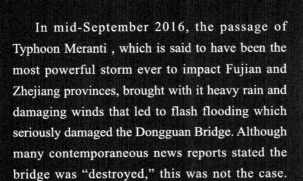
III.1.30 In less than a year and a half, the historic Dongguan Bridge was "reborn." Source: http://www.qzcns.com/qznews/2018/0104/511752.html. Accessed January 1, 2018.

Zhejiang
Covered Bridges

Situated along the central portion of China's eastern coast to the south of the Yangzi River and to the north of Fujian, Zhejiang is among China's smallest, yet topographically most diverse provinces. A common Chinese phrase used to describe the province is *qi shan, yishui, liangfentian*—70 percent mountains, 10 percent water, and 20 percent fields. It is less mountainous and with more fields than neighboring Fujian. While plains and river valleys dominate in the north, southern Zhejiang, which shares topographical features with adjacent Fujian and Jiangxi provinces, is characterized by rugged mountains that until recent years were not easy to access by outsiders. Not only are there many relatively common yet still historically significant and beautiful bridges that share characteristics with others throughout China, Zhejiang, such as Fujian Province, possesses large numbers of the extraordinary woven arch timber bridges introduced in Part II.

The well-watered northern third of Zhejiang is well-known for its stone beam and humpbacked arch bridges that cross the network of canals characteristic of the broader Yangzi River Delta.[1] Covered bridges of many types have a long history in northern Zhejiang as well. Noteworthy is the Yudai ("Jade Belt") Pavilion Bridge that graces the Su Causeway in Hangzhou.

[1] For a comprehensive look at the stone bridges of the Yangzi River Delta, see Knapp, 2008a: 160–79.

III.2.1 With its double-tiered pavilion atop massive stone piers, the Yudai ("Jade Belt") Bridge provides not only a passageway but also a retreat to catch the breezes and enjoy the scenes along West Lake in Hangzhou. Source: ACO, 2006.

While functionally utilitarian covered bridges were located throughout northern Zhejiang as well, no area had more than the historically significant region centered on the port of Ningbo. Known as Mingzhou during the Song Dynasty (960–1279), mercantile Ningbo lies astride the Yong River, which is formed by the confluence of the Fenghua and Yuyao rivers before flowing to the East China Sea. Ningbo has thrived at the center of a network of routes, which involved many bridges, that fed goods from a multiplicity of market towns for transport via local coastal and long-distance ocean junk transport.

Among the surviving old bridges in the Ningbo region are three in Yinzhou District, all of which were documented photographically in the early twentieth century. The smallest is the two-span Dong Bridge crossing the Nantang River in Dongqiao Village within Dongqiao Township and said to date to 960 at the beginning of the Song Dynasty. It has been repaired many times over the centuries. With a single massive stone pier and large abutments comprising blocks of granite, the slightly cambered bridge is formed by sets of parallel wooden beams with a timber gallery above. The bridge itself is nearly 27 meters (88 feet) long with pavilions on both ends that extend the full length to 37 meters (121 feet). In 2006, the Dong Bridge underwent a comprehensive renovation as an historic relic, with most traffic having shifted to a nearby bridge, while maintaining the old and simple style. A New Dong Bridge was built east of Old Dong Bridge, relieving most of the vehicular pressure while pedestrians continue to cross the old bridge.

III.2.2 Photographed c. 1870, this view of the Dong Bridge in Ningbo's Yinzhou District is said to date to the Song Dynasty where it provided an important north–south crossing. Source: Edward Bowra Collection, University of Bristol, Royal Society for Asian Affairs, London.

III.2.4 The portal end of the bridge, with its stepped gables, unfortunately has been blocked partially by an abutting residence. Source: TEM, 2016.

III.2.3 A contemporary view of the restored Dong Bridge. Today, the bridge functions essentially for pedestrian use because of the presence of a new bridge nearby. Source: TEM, 2016.

Also located in Dongqiao Township is the Bailiang ("One Hundred Logs") Bridge, said to date to 1078 during the Song Dynasty, which actually has 124 round timbers supporting it. With a length of 77.4 meters (254 feet) and a width of 6.18 meters (20 feet) spanning the Yin River, it is the longest covered bridge of its type in Zhejiang Province. Six stone piers prop up the large number of long tree trunks that form the parallel beams supporting the gallery. The number of benches along the sides, as well as the extensive assemblage of shrines in the central portion of the bridge, underscore the structure's past significance as an important community space.

III.2.5 The interior of the slightly elevated Dong Bridge shows the narrow wooden benches that line its sides. Source: TEM, 2016.

III.2.6 The Bailiang Bridge as photographed between 1878 and 1880 by Edward Bangs Drew, Commissioner of Chinese Maritime Customs Service. Source: Harvard-Yenching Library © President and Fellows of Harvard College.

III.2.7 The longest covered bridge of its type in Zhejiang, the Bailiang Bridge sits atop six midstream cut-stone piers. Source: TEM, 2016.

III.2.8 Divided into 25 *jian*, the space between four columns, the lengthy corridor is lined with narrow benches that provide stability for the structure as well as places to rest. Although there is an adjacent modern bridge, townsfolk use the old bridge to cross since it is cooler and safer. Source: TEM, 2016.

III.2.9a, b Midway across the span is a lengthy glass-enclosed shrine with a collection of images. Today, there is no evidence of daily ritual occurring within the bridge. Source: TEM, 2016.

Bridges of incredible variety are found in the basins, foothills, and remote mountainous counties of south and southwestern Zhejiang, an area laced with deep gorges and countless streams of various sizes. Some covered bridges in southern Zhejiang are relatively level structures, with gradual approaches or steep steps that reach the flat bridge, just as they are typically found elsewhere in the world. The Tongzhou Bridge in Meijiang Township in Lanxi, which crosses the Mei River, was first constructed as a timber crossing in 1758 before stone arches replaced the wood in 1886. Throughout the Qing Dynasty (1644–1911), this location was at a critical junction linking the five counties of Jinhua, Lanxi, Yiwu, Pujiang, and Jiande. The sizable dimensions of the five gaping arch-shaped openings between the linked abutments and stone piers suggest decisions were made to provide protection against periodic floods even as today the stream beneath is narrow and shallow. The wooden gallery above the stone base is 84.8 meters (278 feet) long with a stone pavement and well-worn wooden benches between the columns that support the roof structure.

III.2.10a, b The imposing and well-preserved Tongzhou Bridge in Lanxi sits atop a stone base that includes five arches. Source: RGK, 1987.

Further south in the rugged mountains, many covered bridges are completely constructed of timber. They rear up abruptly from their stone abutments and soar dramatically as they cross over steep chasms. Local people refer to these dramatically ascending types as "centipede bridges" because of their resemblance to the arch-like rise of a long arthropod's body as it crawls. In actual fact, none of the covered structures, which appear from a distance to be supported by a wooden arch, is atop an actual arch. Rather, the illusionary "arch" emerges from using a series of logs, long tree trunks gathered from the nearby forests, that function as interwoven chords or segments of the "woven arch." In Taishun County, Zhejiang, alone, 958 bridges of various types were counted in 1987. These included rather simple block stone bridges as well as more sophisticated stone beam bridges, stone arch bridges, timber beam bridges, and what were called at the time timber arch bridges.

While stone beam bridges, stone arch bridges, timber beam, and timber cantilevered bridges are the most widespread types found in this region, timber arch structures, now generally referred to as woven timber arch bridges, are numerous and truly outstanding. Considered true "rainbow bridges," this last type indeed comprises matchless structures employing engineering principals found also in neighboring counties of Fujian Province, but seen nowhere else in the world.

III.2.11 When approached from the paths on the flanks of the adjacent hillslopes, the profile of the Xianju Bridge in Taishun County, Zhejiang, is said by local residents to appear like a crawling centipede. Source: ACO, 2005.

Chinese engineers, such as the well-regarded Mao Yisheng and Tang Huancheng, referred to the structure of such bridges as being a "woven timber arch," or "combined beam timber arch" or "interlocked timber arch" to emphasize the use of straight timber members tied together. Yang Hongxun, an architectural historian, suggested combining the terms so that the nomenclature becomes "woven beam timber arch," which aligned it with technological descriptions already accepted among Chinese architectural historians who examine other structures, such as palaces, temples, and dwellings. The basic components of rainbow bridges, as discussed earlier in the Structures section of Part II.1, are quite simple: two pairs of two layered sets of inclined timbers, with each of the sets embedded in opposite abutments, stretch upward towards the middle of the stream. To fill the gap between these two inclined timber sets, a pair of horizontally trending assemblages of timbers is attached. Transverse timbers tenoned to them and/or, some have speculated, tied with rattan or rope, hold each of the sets of timbers together. It is these warp and weft elements that gave rise to the term "woven." X-braces are sometimes used to enhance structural strength. While the downward pressure of the weighty logs compresses all the components together into a tight and relatively stable composition, the equilibrium can sometimes be upset if forces from beneath, such as might come from torrential floods or typhoon winds, push upward. Computer simulation analysis by Liu Jie and Shen Weiping (2005) revealed that this woven composition of logs operates like both an arch structure as well as a beam structure in the mechanical sense. Thus, the technical term describing the configuration, they suggest, is better called a "woven timber arch-beam" structure, with the word "beam" being added to better describe mechanically its form. To further provide stability to the underlying "woven timber arch-beam" structure, additional weight is added by erecting a building on top of the bridge,

thus creating a covered bridge. The heavy timber columns, beams, balustrades, and baked clay roof tiles add substantial weight—a dead load—which strengthens the structure and reduces possible damage from both torrential flash floods and typhoon winds. With the addition of wooden skirts along the side perimeter, moreover, the wooden members of the bridge are also protected from weathering and deterioration. While "woven timber arch-beam" rainbow bridges in Zhejiang and Fujian are similar to each other, there are many minor variations—creative mutations—which may have resulted from trial and error arising from local circumstances. Two bridges in Qingyuan County and three in Taishun County illustrate these similarities and differences.

Rulong Bridge

Qingyuan County claims a glorious history dating back to the Song Dynasty, a time when the imperial family in Hangzhou reached into the mountains for exotic foods and medicines. In an area said to have "10 bridges in a distance of 1 *li*," the Rulong ("Like a Dragon") Bridge is exceptional in a township with many fine extant bridges. The date of construction of this covered bridge, located along a major trade route between Fujian to the south and the Jiangnan region to the north in Jushui Township, is not clear. Records, however, indicate it was renovated in 1625, during the last decades of the Ming Dynasty (1368–1644). The bridge has a clear span of 19.5 meters (64 feet), a length of 28.2 meters (93 feet), and a width of 5.09 meters (17 feet), with nine interior modular bays (*jian*). Its underlying support is very much like that of other "woven timber arch-beam" structures, with its distinction arising from the magnitude and extent of the covered portions above.

In addition to a double layer of overlapping wooden skirts along the sides and along the beams, there are three pavilion-like structures that rise above the roof. On the north end is a three-tiered overhanging gabled structure that served as a bell tower, with two entries. On the south end is a pavilion with three entries from stone pathways. The central elevated structure houses a complex of altars. As discussed in greater detail in Part II.2, the Rulong Bridge was one of five bridges that were part of a protective *fengshui* configuration. In recognition of its significance, the Rulong Bridge was declared a National Historic Site in 2001 and today is heralded as China's oldest timber bridge. Adjacent to the bridge is a temple that is said to date to the Song Dynasty.

III.2.12 Adjacent to a Song Dynasty temple, and among the most spectacular and historic covered bridges in China, the Rulong Bridge dates to the seventeenth century. The three pavilion-like structures rising above the roof are unique. On the north end is a three-tiered overhanging gable with one pavilion serving as a bell tower, a second as a grand double entryway, and the middle one dominated by a complex of altars. Source: TEM, 2007.

III.2.13 The interdigitated parallel log assembly supporting the bridge that constitutes the woven arches includes horizontal members that help lock the timbers into secure positions. Source: RGK, 2005.

III.2.14 Bracket sets of this complexity are very rare within wooden covered bridges. Here, however, they are used to lift the central pavilion roof above the altars in the central bay of the Rulong Bridge. Source: ACO, 2005.

III.2.15 The dimensions of both the beams, shown here, and the columns supporting them are much greater than those on more common covered bridges, clearly attesting to the magnitude of the donations to build the bridge. Source: ACO, 2005.

III.2.16 When ritual ceased in the Rulong Bridge is not clear. After restoration, no effort was made to replace the deities and votive paraphernalia that once populated the altar. Above the empty *shenkan* altar niche is a horizontal board proclaiming the name of the bridge. A coffered ceiling attests to the significance of the space. Source: ACO, 2009.

Houkeng
(Hongjun) Bridge, Qingyuan

Houkeng Bridge is one of the thirteen surviving timber arched corridor bridges (*langqiao*) in Qingyuan County, Zhejiang. Originally built in 1671 and renovated several times over the centuries, the bridge, nonetheless, had fallen into substantial disrepair by the late 1980s. Because of rotting as well as the theft of some wooden structural parts, iron pipes had to be added to prop up the arch. By 2001, when circumstances had become quite dire, significant efforts began to be expended to restore the bridge, but these were initially frustrated because of the shortage of available funding.In reviewing possibilities, it was recollected that the bridge had played a role in a battle between Communist and Guomindang armies on August 30, 1934 and had been dubbed a "Red Army Bridge" during the Great Proletarian Revolution in order to save it from wanton desecration. The desire to preserve a "Red" site rather than merely an old bridge quickly gained momentum under the slogan "Carry Forward the 'Red' Tradition, Promote the Redevelopment of Qingyuan."

The signs around the site today clearly demarcate the bridge's military significance, validating its recent importance, but with minimal acknowledgment of the Houkeng Bridge's significance as an engineering achievement. Indeed, the county's website proclaims that the bridge's name, "Red Army Bridge," first surfaced soon after the 1934 battle nearby. Nonetheless, those involved in the dismantling and reconstruction of the bridge paid great attention to conservation principles, historically accurate rebuilding, and careful documentation of the process. Recognizing its importance, the Houkeng Bridge was nominated for an international award,

and was granted a 2005 Award of Excellence in the UNESCO 2005 Asia-Pacific Heritage Awards for Culture Heritage Conservation program. The press release highlighted "the community's respect for historic engineering principles" and the role of the scholar Zhao Chen and others but did not mention the bridge's "Red" history.

III.2.17 The Houkeng Bridge had deteriorated substantially before its reconstruction began in 2001 due to both lack of maintenance and vandalism. Source: The World Heritage Research Center, Peking University.

III.2.18 The Houkeng Bridge, originally built in 1671, was later christened a "Red Army bridge" because of a nearby battle. Source: ACO, 2007.

III.2.19 Looking out through one of the shaped windows cut into the timbers along the sides of the bridge, the scenery suggests a landscape painting. Source: RGK, 2006.

III.2.20 An Award of Excellence by the UNESCO 2005 Asia-Pacific Heritage Awards for Culture Heritage Conservation Program recognized the careful restoration of the bridge's underlying interior wooden framing and timber arch-beam structure. Source: ACO, 2006.

Santiao Bridge, Taishun

Straddling a rock-strewn ravine between Zhouling and Yangxi townships, where four interprovincial mountain byways converge, the Santiao Bridge is the region's oldest rainbow bridge. Records indicate that there was a bridge here as early as the Tang Dynasty (618–906), which was repaired in 1137 during the Song Dynasty. The bridge seen today was built in 1843 and has undergone a series of renovations over the century and a half of its existence. The only access to the bridge is via the old stone-lined paths that drop out of the mountains to cross the gorge via the bridge. Rising an impressive height of about 10 meters (33 feet) above the bed of the stream, the bridge is 32 meters (105 feet) long with an open span of 21.3 meters (70 feet).

The covered portion includes eleven bays with sawn timber cladding and a relatively simple two-slope tile roof. Transverse and longitudinal drawings of the bridge show clearly the relationship between the stone abutments—seven major and six minor logs—which are tied together by a pair of crosspieces and strengthened with an X-shaped brace to give strength to the arch. Atop this structure are longitudinal members, which then are tied to the mortise-and-tenon building above to form a covered arcade running from end to end. Because the location of the bridge is so well chosen, there is no need to climb steps to cross it. The symmetrical bracket sets extend the eaves well beyond the vertical line of the bridge below. In conjunction with the wooden cladding, this substantial overhang helps protect the underlying wooden structure from the elements.

III.2.21a–c Whether viewed from the boulder-strewn floor of the mountain stream or from any of the paths that drop from the surrounding mountains, the Santiao Bridge occupies a beautiful site. Set deep in a V-shaped valley, the bridge was a critical link in a system of byways connecting southern Zhejiang and northern Fujian provinces. Records clearly show that there has been a bridge here since the Tang Dynasty, and one can see nearby the hollowed-out sockets chiseled into the exposed stone outcrops that indicate the location of earlier bridges. Source: RGK, 2013.

III.2.22 At one end of the wooden corridor of the Santiao Bridge is a shrine that was moved outside during renovation in order to reduce the chance of fire. Source: ACO, 2005.

Beijian Bridge and Xidong Bridge, Taishun

The Beijian Bridge and Xidong Bridge, a pair of nearby bridges cross one of two streams in a town called Sixi. Built initially in 1674, rebuilt in 1849, and then again in 1987, the Beijian Bridge is 51.7 meters (170 feet) long and 5.37 meters (18 feet) wide, with a clear span of 29 meters (95 feet). Although it rises some 11.22 meters (37 feet) above the streambed, which often has a sluggish watercourse passing under it, rushing torrents of water can bring seasonal flooding, as in September 2005 when floodwaters submerged the abutments and wreaked considerable damage but failed to sweep away the bridge. Built in 1570, refurbished in 1745, and taking its current form in 1827, the Xidong Bridge lies a bit closer to the water, with

a length of 41.7 meters (137 feet), a width of 4.86 meters (16 feet), and a span of 25.7 meters (84 feet). The Xidong Bridge is just 500 meters (1,640 feet) upstream from the Beijian Bridge and is sometimes called a "sister" bridge.

Both bridges have external skirts made of sawn timber that disguise the underlying structure, giving the appearance that they are structurally built atop a polygonal arch formed by three timber chords. In fact, the "arch" is an illusion. When one looks up from under the bridges, each superstructure is seen clearly as a set of interwoven tree trunks. While differing in details, both include two pairs of double-layered inclined timbers, which are embedded in stone abutments. Since the sets of inclined timbers do not meet, another two sets of horizontally laid timbers are inserted

III.2.23 The interlinked logs that allow the Santiao Bridge to soar more than 21 meters (69 feet) across the valley bottom are clearly shown in this view from beneath. Source: ACO, 2005.

between them. While tenon joinery and possibly rattan rope initially played some role in tying the system together, it is the positioning and weight of the horizontal timbers that secure the structure. The addition of X-braces helps to further stabilize the woven nature of the interlocked system. Operating together, the timber components function like a stone arch in compression as forces push outward against the abutments.

The internal portions of the covered galleries of both bridges are similar although each has distinctive entryways. The Beijian Bridge is entered on one end via a series of steep steps that lead to a cluster of wooden shops tied to the bridge itself. The Xidong Bridge has a roadside entry that is somewhat like a porte-cochere, a portico-like structure. While the Beijian Bridge is somewhat

longer, with nineteen modular bays compared to the Xidong Bridge with fifteen, both were built using pillars-and-transverse tie beams mortised together. Each pillar is set atop a stone pedestal and rises to directly support a roof purlin. No groundsills tie adjacent frames of individual bays together, but the connecting wooden railings and benches serve as stabilizing components. Along both sides of the bridges, projecting tie beams, some tiered with supporting struts, elongate the structure beyond the side walls, in the process creating substantial curved eaves overhangs that shade the timbers beneath from rainfall. Within both bridges are intricate wooden alcoves containing images of local gods and goddesses.

While just a little more than a decade ago Sixi Town was a quiet place accessible only by a winding road, today it is connected by good quality highways to both Wenzhou on the coast and Lishui and Hangzhou to the north. Where once only country inns were available for visitors, there are today several international hotels. Beyond its clean air, bucolic vistas, Sixi and the surrounding more remote areas have become nationally famous for their covered bridges. Indeed, the area has benefited from promotion on television and in the press as a venue for "destination weddings" for individual couples or groups, which involves both formal and informal photography. Sixi Town itself is now a tourist mecca, with a covered bridge museum as well as restaurants and shops with myriad *langqiao* souvenirs along a newly constructed "traditional" street.

III.2.25 A close-up view of the interdigitated logs supporting the Beijian Bridge. Source: ACO, 2013.

III.2.24 The Beijian Bridge is considered by many to be Taishun's most beautiful covered bridge. Although rising more than 11 meters (36 feet) above the water below and spanning 26 meters (85 feet), the bridge nonetheless is periodically assaulted by rushing floodwaters. Source: ACO, 2005.

III.2.26 The languid and shallow stream that passes beneath the Beijian Bridge belies the fact that the stream sometimes erupts in flood that reaches the upper portions of the abutments. Source: RGK, 2013.

III.2.27 These markings along the steps leading to the Beijian Bridge indicate the height that the floodwaters rose to on September 1, 2005. Source: RGK, 2006.

III.2.28 The open western end of the Beijian Bridge, which provides an entryway to the steps leading to the span, included shops that once were busy. It protrudes from the main bridge structure but is attached to it. Source: ACO, 2005.

III.2.29 Although the Beijian Bridge is heavily visited today by tourists, it still serves an important route for villagers as they carry freshly harvested tubers from their fields. Source: RGK, 2013.

III.2.30 Taishun and its covered bridges have become sites for weddings. January 2017 was a memorable wedding event for ten couples. Source: http://news.66wz.com/system/2017/01/09/104953881.shtml. Accessed January 10, 2017.

III.2.31 The elegant lines of the Xidong Bridge, which is considered a "sister" of the soaring Beijian Bridge, are widely admired. This end has a portico-style covered entryway. Source: ACO, 2005.

III.2.32 The entry from the portico reveals the generous use of cut stone and the timber framework that continues through the bridge. Source: RGK, 2013.

III.2.33 The interior framework utilizes mortise-and-tenon joinery to link all the timbers. Source: ACO, 2005.

III.2.34 At the central bay of the Xidong Bridge there is an octagonal-shaped caisson above what was once an imposing altar. Source: ACO, 2005.

III.2.35 At the opposite open-sided end of the Xidong Bridge, the steps are gently inclined. Although the roofline is flared, there is no portico. Source: ACO, 2005

Xuezhai Bridge, Taishun

The impressive Xuezhai Bridge, named after the Xue family whose contributions and power led to its construction in 1857, was built to link two sides of a stream in Sankui Town, Taishun County. Along the immediate approach to the bridge, the stone stelae present facts concerning the building of the bridge and the generosity of individuals and families who funded its construction. However, it is left to local lore to reveal the complications and animosities that arose with both the building and renovation of the bridge. Records show that there was a precursor span called the Jinxi ("Embroidered Stream") Bridge on this site from as early as 1512, and that flooding periodically led to damage and rebuilding amidst prolonged and recurring community tensions as well as philanthropic competition. After a great flood in 1579, however, there were insufficient resources to rebuild and the town had to make do with a nearby smaller bridge. Meanwhile, the Zhang family purchased one bank of the stream on which the earlier bridge had been built, a location that was believed to have the attributes of the tortoise-snake, according to the canon of *fengshui*. When the Xu family decided, in 1739, to build a *wugong* or "centipede bridge," the local name for a soaring wooden covered bridge, the Zhang family objected because of the widespread belief that centipedes devour snakes and tortoises. If the Xue family succeeded, this would mean that the Zhang family would be diminished. As a result of the feud, it was not possible to build a centipede bridge until 1857, after the Xue family gained the support of all the other clans in the village and after the Zhang family had sold the land.

While the overall length of the bridge is 51 meters (167 feet), the span is only 29 meters (95 feet), which rises like a high arch some 10.5 meters (34 feet) above the creek below. The steep set of cut-stone steps leading to the bridge itself gives pedestrians the sense of crossing an arch-type bridge because of the dramatic rise, but a view from below shows that the underlying structure is a system of interlocked timbers. The massive stone abutments formed by the buttressing stairs take the lateral thrusts of the massive timber frame. As the illustrations reveal, the fifteen structural bays are quite simple and regular.

With its upturned eaves, the roofline looks much like that of a country temple. In recent years, much repair work has been done on the bridge so that the modular nature of the wooden framework is quite apparent. At one time, the soaring Xuezhai Bridge dominated its site, with only a large camphor tree beside it. Over time, the bridge became lost among drab, unfinished multistoried buildings that cluster around them and diminish the beauty of this community emblem. Tragically, the Xuezhai Bridge and two other historic covered bridges in Taishun were washed away by flash floods during Typhoon Meranti on September 15, 2016. A restored bridge, which the Chinese call "reborn" bridge, was opened in October 2017.

III.2.36 Once a bucolic scene, with only an ancient camphor tree growing out of the riverbank, the Xuezhai Bridge over time was "lost" among dozens of looming multistoried brick buildings. Source: RGK, 2015.

III.3.37 The sloping steps rise to the floor of the bridge, which continues to incline since the structure is elevated high above the stream below. Source: ACO, 2005.

III.2.38 The complex interdigitized log structure is clearly shown in this photograph. Source: ACO, 2005.

III.2.39 The Xuezhai Bridge connects two areas of the town, providing a critical link between them for not only pedestrians but also those simply wanting to sit in a cool spot to rest or chat. Source: ACO, 2005.

III.2.40 Resulting from the passage of Typhoon Meranti on September 15, 2016, flash floods ravaged the embankments supporting the Xuezhai Bridge. This news source includes a video of the bridge being washed away. Source: https://www.thepaper.cn/newsDetail_forward_1529349. Accessed September 15, 2016.

III.2.41 Except for the stone steps leading to the historic bridge, all of the timber structure was washed away. Source: http://news.66wz.com/system/2017/12/16/105050443.shtml. Accessed September 18, 2016.

III.2.42 Carrying the adorned ridgepole during the reconstruction of the Xuezhai Bridge in mid-September 2017. The *shangliang* ritual of raising the ridgepole followed traditional practices. Source: https://www.weibo.com/ttarticle/p/show?id=2309404152553679018389. Accessed September 16, 2017.

Huizhou: Anhui and Jiangxi Covered Bridges

The region historically known as Huizhou was surprisingly both isolated and poor and accessible and cosmopolitan because of the relationship between its sprawling mountains and dense system of rivers. In terms of today's political divisions, the Huizhou region includes the southernmost portions of Anhui Province plus Wuyuan County in northeastern Jiangxi Province. Dominated by the lofty Huangshan or Yellow Mountains, divided by countless hillslopes, the region boasted hundreds of remote, relatively self-sufficient villages until its transformation began during the Song Dynasty (960–1279). During this period, a distinctive mercantile system emerged as the Southern Song capital moved from Kaifeng in the north to the city of Hangzhou in neighboring Zhejiang. Utilizing the prolific system of mountain-fed tributaries that entered the Xin'an River, *keshang* "traveling merchants" and *Huishang* "Huizhou merchants" spread themselves widely, not only in Hangzhou but also into China's other great metropolitan centers of the Jiangnan region in the lower portions of the Yangzi River. Here they amassed wealth from trade and pawnshops, sometimes even purchasing official titles that made it possible to improve their social status by becoming gentry-literati. Long-distance trade, first in timber, tea, lacquer, and especially salt, then later including the "four treasures of the scholar's studio"—paper, writing brushes, ink sticks, and ink slabs used by calligraphers—came to represent significant commercial resources for a distinctive and much-heralded group called Huizhou merchants.

Relatively unknown until recent times, the architectural heritage of Huizhou merchants is usually defined in terms of residences, ancestral temples, and academies, all similar in style because of their whitewashed walls and gray tiles, as well as imposing stone memorial archways called *paifang* and *pailou*. Yet, tucked within some of the old villages of Huizhou are bridges of great distinction, not only broad ones with multiple arches but also many covered with timber structures of various sizes. Many of these bridges are mirrored in roadside pavilions called *luting* and *liangting*, whose structure and purpose are similar even though they do not cross water. While the residences Huizhou merchants constructed clearly embody their concern for the families they left behind and their own hopes for a retirement sanctuary in old age, it was through the building of schools, byways, roadside pavilions, and bridges that their civic consciousness was best seen. Family genealogies, which outline the history of a lineage in terms of birth and death records of all its members, also detail acts of public philanthropy, such as the construction of bridges and roadside pavilions. While details of such charity may no longer be remembered clearly by villagers, the presence of a covered bridge or pavilion is often accompanied by stone stelae that record details of its initial construction along with a listing of those who contributed towards its periodic restoration. Whether small or large, covered bridges in Huizhou are all relatively unassuming structures when compared to the magnificent corridor bridges

of Guangxi, Fujian, and Zhejiang. None stand out as having sumptuous structures piled above them or are distinctive because of their innovative understructures. For the most part, each is merely serviceable in that it functions to span waterways of various widths while providing a space for villagers requiring a place to rest.

III.3.1 The humble Zhongshu Bridge in Likeng Village, Wuyuan County, Jiangxi, is an example of a *luting*. Said to date to the latter part of the Northern Song Dynasty (960–1126) to provide a resting place for villagers, today it serves as a focal point for photography by tourists visiting this historic village. Source: ACO, 2005.

Huanxiu Bridge

Although less known until recently compared to the nearby Huizhou district UNESCO World Heritage village sites of Hongcun and Xidi in southern Anhui Province, Chengkan Village is an exceptional maze-like settlement. Located some 40 kilometers (25 miles) from Huangshan City,[2] it traces a settlement history that reaches to the Tang Dynasty (618–906) and lays claim to being a veritable museum of old Hui-style buildings. Indeed, Chengkan is a treasury of rather simple, yet sometimes stunning, architecture with more than 200 structures—houses, ancestral halls, memorial arches, pavilions, and bridges—from the Qing Dynasty (1644–1911), as well as 20 from the Ming Dynasty (1368–1644), and at least one from the Yuan Dynasty (1280–1368). Over time, Chengkan came to be known as the village with "three streets and ninety-nine lanes," a tight checkerboard settlement with its back and sides embraced by overlapping ranges of sinuous mountains and its front facing east towards the meandering Zhongzhong River that threads through the village. This topographic configuration shelters Chengkan from cold winter winds blowing from the northwest and facilitates good drainage, a superior site, and an auspicious village acknowledged by villagers since it accords with optimal *fengshui* elements.

While some of the old Huizhou-style dwellings in Chengkan rival those in other villages, its unassuming covered bridge is unique. Being but a modest intimation of what it once was, the Huanxiu Bridge across the Zhongchuan River seen today has a layered history. First built during the Yuan Dynasty by the widow of a young traveling merchant to memorialize him, the original bridge had five spans, each comprised of several cantilevered stone planks. During the Qing Dynasty, a member of the dominant Luo lineage built a structure on top of the multiple spans for villagers to use as a place to relax. Over time, as the broad stream was filled in, only two stone-lined spans remained, with a single granite deck retaining its austere shaded gallery. The well-worn benches have for centuries provided seats for grandparents to chat as they watch their grandchildren and for villagers in general to catch the cool breeze that flows with the course of the stream.

[2] The name Huangshan City was adopted only in the late 1980s in an effort to gain from the fame of the nearby Huangshan Mountains. Until then, for a thousand years the city had been called Huizhou. In recent years, efforts have mounted to reclaim the historic name, but as of mid-2018 this has not yet been settled. http://www.bjreview.com.cn/Nation/201606/t20160614_800059318.html

The Huanxiu Bridge suffered in June 2013 when the covered portion and its deck collapsed as a result of a flash flood. While the stone components fell nearby, wooden pieces were swept downstream. Villagers subsequently were able to salvage some 75 percent of the original wooden pieces,which led relatively quickly to full reconstruction of this Yuan Dynasty covered bridge in November 2013.

III.3.3a, b In June 2013, when floodwaters rose, all the wooden components that were not anchored to the stone beams were washed away. Source: https://www.chinadaily.com.cn/life/2013-08/02/content_16866720.htm. Accessed August 6, 2013.

III.3.2a, b The Huanxiu Bridge in Chengkan Village seen in recent decades is but a remnant of a longer covered bridge that existed during the Qing Dynasty. Although short, the bridge has continued to provide a shady and breezy location for villagers who cross it. Source: ACO, 2005.

III.3.4 With some 75 percent of the original wooden components salvaged, the Huanxiu Bridge was rebuilt. Source: http://vip.people.com.cn/do/userbuy.jsp?picId=2819896&aId=370659. Accessed December 5, 2013.

Caihong Bridge

No bridge is promoted more in the historical Huizhou region than the Caihong ("Rainbow") Covered Bridge in Wuyuan County, Qinghua Township, in the northeastern corner of Jiangxi Province. Although called a "rainbow," the bridge neither soars nor is arched; indeed, it is described as "resting like a rainbow across the water." While overly touted as China's "most beautiful covered bridge," Caihong Bridge nonetheless has a charm derived more from its setting than its character. Said to have been build some 800 years ago during the Southern Song Dynasty (1127–1279), with a length of 140 meters (460 feet) and width of nearly 7 meters (23 feet), the longest covered bridge in Huizhou, it is nonetheless an important old structure. A pair of substantial abutments on both ends as well as four midstream boat-shaped piers 14.4 meters (47 feet) long and 8 meters (26 feet) tall, all made of cut stone, support the six-span wooden corridor bridge above. While the rear of each boat-shaped pier is square like the stern of a skiff, the upstream end is pointed in shape, like a prow, referred to locally as a "swallow's beak," a shape said to boost flow-through during seasonal flooding. Flow-through is also facilitated by the greater distance between the middle set of piers than the openings at the ends, the distance varying between 9.8 meters (32 feet) and 13 meters (43 feet). The visual rhythm of the long covered wooden framework corridor above fluctuates in both elevation and plan as the wooden structure widens and is elevated above each pier, permitting surprisingly broad spaces for each of the open pavilions. Above the midway pier, a masonry building with tables and benches made of cut stone also houses an elaborate shrine with a statue of Yu the Great, the tamer of floods. While the underlying masonry work is finely done, the carpentry above, while functional, is rather rudimentary, even crude. Today, the Caihong Bridge is the anchor for a scenic area set in the middle of an active village. Here, farmers go about their lives, including passing back and forth across the bridge, as tourists stop to capture images with their cameras of antique farm equipment and rural life that is slowly being transformed by their presence. Visitors can rent a bamboo raft to enjoy the river and the views of the colorful covered bridge.

III.3.5 "Resting like a rainbow across the water," the Caihong Bridge is a multiple-span timber beam bridge with four midstream stone piers, with the cutwater edge pointing upstream. Source: ACO, 2005.

III.3.6 Viewed from the downstream side, the bulky piers are quite broad, each serving as the base for a spacious pavilion above. Source: ACO, 2005.

III.3.7a, b The approaches to the Caihong Bridge differ. On one end, there is a series of steep stone steps that reach a shop that intrudes, covering half of the portal. On the other end, an inclined stone path facilitates the climb for villagers. Source: ACO, 2005.

彩虹橋

b

長虹臥波

雙橋薈彩虹

兩水夾明鏡

III.3.8 As seen here, the timber components are all rather roughly hewn. All around the vicinity of the bridge are planted fields, with farmers regularly transiting the bridge even as tourists snap photographs. Source: ACO, 2005.

III.3.9 The shrine at the center of the bridge has a mere three images on display. There is no evidence that villagers participate in any ritual here. Source: ACO, 2005.

Gaoyang Bridge

The streamside pathway that leads into Tangmo Village in Qiankou Township, Huangshan City, Anhui Province brings one quickly to an exceptional covered bridge. Constructed between 1723 and 1735 and restored in 1996, the Gaoyang Bridge straddles the tightly constricted Xi Stream that threads its way through the village. Constructed upon a double-arched stone base, it is topped with a compact five-*jian* building that functions as both a teahouse and a performance stage because of its width. This is the only one of nine bridges in the village that is covered. Although said to have originated in the Yuan Dynasty, the current form dates from 1557 during the Ming Dynasty. Since the structure is so substantial, there is debate as to whether it once served as a temple or ancestral hall. Today, a teahouse occupies the space, with service geared more to wandering visitors who arrive by bus or car than village residents. In the evening, after most of the tourists have left, others who are spending the night in local B & Bs enjoy the atmosphere. Tangmo, like many old Huizhou villages, is in a remarkable state of preservation, with an overlay of tourism-related elements that are heavily promoted online.

III.3.10 Space is at a premium in Tangmo Village, with buildings constructed along the stream, which is bridged with stone planks at many locations. At one site, a double-arched stone bridge has above it a substantial building. Source: ACO, 2005.

III.3.11 The substantial timber framework that defines the interior spaces suggests that the structure might once have been a temple. Today, it functions day and night as an impressive teahouse. Source: ACO, 2005.

Bei'an Bridge

Among the most substantial covered bridges, with a length of 33 meters (100 feet) and width of 4.7 meters (15 feet), the Bei'an Bridge, which was constructed in the middle years of the Ming Dynasty, crosses Mianxi Stream in Shexian County, Huangshan City, Anhui Province. With its three stone arches and two midstream piers, the covered portion is divided into eleven bays consisting of a wooden framework with solid walls of fired brick on both sides. Above the entry on one end are the characters 谦庵旧址 , indicating this was the former site of a modest nunnery. Eight large rectangular windows are cut into the east side, with another eight on the west wall in various auspicious shapes, including a full moon, flower pots, cassia leaves, and bottle gourds. A balcony-like feature made of wood that slants outward, called a *meirenkao*, which is suitable only for sitting and leaning out to take in the view, is found on one side of the bridge. *Meirenkao* are typical sitting areas overlooking either a garden or small courtyard in Huizhou dwellings. Like many larger bridges, the Bei'an serves not only as a place to transit but also has a Buddhist shrine. On many mornings, it is also a place where itinerant merchants display what they have to sell to villagers. Strangely, except for the *meirenkao*, there are no boards along the side for sitting, which perhaps had not been put in place after renovation. In 2013, the State Council listed the Bei'an Bridge as a National Historical Cultural Site.

III.3.12a, b Viewed either from a distance or close up, the Bei'an Bridge clearly has a triple stone arch base with a masonry structure above it. The whitewashing of the exterior walls is similar to that applied to homes in the region. Source: ACO, 2005.

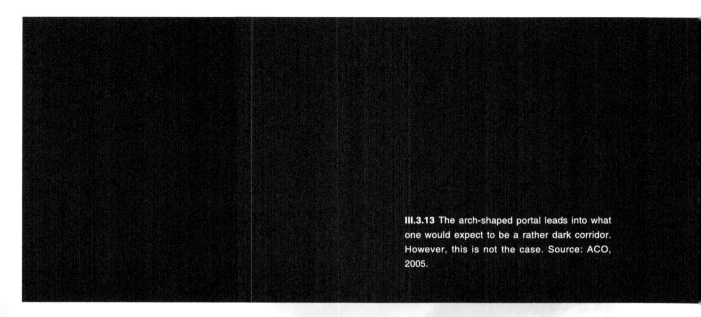
III.3.13 The arch-shaped portal leads into what one would expect to be a rather dark corridor. However, this is not the case. Source: ACO, 2005.

III.3.14 The rectangular and auspicious shaped windows all mimic the type associated with Chinese garden wall openings. Together, they bring abundant light and air into the corridor. Source: ACO, 2005.

a

III.3.15a, b On one wall of the bridge, there is a single *meirenkao*, a wooden addition suitable for sitting and taking in the view, even for young children. Source: ACO, 2005.

III.3.16 Of the sixteen windows along the sides of the Bei'an Bridge, Shexian County, Anhui, eight are rectangular and eight, like the one shown here, have auspicious meanings. A Chinese bottle gourd is pronounced *hu*, which is homophonous with *fu*, meaning "good fortune." Source: ACO, 2005.

Guangxi, Guizhou, and Hunan (Dong Minority) Covered Bridges

Of China's 55 ethnic minority groups, until recently only the Dong (Gaeml/Kam) in Guangxi and Guizhou provinces have been celebrated for their covered bridges. Into the second decade of the twenty-first century, travelers' accounts, even those of backpackers, and news reports basically only focused on comparatively accessible Dong villages and their striking timber architecture. This may have been because the somewhat exotic Dong minority villages in northern Guangxi were not only near enough to the tourist mecca of Guilin but were still relatively off the beaten track of tourism at the time. Even the material culture of the Dong and other ethnic minority groups in less traveled areas of adjacent Guizhou and Hunan was little known and poorly documented.

As analyzed by Xing Ruan and illustrated below, the Dong have an "architecture-based culture" in which life and building culture are inextricably interrelated (2006: 23–37). Moreover, we now know in the second decade of the twenty-first century that other ethnic minorities like the Tujia also have excelled in defining their settlements, called *zhai*, using timber for many structures, including covered bridges, most of which are *fengyuqiao* "wind-and-rain bridges." Those constructed by the little known Tujia (Bifzivkar) minority in today's Chongqing Municipality and Hunan Province will be discussed in Part III.5. Timber covered bridges and associated wooden structures of the Bai and Hui in Yunnan Province will then be presented in Part III.6. Aside from these four ethnic minority

groups, the Miao and Bouyei (Buyi) also still construct covered bridges, but most are in areas inhabited by larger and dominant ethnic minority groups, making it difficult to pinpoint any special characteristics. We have been unable to determine whether other non-Han ethnic minority groups like the Zhuang, Yi, Naxi, Lisu, Yao, and Li constructed covered bridges within their village communities in the past. One reason for this is that in many counties each group inhabits its specific local environmental niche. For example, in a given area, one ethnic group is concentrated in a valley bottom and spread along tributaries, while another is further up the hillslopes, and yet another occupies the rugged eroded upper reaches of mountains. Moreover, often living relatively near to one another, local ethnic minorities have long influenced each other, with the result that there has been a sharing of both tangible and intangible elements of cultures leading to hybridity. Naturally, a precondition for constructing *fengyuqiao* is the need to cross a stream associated with a village.

This recent awareness that six ethnic minority groups have covered bridge traditions is the result of several factors. First, centrally funded infrastructure projects, like the expansion of interprovincial highways and railways, has opened traditionally insular communities to tourists with the avowed purpose of relieving local poverty. Now that once remote villages and towns throughout Guizhou, Hunan, Hubei, and Chongqing Municipality, indeed most of China, are linked via modern highways and high-speed railways to the more cosmopolitan areas of the country, there has been a rapid expansion of Chinese domestic tourism penetrating areas once thought of as remote because of the difficulty of travel. Travel reports via Chinese language blogs and websites continue to reveal previously unknown or not widely known tangible and intangible elements of minority folk culture—ethnic festivals, songs, dances, and native costumes—as well as unique architectural features that include stilt houses, drum towers, and covered bridges.

Many of these cultural features are residual elements from the past that are authentic. Sometimes, the features have been altered or constructed anew because of the commodification of culture, in the process creating stereotypical markers of ethnic identity that highlight exotic elements, the "othering" of ethnic minority communities to satisfy the voyeuristic interests of visitors. In some cases, villages have undergone such an expensive and thorough facelift that they have become ethnic theme parks, with large parking lots, entry gates, pricey tickets, guest houses, obligatory performances in a designated entertainment area that sometimes includes bars and cafes, as well as newly built replicas of architectural features, including covered bridges as locations for photography and cultural performances. While Chinese tourists generally arrive in groups by bus and are funneled along a prescribed route, those who come unescorted are free to wander through minority villages to experience the authenticity of daily life. The architectural icons are frequently lit up at night, not only to make them accessible for tourists wandering about but also to highlight their structural elements. While these comments apply to many villages still undergoing renovation, the makeover of Fenghuang Town in Hunan as well as villages around Kaili and Zhaoxing in Guizhou has been transformative. Still, while those who visited these locations more than a decade ago and have returned to comment on the "touristy" upheaval,

first-time visitors still post on TripAdvisor comments such as "Go before it is too late."

The discussion below and in the following sections on other exemplary covered bridges attempts to differentiate "wind-and-rain" covered bridges for different ethnic minority groups, but it must be admitted that it is not always possible to determine clearly differentiating traits. This is because most ethnic minorities live among others groups, which all increasingly share traditions today. Perhaps in the distant past there were sharper differences, but today attributes are shared.

Dong Wind-and-Rain Covered Bridges

With a population of about three million, the Dong live in villages in the rugged region linking northern Guangxi, southern Guizhou, and southern Hunan provinces. Featured in this section are the following wind-and-rain covered bridges: Guangxi (Yongji/Chengyang, Batuan, and Sanjiang), Guizhou (Xiaohuang and Diping), and Hunan (Longjin). Others are discussed and illustrated throughout the earlier texts.

In Dong villages, which generally straddle streams, several types of buildings stand out as signature public structures arranged in well-defined compositions: altars or shrines, village gates, drum towers, opera stages, and wind-and-rain bridges. While each of these Dong building types is distinctive individually, they collectively provide a striking picturesqueness in which buildings, agriculture, and the natural landscape are in harmony. According to Xing Ruan, "It is architecture that 'speaks' to them [the Dong], and it is an architecture that is primarily for its inhabitants. The built world indeed is the extension of their body and mind; their experience with architecture is figurative, and their understanding of the built world is allegorical" (2006: 10).

Any Dong building, whether a bridge, drum tower, or house, is usually constructed using timber from a single tree species called "eighteen-year China fir" that matures in about eighteen years. Trees of this type are frequently planted when a child is born, with the expectation that over eighteen years, as the child matures to the age of marriage, the trees will have matured to a size suitable for building a home for the newlywed couple. A multistoried drum tower built of fir is viewed as an "umbrella" to shelter villagers. In fact, when a drum tower is destroyed by fire or accident, the Dong raise the trunk of a large fir tree on the drum tower site as a transitory replacement before a new one is built.

Wind-and-rain bridges are especially noteworthy for their wooden covered super-structures that allow the building to serve both as a covered corridor and as a pavilion for leisure. In terms of structure and overall composition, a wind-and-rain bridge is constructed with four parts: stone piers, an inverse pyramidal frame made of massive logs held together by tenons that serves as cantilevered support, an open or semi-enclosed corridor (sometimes with a shrine inside), and a roof. Usually each pier is crowned with a pavilion with a quadrangular or hexagonal roof with multitiered eaves. Each pavilion not only adds weight to the structure at locations needed to stabilize the overall structure, but also contributes to the beauty of the bridge. The entire bridge structure, except for the stone piers, is built of timber without nails using mortise-and-tenon joinery, just as vernacular village dwellings have been built. In connecting a village with the world beyond, each wind-and-rain bridge is located either at the "head' of a village, that is, an upstream area, and/or downstream at the "tail" of the village. Bridges are not commonly built near the center of a village since such a location is considered a "belly" that must be avoided in order to prevent pestilence. Whenever a bridge is located at a more central location, it is usually because of a need to link propitious "dragon veins."

Yet, Dong wind-and-rain bridges serve more than a structure to span a stream. Each is a public place that offers shelter for weary travelers and nearby farmers, protecting them from the elements—wind and rain. In addition, it is to the bridge that villagers retreat on hot or rainy days, as well as couples looking for romance under the moonlight or in darkness. As with many covered bridges elsewhere in China, there are altars to gods such as Guan Yu, also called Guandi and Guan Gong, a compassionate, courageous, and virtuous general. Guan Yu, who is shown as a red-faced armor-clad warrior with a long, lush beard, is worshipped in many incarnations: a Daoist guardian deity, a Buddhist bodhisattva charged with protecting the Dharma, and an heroic historic figure thought to be just and righteous. In southern China, moreover, many see Guan Yu as an alternative God of Wealth in that he is capable of providing blessings to those who are upright while protecting them from those who are dishonest. Futhermore, bridges, like other buildings, are usually sited carefully using *fengshui* principles, since villagers believe that a properly located bridge can protect the wealth of a village from being drained away by its streams.

GUANGXI

Yongji (Chengyang) Wind-and-Rain Bridge

In three rural townships in the Sanjiang District at the northern tip of Guangxi Province, there are more than 110 wind-and-rain bridges. Among the most representative and clearly the most famous is the Yongji Bridge, also generally called the Chengyang Bridge, which spans the Linxi River in Ma'an Village. Constructed between 1912 and 1924 with the support of villagers living in eight villages called *zhai*, the bridge is 77.8 meters (255 feet) long, 11.5 meters (38 feet) high, and 3.8 meters (12 feet) wide with five piers and four 17.3-meter (57-foot)-wide openings. In 1953, the bridge was recognized as a provincial-level heritage site and in 1982 was granted national heritage status. Sadly, much of the bridge was destroyed in 1983 because of flood, but this disaster spurred extensive renovation that, even after nearly a quarter century, has given the Yongji Bridge a strikingly new, yet rather weathered look.

Three cantilevered layers of fir logs, a series of projecting horizontal beams 7–8 meters (23–26 feet) in length, are laid longitudinally across the top of each of the five stone piers that each measure 2.5 meters (8 feet) wide by 8.2 meters (27 feet) long. Between the four levels of cantilevered logs, which are held firm by tenoned timbers, are thin spacer logs that together not only stabilize the support but also give it some level of flexibility. These then support a continuous overhanging wooden corridor built of interlocked columns and beams that divide the interior into 19 bays or *jian*. Five pavilions with stacked flying eaves rising above the five piers endow the bridge with a distinctive architectural rhythm. Arranged symmetrically, the central pavilion is the tallest at 7.8 meters (26 feet), those on both sides at 7 meters (23 feet), with the two outer pavilions at 6.5 meters (21 feet) above the bridge. The middle taller pavilion is topped with a hexagonal structure, reminiscent of a drum tower, while the adjacent two pavilions have pyramidal hipped roofs with four slopes. The end pavilions have rectangular gambrel roofs, that is, a double slope roof with the upper slope having a lesser pitch than the lower, rising high with five layers. All of the roofs are covered with gray tiles of the sort found on dwellings and temples. Wherever there are eaves, just as on similar drum towers, one finds colorful painted images of mountains, rivers, flowers, birds, fish, and other animals. Looking into the upper reaches of the central hexagonal pavilion from the inside of the bridge, one sees clearly a sunken coffered ceiling.

With the coming of domestic tourism to the Sanjiang region, the Yongji Bridge no longer bears the traffic it once did, in as much as a nearby modern bridge has been constructed to carry vehicular and animal traffic. Today, the colorful bridge is open only to pedestrians who can sit on the wood plank benches along the covered corridor to enjoy the breeze. Doing so, they sit among countless villagers selling homespun fabrics and embroidered Dong-style clothing.

III.4.1 Viewed from a nearby hillside, the Yongji Bridge, otherwise known as the Chengyang Bridge, is an iconic element along the Linxi River. Source: TEM, 2007.

III.4.2 With a waterwheel made of bamboo in the foreground, the bridge rises from three midstream stone piers, each with a multitiered tower above it. Source: TEM, 2007.

III.4.3 In order to be above periodic flood stages, tall piers raise the bridge to a level that demands a set of stone stairs to reach it. Source: ACO, 2006.

III.4.4 Stacked logs resting on the piers provide cantilevered support for the timbers above. Source: TEM, 2007.

III.4.5 A close-up view of the tiered entry pavilion with upturned features at the end of the spine. Source: TEM, 2007.

III.4.6 While traditionally the benches within the bridge were used for the comfort of villagers, today they provide space to display items for sale to tourists. Source: TEM, 2007.

III.4.7 The timber framework within the bridge corridor. Source: TEM, 2007.

III.4.8 There are picturesque views of the Linxi River from inside the bridge. Source: ACO, 2006.

Batuan Wind-and-Rain Bridge

While the Yongji (Chengyang) Wind-and-Rain Bridge is outstanding for its size and ornamentation, the Batuan Bridge in Dutong Township, a mountain range away, stands out because of its two separate corridors, a lower narrow one just 1.8 meters (6 feet) wide at grade level through which animals can be led across, and an upper wider one 3.9 meters (13 feet) wide, which is reached by stone steps for pedestrians and those wanting to tarry. Built in 1910 as a unique double-passage structure, the 50-meter (164-foot)-long span rises above a narrow section of the Miao Stream at high locations along its bank. While the stream appears much of the time to be shallow and sluggish, the water is far from languishing

during late spring and summer, as can be attested by the significant accumulations of rubble stone and gravel along its banks and the well-worn nearby rock surfaces. Stone abutments on both ends extend well beyond the stream's bank to offer supplementary support to the massive cantilevered logs that reach toward the single midstream pier. Three hipped-roof pavilions, the central one being somewhat taller and more elaborate than the matching pair on each side, are symmetrically placed above the linear roofline, highlighting the covered corridor and, at the same time, mimicking the roofs of village houses in the distance. Until recently, few outsiders visited the Batuan Bridge since it was located in a village difficult to reach. The centrality and significance of the bridge to villagers are attested to by the steady traffic of humans and animals across it as they travel between their homes and stables in the *zhai* and the terraced fields on the nearby hillslopes and valley floors.

III.4.9 Footpaths between villages carry both pedestrians and sure-footed animals to the elevated bridge that crosses the Miao Stream. Source: ACO, 2006.

III.4.10 Both entries to the bridge are highly decorated with multitiered towers. Left center is the wide portal for pedestrians that is reached from a gently rising path. The children are standing at the lower entry for animals. The cantilevered logs are visible above the pier and projecting from the two abutments. Source: ACO, 2006.

III.4.11 Viewed head on, the lower channel that accommodates the crossing by animals is separate from the corridor above where villagers can rest or pass from one side to the other. Source: ACO, 2006.

III.4.12 In addition to the tiled roof, a projecting skirt-like overhang helps protect the timbers beneath. Source: ACO, 2006.

III.4.13 Lined with benches, the central corridor is framed with dovetailed as well as mortise-and-tenoned timber members. Source: ACO, 2006.

III.4.14 A decorative caisson beneath one of the towers. Source: TEM, 2007.

III.4.16 Overall, the timber framework employs hardwoods with substantial dimensions. This assemblage reaches out from the main corridor to support the special lane for animals that is beneath. Source: TEM, 2007.

III.4.15 The ritual niche is much smaller than expected in a bridge of this size. Rather strangely the two images—Guan Gong, also known as Guan Yu, and his Three Kingdoms period fellow general Zhang Fei—are usually displayed as Door Gods on the outside of a dwelling at the New Year rather than in a shrine. Source: TEM, 2007.

Sanjiang Wind-and-Rain Bridge

The massive wind-and-rain bridge in the city of Sanjiang was opened at the end of December 2010. This urban bridge is a signature structure within the seat of the Sanjiang Dong Autonomous County that has many distinctive traditional *fengyuqiao* features. While usually described as covered, as the aerial view demonstrates, the bridge is surmounted by seven drum tower-like pavilions that straddle the otherwise open roadway. Spanning the Rong River with a length of 368 meters (1,207 feet) and a width of 16 meters (52 feet), only the pedestrian walkways on both sides are covered. Like other newly built *fengyuqiao*, the one in Sanjiang is brightly lit at night. While the supporting structure beneath is a prestressed concrete open-spandreled arch bridge with piers supporting long approaches, the timber superstructure above models traditional forms with *chuandou* mortise-and-tenon joints.

III.4.18 This portal view emphasizes both the eight tiers of the entry as well as the double-lane roadway and the pedestrian corridors along the edges. Source: TEM, 2017.

III.4.17 This aerial view during construction in October 2010 reveals the complexity of the timber framework that ran the full length as well as constituted the multiple towers. Source: http://travel.sina.com.cn/china/2013-09-22/1153218186.shtm. Accessed September 22, 2013.

III.4.19 When viewed from a nearby road, it is clear that the understructure of the Sanjing Bridge is a modern prestressed concrete arch with open spandrels. Source: TEM, 2017.

III.4.20 On this quiet morning, both the pedestrian and traffic lanes were virtually empty. All of the framework above the masonry deck is composed of timber. Source: TEM, 2017.

III.4.21 At the center of the Sanjiang Bridge, above the roadway, is a towering drum tower-like structure whose height is accomplished with intersecting timbers. Source: TEM, 2017.

III.4.22 The interplay between the six tiered sets of towers is shown clearly in this oblique aerial view of the Sanjiang Bridge. Source: http://www.globaltimes.cn/content/607563.shtm. Accessed December 31, 2010.

III.4.23 At night, the Sanjiang Bridge is brilliantly illuminated as both a focal city icon and an attractive place to stroll or rest. Source: https://kknews.cc/travel/kzrjyn8.htm. Accessed February 13, 2016.

GUIZHOU

Xiaohuang
Wind-and-Rain Bridge

While the better known Dong covered bridges in Guangxi Province share certain characteristics, which are commonly viewed as being distinctively Dong, once one travels westward into Guizhou Province different patterns emerge. No covered bridge there is more striking than the one in Xiaohuang, a village of about 3,500 people in Congjiang County, which is encountered in the approach to the village on the county highway. The buildings in the *zhai* rise as rows up the hillslope adjacent to a stream that passes through the village. Somewhat reminiscent of a covered bridge in Kaili and a smaller one in Xiaohuang,

which may have been the model for the long bridge, Xiaohuang Bridge has a variety of striking wooden pagodas atop that mimic those on the tops on the village drum tower. The long bridge is entered from the main highway via an elongated stone causeway that then traverses an arch-shaped masonry bridge where it terminates in paths that lead into the hills or back into the village. A large entry portal with an abandoned ticket booth connected to the bridge is adjacent to an expansive but empty parking lot. Together, these suggest that anticipated tourism plans were not realized. The anticipation for increased tourist visitation stems from the naming of Xiaohuang as a Village of China's Folk Art by the Ministry of Culture in 1996, which acknowledged the fame arising from their singing of polyphonic folk songs called Grand Songs *da ge*.

III.4.24 The entry to Xiaohuang Village, with a prominent multitiered cupola above it, also serves as the entrance to one end of the bridge, which is to the left. As a toll gate with an expansive parking area adjacent to it, these were built to meet the needs of an expected flood of Chinese tourists that has not materialized. Source: TEM, 2017.

III.4.25 Although long, the Xiaohuang Bridge actually only spans a narrow stream, with most of the structure built as a causeway across the paddy fields. This view is from the end opposite that of the formal toll booth entry to the village. Source: TEM, 2017.

III.4.26a–c Mimicking the pinnacles found above village drum towers, a series of different cupolas punctuate the roofline of this long bridge.

III.4.27 The long corridor includes a stone path for pedestrians and wooden benches for those who prefer to sit and enjoy the breeze and scenery. Source: TEM, 2017.

III.4.28 Looking towards this large Dong village, those crossing the bridge can see the distinctive drum tower that rises above such communities. Source: TEM, 2017.

Diping
Wind-and-Rain Bridge

Located in the southern corner of Liping County, Diping Village is easily accessed via a highway from the Congjiang County seat some 100 kilometers (62 miles) away. With the extended village spread across three hamlets linked by footpaths, the covered bridge has served as a critical link among them since 1882–3 in crossing the Nanjiang River. In 1959, the old covered bridge was destroyed in a fire, then rebuilt in 1964, only to suffer major damage in 1966 at the beginning of the Cultural Revolution. In 1981, the bridge was granted protection by the county government, then in 1982 by the Guizhou Provincial Government. The Diping covered bridge was fêted in 1997–8 as one image of four postage stamps featuring Dong architecture at a time when few outsiders visited remote Guizhou. Finally, in 2001, the State Council granted it national protection. Though spanning a gully and rather high above the stream, the bridge was flooded in 2004 to the degree that extensive restoration work took until 2006 to be completed.

III.4.29 To celebrate Diping Bridge's restoration in 2006, the Postal Administration issued a stamp depicting it. Source: RGK Collection.

To access the bridge from the Diping hamlet, one must climb a series of stone steps, walk 100 meters (328 feet), and then descend a dozen more steps before entering the wooden gallery. With a style like larger Dong covered bridges in Guangxi Province, the Diping Wind-and-Rain Bridge is 56.6 meters (187 feet) long, 4.5 meters (15 feet)

wide, and lifted about 10 meters (33 feet) above the stream by abutments and a single stone pier. Atop these stone supports, an assemblage of China fir logs form cantilevers that extend about 2 meters (6 feet) before large beams complete the remaining gap. Wooden flooring is then tied to a series of timber bents, each comprising four columns with a *chuandou* set of pillars and beams that lift the roof without the use of any metal nail or other fastener. A 1-meter (3-foot)-high balustrade along the

perimeter is sheltered by an eaves overhang capped with roof tiles. When viewed from a distance, this row of eaves and those extending along the cantilevers give the appearance of a double set of eaves, which together shelter the structure from rain while allowing wind to penetrate it. Wooden benches are spaced between the pillars and run the full length of the corridor. Above the entry on each end is a multitiered tower with triple eaves that each reach about 3 meters (10 feet) above the tiled roof. A prominent tower reminiscent of a drum tower with four eaves and a protruding cap rises some 5 meters (16 feet) above the roof at the location of the stone pier. Together with the eaves above the cantilevers and along the side of the bridge, the three towers appear from a distance to be taller than they actually are. When viewed from inside, the central tower has a coffered ceiling that is decorated with paintings celebrating the musicianship and festivals of the Dong.

III.4.30a, b The Diping Bridge exemplifies classic Dong bridge construction using large-scale log cantilevers, presumably held down by the multistoried towers on each pier. Source: TEM, 2017.

III.4.31 As is typical, the cantilever structure is protected by eaves covered with clay tiles that only partially cover the sides, allowing for air circulation. Source: TEM, 2017.

III.4.32 The steep stone steps to access the crossing do not deter those riding motorbikes. Source: TEM, 2017.

III.4.33a, b Several Dong women return to their homes from shopping through Diping Bridge, several bays of which are elaborately decorated. Source: TEM, 2017.

"三月三" 抢花炮

III.4.34a (previous spread), b, c Beneath the central tower of the Diping Bridge is a coffered ceiling with murals that depict Dong festivals, including music performances. Other related images are found in Part II.2. Source: RGK, 2017; TEM, 2017; TEM, 2017.

夫妻常樂歌養心

Yinglong
Wind-and-Rain Bridge

Gaojin Village in Maogong Township, although a small settlement of only 110 households in three hamlets, once had eight bridges with six surviving today. Of them, the most outstanding is the Yinglong Bridge, here called a *huaqiao* or "flowery bridge" rather than a *fengyuqiao* "wind-and-rain bridge" and which was earlier celebrated by the Postal Administration along with the Diping Bridge. The postage stamp, which was shown earlier as II.1.82, does not reveal its location but simply states "*fengyu qiao* in a field." Said to have been first constructed in 1765, probably as an element in the scripting of a *fengshui* composition, the small Yinglong Bridge has assumed outsized mythic significance to villagers. Over the years, the paths within the village and beyond were lined with slate. High on a nearby mountain is a carving of a protective lion. Together with an impressive eighteenth-century opera stage and drum tower in the village, the Yinglong covered bridge provides a signature culture landscape more complete than comparatively sized villages.

Restored in 1846 and then more recently rebuilt in 1980, the bridge is situated close to the ground over a narrow stream and is approached via a level path on one end and two sets of steps leading in different directions on the other. The stone abutments of the bridge support stone slabs as flooring, a highly unusual form. These stone slabs are 5.5 meters (18 feet) long, 1.2 meters (4 feet) wide, and 20 centimeters (8 inches) thick.

III.4.35a–c The Yinglong Bridge in Gaojin Village is highly unusual in that its base is a stone slab 5.5 meters (18 feet) long and 20 centimeters (8 inches) thick. Source: TEM, 2017.

a

327   PART III China's Exemplary Covered Bridges

III.4.36 From inside the Yinglong Bridge looking back across the fields to the drum tower and village dwellings. Source: TEM, 2017.

III.4.37 The old opera stage in the village dates to the reign of the Qianlong Emperor (1736–96) during the Qing Dynasty. Here it was being used as a banquet space for men after a wedding. Source: TEM, 2017.

HUNAN

Longjin
Wind-and-Rain Bridge

While all the Dong wind-and-rain bridges discussed above sometimes have periodic commercial activity that ranges from a local farmer selling produce to an individual offering handcrafted goods, the Longjin Wind-and-Rain Bridge in the county town of Zhizhiang, Hunan, is a veritable marketplace, with Chinese life in all its richness on display. Records reveal that a bridge has spanned the Wushui River at this critical link between Hunan and Guizhou provinces since 1591 during the Ming Dynasty. Numerous structural and functional changes that are only vaguely known were carried out in 1602, 1633, and 1777 due to flood or fire. At some point after 1937, the Nationalist army destroyed what is described in records as a wooden covered bridge, and it was

subsequently rebuilt with stone piers and a wooden plank floor to serve principally as a link in the supply route along a strategic highway. During the Sino-Japanese War between 1937 and 1945, the bridge was bombed daily since it was near a Nationalist air base and was at a key transportation junction. With no date specified, local lore recounts that one day 27 Japanese planes attacked the bridge, destroying it and leaving it lying in the river until it was rebuilt after Liberation in 1949. With this rebuilding, an extensive market was established within it.

More recently, in 1998–9, the bridge was completely rebuilt as a covered bridge with flourishes that distinguish it as a Dong wind-and-rain bridge. While the piers and the deck of the bridge were constructed using prestressed concrete, all of the superstructure is timber without the use of nails. The length of 146.7 meters (482 feet) and an overall width of 12.2 meters (40 feet) accommodates a broad 5.8-meter (19-foot)-

wide pedestrian passageway at the center. Accompanying this rebuilding was the installation of approximately a hundred market stalls, transforming the span into a lively market for the Dong and Miao minority groups who inhabit the extensive residential areas on both sides of the bridge. Virtually anything that locals require can be purchased on the bridge. There are even several open-air dentist "offices," allowing passersby to see what is being carried out on patients. There are seven airy open areas among the stalls for folks to relax, play games, or just sit and chat. Beyond serving the needs of locals, the bridge has become a tourist hotspot as it proclaims itself "the longest covered bridge in China," a claim that now is contested with other new structures. Nearby is the largest Mazu Temple in interior China, as well as a collection of Dong drum towers and stilt houses that attract domestic tourists.

III.4.38a, b Because Longjin Bridge is essentially a market and community center over water, its dimensions outside and inside are broad and high. With such massive dimensions, Longjin's roof structure is unusually robust, even including steps into a tower. Source: TEM, 2017.

b

III.4.39a (previous spread), b Although appearing to be a long wooden covered bridge from a distance, a closer view reveals that the Longjin Bridge is a vast multitiered wooden structure on a reinforced concrete deck supported by concrete piers. Source: TEM, 2017.

III.4.40 A group of retired men play cards in an open area on the Longjin Bridge. Source: TEM, 2017.

III.4.41 The bridge includes several open-air dentists' offices that offer patients little privacy. Source: TEM, 2017.

III.4.42 Viewed from the Longjin Bridge, visitors will be captivated by several large and small drum towers, attesting to the rising tourism of the Zhijiang area. Source: TEM, 2017.

Chongqing and Hunan (Tujia Minority) Covered Bridges

Although less known than the Dong ethnic minority even as they have a significantly greater population, the Tujia (Bifzivkar), who live in mountainous borderlands straddling Hunan, Hubei, and Guizhou provinces as well as Chongqing Municipality, also have a covered bridge-building tradition. Principally inhabiting once remote autonomous counties where they intermingle with both the Miao and Dong, they share many cultural traits that reflect the dramatic nature of assimilation. Over the past decade, as domestic tourism has surged, the beauty of the Zhangjiajie Mountains and the isolated villages throughout this region have been accompanied by major efforts to construct buildings, including covered bridges, that are markers of Tujia communities. The promotion of tourism among the "colorful minorities" has meant displays of recreated songs and dances, the performance of the exotic for Chinese tourists, with new covered bridges and other architectural features serving as stage settings.

In the past, most of the Tujia covered bridges in the mountainous areas were rather simple structures made with readily available stone and timber, unlike either the more dramatic and better-known Dong bridges or the new Tujia *fengyuqiao* wind-and-rain bridges. In recent years, the Tujia have carried out the feverish construction of new *fengyuqiao* that not only rival those of the Dong but aspire to eclipse them. One noted characteristic of Tujia covered bridges that distinguishes them from Dong covered ones is that they have upturned corners where the side eaves join. These upsweeping rooflines mimic those found on their dwellings.

III.5.1 While upturned eaves are generic elements of Chinese architecture, those found on Tujia minority structures are more pronounced. Source: Li and Zhang, 1994: 182.

Like wind-and-rain bridges elsewhere, those of the Tujia serve other purposes besides being a link across a stream. The fact that covered bridges serve also as markets is underscored because in the Tujia language "going to market/fair" *gan chang* is usually expressed as "going to bridge" *gan qiao* (Li and Zhang, 1994: 24).

CHONGQING

Kezhai
Wind-and-Rain Bridge

A fine example of a traditional workaday wind-and-rain bridge built without fancy roof ornaments within a Tujia area is the Kezhai Wind-and-Rain Bridge in Qingxichang Town, Shoushan County, Chongqing Municipality. Originally called the Yongxing Bridge and Zhongling Bridge, it is said to date to 1458 and was rebuilt at least ten times. Five piers lift the bridge structure above the stream to the degree that stone steps must be mounted to enter and cross. A distinguishing characteristic of the bridge is that the triple overlapping eaves along the sides open the interior to both sun and air but not to damaging rain. It is said that during the late Qing Dynasty (1644–1911) there were five levels of eaves, but these were reduced to three in 1952 when the bridge was renovated. The bridge is approximately 60 meters (197 feet) long and 6 meters (20 feet) wide. While the interior structure utilizes a *chuandou* mortise-and-tenon structure, a striking feature of the bridge is that 93 stone slabs form the central pavement atop a timber surface. Both sides of the bridge are lined with narrow benches without backs that together with the open, yet sheltered sides provide a breezy location for villagers.

III.5.2 The substantial portal of the timbered Kezhai Bridge includes a boxed-bond brick façade with a scalloped ridgeline and an arch-shaped opening. Source: RGK, 2017.

III.5.3 Resting on five piers that span a broad river channel, which much of the year has a low volume of water passing through it, the Kezhai Bridge has a triple eaves overhang along the sides. Source: TEM, 2017.

III.5.4a, b As these views reveal, many of the timbers supporting the bridge are rotting and sagging, thus require replacement. Source: TEM, 2017.

b

III.5.5 Even as the structure of the bridge is deteriorating, it provides a cool location for local villagers to rest. The rough-hewn boards placed above the timber beams also support a weighty cut-stone walkway down the center of the corridor. Source: TEM, 2017.

III.5.6 The timber framework of sections of the gallery has been rebuilt using a mixture of new and old wood, providing some seating. Source: TEM, 2017.

Tiansheng
Wind-and-Rain Bridge

Built in 1849 with four stone piers, each approximately 20 meters (66 feet) high, the Tiansheng Wind-and Rain Bridge is 55.65 meters (183 feet) long and 7.35 meters (24 feet) wide and is located along a route from Xiyang via Xiushan to Changde in Hunan Province. Entry is through a brick façade with a double set of eaves extending along each side. Though renovated in 1964, the most recent renovation began in March 2017 utilizing giant creosoted beams from Russia's Siberia.

III.5.8a, b The rebuilding of the timber-framed gallery structure mixed new and old wood and used mortise-and-tenon joinery. Source: TEM, 2017.

III.5.7 Continuing restoration work of the Tiansheng Bridge involved the strengthening of the portal. Source: RGK, 2017.

III.5.9 The enormous creosoted beams added along the axis of the bridge were all imported from Russia's Siberia. Source: TEM, 2017.

Canglang (Zhuoshui) Wind-and-Rain Bridge

The most striking modern Tujia *fengyuqiao* wind-and-rain bridge is in Zhuoshui, Qianjiang District, Chongqing Municipality, formerly Qianjiang Tujia and Miao Autonomous County, where the Canglang *fengyuqiao* is now heralded as "the longest covered bridge in the world." While this is an impressive structure, there are unanswered questions about it. Local authorities state that the site had a covered bridge from 1591 onward. However, there is no known descriptive or illustrative information about the original bridge and its reconstructions over four centuries. Surprisingly, a 2011 book titled *Chongqing qiaoliang zhi* [Records of Chongqing Bridges], which included information concerning past and standing covered bridges throughout the municipality, including Qianjiang, contains no information concerning the original old bridge or a replacement that was reported to have been constructed on cement piers in 1999. The very long current bridge leads to little more than fields. If there had been a bridge at that location since 1591, it would have been much shorter since the stream crossing at that time was narrow.

We know more recent history since it was widely reported in late November 2013 that the "longest covered bridge in Asia," at 303 meters (994 feet) in length and 5 meters (16 feet) in width, was destroyed as a result of a massive fire that not only ripped through the wooden structure but dropped it (but not its reinforced concrete base and piers) into the Apeng River where it was strewn as charred driftwood. Dramatic photographs of this fire were circulated worldwide and provided glimpses of what, indeed, was a long bridge that connected the old town with open fields. Interestingly, news reports at the time rued the fact that the lost Zhuoshui Bridge was second in length only to the 391-meter (1,283-foot)-long Hartland Covered Bridge in Canada.

III.5.10 Even before the disastrous 2013 fire, the Canglang Bridge was impressively long. Source: https://www.backchina.com/blog/250647/article-191233.html. Accessed December 1, 2013.

III.5.11a–c The spectacular night-time fire, whose origin is unknown, consumed the wooden structure above the prestressed concrete deck, leaving behind only charred remnants that were not usable during reconstruction. Source: http://news.163.com/photoview/00AP0001/40509.html#p=9EPBHH5300AP0001. Accessed November 28, 2013.

In May 2014, a decision was made to rebuild the destroyed covered bridge, including lengthening the original 303 meters (994 feet) to 310 meters (1,017 feet), in addition to adding three significant components to the covered gallery so that it would indeed become "the world's longest covered bridge." To accommodate this, a channel was dug that allows the Apeng River to sweep across a midstream island, with the effect of two stream crossings connected and extended by causeways. As the image here shows, this was to be accomplished by continuing the gallery across three extensions: a 105-meter (344-foot)-long four-story bell tower, a 93-meter (305-foot)-long "surging rainbow" over the Puhua River, and a 146-meter (479-foot)-long "flying dragon" section that is more concourse than bridge in as much as it simply crosses land and not water.

After all the sections were completed in September 2017, the total length of 658 meters (2,159 feet) was sufficient to make the bold claim that it is indeed "the longest covered bridge in the world" and significantly longer than Canada's Hartland Covered Bridge.

This new bridge is a signature component of the 5A Tourist Development Area focusing on Zhuoshui Old Town, which includes at its entrance the upscale Tianlai Bamaodao Hotel complex and numerous less costly inns for visitors nearby. As can be seen in the images above, the upswept rooflines clearly distinguish Tujia *fengyuqiao* from those constructed by the Dong ethnic minority group. Nonetheless, both utilize sophisticated mortise-and-tenon joinery in the timber framing of both dwellings and bridges.

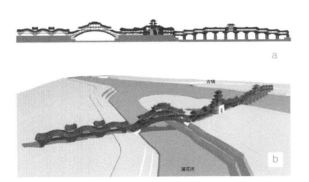

III.5.12a, b Schematic drawings of the proposed bridge. Replacement for the original bridge, which was lost to fire, is the section on the right with a single tower along it. Source: RGK Collection.

III.5.12c This aerial view from the opposite angle from the drawings above reveals the full extent of the Canglang Wind-and-Rain Bridge. Source: http://www.qjzsjq.com/mobile/item.asp?id=925. Accessed March 13, 2019.

III.5.13 The entrance to the Canglang Bridge from Zhuoshui Old Town. Source: TEM, 2017.

III.5.14 This is the first of many interconnected corridors along the bridge, some of which involve steps as visitors move from one level to another. Source: TEM, 2017.

III.5.15 The third section of this lengthy bridge has been poetically named the "Surging Rainbow" section. Source: TEM, 2017.

11.5.16 At dusk and after dark, the Canglang Bridge comes to life with a brilliant, often wave-like extravaganza of colored lights that draws the eye well beyond the original crossing. Source: TEM, 2017.

HUNAN

Reba Laochehe
Wind-and-Rain Bridge

A striking Y-shaped bridge is found in the Xiangxi Tujia and Miao Autonomous Prefecture, Longshan County, in the Wuling Mountains of western Hunan Province. Said to be one of the oldest Tujia settlements and dating to the Ming Dynasty (1368–1644), the small village of Laochehe includes an impressively large replica of a traditional Tujia *fengyuqiao* connecting three hamlets across the Dianfang and Xihe streams. Constructed in 2008 on a series of reinforced concrete piers and with a concrete base, this 288.8-meter (948-foot)-long bridge was for a short time billed as "the longest wind-and-rain bridge in the world." Where the three legs of the timber covered bridge come together, there is a tiered pavilion also of wood.

The promotion of tourism in the broader Xiangxi Region of which Reba Laochehe is a part, continues with visitors drawn principally to the Zhangjiajie Sandstone Peak Forest National Geopark, China's first national park and a UNESCO World Heritage site. With its impressive ageless jagged quartzite sandstone pillars, ancient forests, rivers, and waterfalls, as well as the 2016 completion of the Zhangjiajie Grand Canyon Glass Bridge, billed as the longest (430 meters, 1,411 feet) and highest (300 meters, 984 feet) glass pedestrian bridge in the world, this once remote region is today known for its contemporary hyperbole. The worldwide success of the epic science fiction film *Avatar*, some of whose scenes drew inspiration from Zhangjiajie, put a spotlight on the region. Within the region also is Fenghuang, the well-preserved and celebrated rivertown that became a UNESCO World Heritage site in 2008. In an attempt to benefit from the overflow of visitors, small towns and villages like Reba Laoheche have devised creative strategies that include the construction of dramatic and expensive *fengyuqiao*

to help them transform once relatively poor areas into areas linked to the world economy through tourism.

III.5.17 No other covered bridge in China, historic or modern, has this Y-shaped configuration. Cleverly designed and connecting three hamlets, the three covered corridor arms rest on reinforced concrete piers and base. Source: http://www.sohu.com/a/149651092_11659. Accessed May 17, 2017.

III.5.18a–c Although resting on a concrete slab, the Y-shaped gallery models a traditional covered bridge, from its pebble surface to its tiered timber framework and seating. Source: Eunice Hau Yee Eng.

Yunnan (Bai and Hui Minority) Covered Bridges

While it is well-known that Yunnan, which is nearly as large as the US state of Montana, has more ethnic minority groups than any other Chinese province—25 of the 55 official groups—few are aware that the province and surrounding areas have a long-standing covered bridge tradition. The most extensive distribution of covered bridges is in the counties within and adjacent to the Dali Bai Autonomous Prefecture in northwestern Yunnan, a broad transitional region situated between the dramatic terrain of the Tibetan Plateau to its west and the rugged landscapes of the Yungui Plateau to its east. Another significant cluster is in the Tengchong/Baoshan area along the border with Myanmar (Burma). Crossing the vast Yunnan region from north to south are the incised parallel valleys of many of Asia's great rivers, the Jinsha (upper reaches of the Yangzi/Yangtze), Lancang (Mekong), and Nujiang (Salween). While none of these three major rivers is known to have been crossed by any type of bridge in the past, their numerous tributaries within the drainage basin were bridged in order to facilitate movement along routes that were part of an extensive network of commercial trails known as the Tea-Horse Road or *chamadao*. Like the Great Wall, which actually consists of many intersecting as well as parallel walls, the Tea-Horse Road network incorporated major routes in addition to many interconnecting feeder footpaths.

Tea-Horse Roads

Less known than the fabled Silk Roads that connected China with regions to the west as far as Rome, the Tea-Horse Roads in southwest China, often simple paths, some paved with stones and others mere animal tracks, similarly served as conduits for commercial and cultural exchange. Although sections of the Tea-Horse Roads go back millennia, the network only began to multiply its routes and significance from the Tang Dynasty (618–907) onwards. It functioned continuously, although in decline, well into the middle of the twentieth century. Rather than silk, the catalyst for commerce was tea that was produced in southern Yunnan Province as well as in Sichuan Province in exchange for Tibetan horses and ponies. Salt also increasingly was a commodity transported from interior China along the Tea-Horse Road into Tibet and even beyond the Himalayas. While tea is not produced in Tibet, it essentially became a luxury commodity for elites there during the Tang Dynasty. By CE 1000, the beverage had become a staple for the population at large. As early explorers discovered, Tibetans transformed tea, which even the Chinese saw as more than a beverage, into a food and tonic with yak milk and butter, ground barley, and salt added via a churning process. Even today, Tibetans consume scores of cups of yak butter tea each day to stay hydrated, reduce stress, revitalize their energy, and aid in the digestion of their meat and cholesterol-laden diet rich in fats, oils, and salts. Traded in Tibet for tea and salt, unmounted yet sure-footed Tibetan ponies walked as a team east on the same paths that tea moved west. Once deep in China, they were employed by the Chinese for military expeditions against the nomadic tribes in the north. In addition to the exchange of goods, cultural exchange flourished due to the movement of monks and migrants along the well-trodden routes. The emergence of myriad bazaars and market towns of many sizes along the routes is testament to the intensity of the cultural interactions that occurred.

The demand for tea was satisfied by the overland transport from southern Yunnan of great quantities of fermented Pu'er tea in addition to Ya'an tea from western Sichuan, both teas named after the areas in which they were grown and each being the entry point for one of the prominent routes. From these two tea-producing centers, porters wearing straw sandals carried heavy loads of "brick tea" along zigzagging mountain trails and across numerous streams, only some of which were bridged. As can be viewed in early twentieth-century photography, porters carried T-shaped iron-tipped walking sticks that helped them balance their loads as they traversed rocky paths with strenuous ascents and sometimes precipitous descents. The sticks also allowed the porters to rest without unloading. Since porters were paid by weight, the strong among them carried as much tea as possible. Along the way, handlers facilitated the loading and unloading of tea in a type of relay in which fresh porters replaced those who had worked a previous leg. On some routes, yak, pony, and mule caravans supplanted the processions of porters. Once tea was delivered, porters returned with less heavy but equally valuable loads of medicinal herbs, aromatic musk, and wool and horn from various Tibetan animals. On some less rugged intermediate routes, porters were supplemented by muleteers guiding cargo-laden caravans of yaks and mules with tea strapped to their backs. Covered bridges and bazaars provided safe locations for rest along the way.

TEA-COOLIE CROSSING A SUSPENSION BRIDGE
His load weighed about 160 lbs

a

III.6.1a Whether in Yunnan or Sichuan, tea-bearing porters had to cross suspension bridges that linked the mountain tracks across which they moved. Source: Kendall, 1913: facing p. 152.

III.6.1b Horse and mule caravans often carried tea into Tibet. This tradition is heralded in the museum displays in the Muslim village of Donglianhua, Yunnan, where it is claimed that once there were 350 animals and countless drivers involved with the caravans. Source: RGK, 2016.

b

Pu'er tea from southern Yunnan and Ya'an tea from western Sichuan are unlike the crisp loose green teas from eastern China. Indeed, much of Pu'er and Ya'an tea is picked from trees rather than the hillside bushes common in China's eastern tea-producing areas. After drying and rolling, Pu'er and Ya'an tea leaves undergo a fermenting process that is part of a multi-stage progression of aging which adds a pungency to the flavor that some say is suggestive of fine wine. Unlike favored green teas that have always been prized for their freshness, Pu'er tea leaves especially are esteemed for their age. In contrast with other teas, Pu'er tea and Ya'an black teas are transformed through the action of molds, bacteria, and yeasts. Rather than being sold as loose leaves, Pu'er and Ya'an teas historically have been compressed into cakes of different forms, among which are round, square, oblong, as well as cylindrical, ball, and thin disk shapes. Stacked and carried by humans and animals, the semi-permeable packaging around the cakes led to further alteration of the properties of the tea due to interactions with the sweat of both animals and humans as well as changing temperatures and humidity during transit. With its deep, rich flavor and its suitability as a digestive, Pu'er tea, known to those who speak Cantonese as *bo-leycha* (tea), is usually consumed after a heavy or greasy meal not only in Tibet but throughout southeastern China.

While the full extent of the network is no longer traversed, sections are still utilized by villagers and their animals as they tramp to and from market towns. In 2005–6, Jeff Fuchs and his team trekked more than seven months over 5,000 kilometers (3,107 miles) along the route of the Tea-Horse Road in Yunnan, Sichuan, Tibet, Nepal, and India. Fuchs remarked that the lines of the old route could be discovered in most places, but that by "the 1960s, that omnipotent intruder, the paved road, cut both time and distance for traders, making the dirt paths, the unheralded mules, and the muleteers themselves obsolete" (2008: 7).

Today, some limited routes have been marked for adventurous trekkers seeking less demanding challenges than those encountered by Fuchs to penetrate areas of China that are still reasonably wild. Once bustling markets along the Tea-Horse Road have been rebranded as tea-horse bazaars, such as Kangding in Sichuan and Shaxi (Sideng), Mapingguan, Shuhe, Lijiang, Dali, Weishan, Donglianhua, and Tengchong in Yunnan, to satisfy the increasingly curious domestic tourist industry. Tea-horse tours along what is always now called an *ancient* route are touted as opportunities to

III.6.2a, b One of the few remaining rattan bridges in southwest China, the Songshui Rattan Bridge in Yunlong County, Dali Prefecture, Yunnan, has been preserved in a small roadside park. Source: TEM, 2016.

enjoy breathtaking natural scenery and satisfy any yearning for ultimate discovery and adventure.

It is not known how many covered and uncovered bridges once served as critical nodes to help thread the network together. Still, today it is possible to access some of the significant bridges that remain as well as the market towns that are markers of a time when the tea-horse trade flourished. In the countryside or near towns, these include not only covered bridges made of timber and stone bridges but also iron suspension bridges and crossings using woven rattan. Old photographs, moreover, record that transiting a river was sometimes not over a bridge of any type but via a sling-style rope or in a yakskin or goatskin boat. Some of the covered bridges are workaday bridges utilizing timber beams with rather simple covers. Other covered bridges soar as a result of impressively assembled sets of angled cantilevered beams. As elsewhere in China where covered bridges were located along trading routes, they provided shelter for porters during inclement weather as well as a place to sleep or rest that was cool in summer.

b

Ethnic Minorities and Covered Bridges

A valid question in approaching the topic of covered bridges in Yunnan is to what degree these structures express local building traditions of specific ethnic minority groups rather than infrastructure that duplicates those found elsewhere in metropolitan China. As the discussion below addresses, there are covered bridges with distinct ethnic minority characteristics, but these were built by only a few of the many minorities found in the region. Most ethnic minorities have no covered bridge-building tradition. There are several reasons for this.

Yunnan, as mentioned earlier, is home to some 25 ethnic minority groups that today are outnumbered in the cities and larger towns by Han in-migrants, some of whom have been in the province for generations or longer. A veritable kaleidoscope of ethnic minorities with widely varying population densities are settled in the villages and towns that shape this region. Few of the groups are dominant over an extensive geographic area. More generally, a region will have two or more ethnic groups living in settlements near to one another but distinctly separate in counties that are administratively autonomous with identification to two minorities. Some of these mixed autonomous counties and prefectures will be mentioned below. Reflecting patterns that were common early in the twentieth century and continue to some degree today, a majority of Yunnan's ethnic minority groups live vertically stratified along the slopes of mountains. Some of them continue to practice slash-and-burn farming as they traditionally did. The Blang in the mountains of southern Yunnan still pick and process Pu'er tea. The Yi, who numerically dominate among the ethnic minority groups in Yunnan, typically live far up in the mountains where they scrape out a living in a harsh environment. Today, it is still common to see ethnic minorities wearing their colorful dress hiking down mountain trails to attend periodic

markets in the valleys, some of which are held within or adjacent to covered bridges.

Of the ethnic minorities, the Bai, Dai, Hui, and Miao, like the Han, occupy the lowlands and practice wet-rice farming. Some, but certainly not all, have a history of being engaged in long-distance trade. Of these four, the Bai and the Hui especially have undergone a high degree of assimilation, sharing many cultural traits with Han Chinese even as they maintain significant distinguishing cultural traits. In general, as anthropologists have stated, there is so much cultural mixing in southwest China that it is impossible to ascertain the degree to which material culture is derivative of Han patterns or independently developed. Thus, whether a specific covered bridge design and construction epitomizes Bai or Hui or some other ethnic minority culture cannot be determined precisely. This is especially true of older covered bridges. On the other hand, new covered bridges, which are multiplying throughout Yunnan as in neighboring Hunan and Guizhou, have features that mark them as distinctly Bai or Hui. As discussed in other sections, two other ethnic minority groups also have long-standing covered bridge building traditions—the Dong in Guangxi and Guizhou and the Tujia in western Hunan and in Chongqing Municipality that was once part of Sichuan.

Weishan Yi and Hui Autonomous County, Donglianhua Village

Although many towns and villages throughout Dali Prefecture and adjacent prefectures through which the tea-horse network passed are inhabited by ethnic minority residents who are ethnically Bai, there are pockets of others, such as in the important Muslim village of Donglianhua and in a cluster of nearby Muslim hamlets in Weishan County. Located 35 kilometers (28 miles) south-southwest of the old town of Dali, Donglianhua is strikingly different from other Yunnan villages in Weishan County. First is the fact that a minaret rises above the rooftops of the Ming era mosque that has a prayer hall accommodating some 1,000 worshipers and, secondly, an impressive multitiered entry gate. A much larger mosque serving 6,000 people stands in another village with 20 smaller mosques elsewhere in Weishan County. The Muslims here are described as Hui, an ethnic minority identified by adherence to the Muslim religion but linguistically and culturally similar to other Chinese.

Donglianhua was settled by Muslim soldiers who had entered Yunnan Province as members of Mongol armies during the latter part of the Yuan Dynasty (1280–1368) and then stayed on after the Chinese Ming Dynasty (1368–1644) was established. While there are buildings from these early periods in the village, most of the structures are from the late nineteenth and early twentieth centuries. In style and ornamentation, they embody the fusion of traditional Chinese forms with Muslim elements. Three large manor houses with multiple courtyards were built by three Ma brothers, descendants of earlier traders, who in the early twentieth century became the village's most successful caravanners, with trade towards the north as well as south into Burma.

Although established well after the laying out of the tea-horse caravan routes, the village of Donglianhua and its Muslim families came to play a major role in commerce as part of transnational trade that was centered in the larger town of Weishan. Donglianhua itself was a post with a large number of stables for more than 350 mules and horses, experienced drivers from 50 families willing to go great distances, and storehouses for goods. While today there is little evidence of this storied past in the village itself, a Museum of Donglianhua Horse Caravan Culture within the largest Ma residence displays artifacts and detailed boards in Arabic, Chinese, and English proclaiming the village's significance as an important trading base on several routes of the Tea-Horse Road.

Interestingly, as a reprise of its historical role, Weishan and Donglianhua served during World War II in transporting goods "over the hump" along the Burma Road to China.

Yongji Bridge

Outside the museum, the one artifact that is testament to trade is the Yongji Covered Bridge which straddles the Xunjian River. While the bridge has been bypassed by a modern bridge and new roads, thus detached from the routes that once gave it prominence, it is not difficult to work out its likely role. A route via the Yongji Bridge provided a shortcut from Weishan to Yongping and then onward to Baoshan and into Burma. Along these old caravan routes, there still are some remnant arched bridges constructed of stone with approaches paved with rubble stone. Where a broad stream is to be crossed, iron chain suspension bridges with thin planks on them were sometimes built, with some still used by villagers.

The Yongji Bridge is supported structurally by a simple cantilever system that is assisted by independent polygonal arches which fit into the abutments. There are two cantilever packages, a short one utilizing stone beams and a longer one comprising five slender logs supported by four angle braces. Oversized stone pavilion-like entryways give prominence to the bridge, whether approached on the level or via stone steps on the southern end. The narrow 3.8-meter (12-foot) width has a raised path for animals along the center. Overall, the bridge is 15.6 meters (51 feet) long with nearly a third given over to the entryways. The bridge corridor has five long and substantial beams that run its full length to support the rafters and roof tiles. Rising at each position, where there is a column, is a crosspiece with etched cloud-like ornamentation. Some Chinese sources declare that the ornamentation within as well as that of the entryways is reflective of Bai culture.

III.6.3a, b Though a seemingly modest bridge, the Yongji has two handsome stone entries. Anyone using the Tongji Bridge, including porters and horses bearing tea, had to negotiate steps on each end. Since it is now bypassed by an adjacent road bridge, the Yongji Bridge enjoys a quiet retirement in a park-like setting. Source: TEM, 2016.

永濟僑

a

III.6.5 The cantilever system of the Yongji Bridge is quite modest but combines a set of short stone cantilevers with a longer wooden set. The two angled posts are the lower ends of the polygonal arch structure. Source: TEM, 2016.

III.6.4a, b These views of the interior not only reveal the ingenious structural polygonal arch support but also the careful restoration of the timber framework, including intricately carved components. Source: TEM, 2016.

Baoshan City, Tengchong County

Western Yunnan, which abuts the border with Myanmar (Burma) and is at the southern terminus of the Hengduan Mountain range, includes Tengchong, an historically important trading center. Although clearly remote when viewed from the metropolitan areas of eastern China, western Yunnan has served at least since the Han Dynasty (206 BCE–CE 220) as a transit hub for international commerce with Southeast Asia, South Asia, and even Southwest Asia. Tengchong, and the surrounding Baoshan area, has long had a reputation for its jade culture in terms of processing, carving, and sales. More recently, imported Burmese amber has gained status there as well.

Throughout this rugged region, there are significant covered bridges, suspension bridges, and stone bridges, some of which date to the Ming Dynasty. In addition, there traditionally were many makeshift timber bridges, virtually all uncovered and utilizing simple cantilevers, laid across streams in order to meet seasonal needs.

One collection of seven bridges in the Mangbang basin south of Tengchong, situated along the Longchuan River, a tributary that flows meanderingly to the Irrawaddy in Myanmar, has been described as resembling the seven stars that comprise the Big Dipper. Whether this was a siting rooted in *fengshui* or merely accidental cannot be affirmed. Most are still being used but a few have been abandoned.

From north to south, these seven covered bridges are locally named Minfu, Xiangyang, Shenzhu, Yezhujing (Chengde), Yongshun, Gao, and Tongji (Shunhe). Four of them—Minfu, Yezhujing (Chengde), Yongshun, and Tongji (Shunhe)—employ cantilevered structures that allow them to soar as "rainbow bridges." A fifth, Gao Bridge, is a beam bridge supported by stone piers with a level crossing. The Xiangyang Bridge is a suspension bridge and the Shenzhu Bridge is

an arched bridge constructed of volcanic lava rock. The discussion below will only address the covered bridges.

For the most part, as the photographs reveal, the covered bridges are quite dilapidated, signifying the lack of ongoing maintenance to meet needs, which suggests reduced use. These and other wooden covered bridges in the Tengchong and Baoshan area utilized in their construction easily available timber from tall, deciduous catalpa trees.

Yezhujing (Chengde) Bridge

Seen from a distance, the Yezhujing ("Wild Boar Bowed") Covered Bridge, which is also known as the Chengde ("Complete Virtue") Covered Bridge, soars some 10 meters (33 feet) above the water in a gorge along the Longchuan River, which is a prominent tributary of the Jinsha River that itself comprises the upper reaches of the better known Yangzi/Yangtze River. This is a region that is prone to torrential rains between June and September, which lead to rapidly rising rivers and, in times past, frequently massive flooding. Today, while dams and reservoirs with associated hydroelectric facilities mitigate the potential for catastrophic flooding, the placement and rise of the Yezhujing Covered Bridge reminds us of how settlers in

the past dealt with the capriciousness of weather during the wet months.

Though iron suspension bridges placed high above the incised riverbed have a longer history in this and adjacent regions than covered bridges, extant covered bridges for the most part also are located high on hillslopes connecting paths that avoid the possibility of any flooding. Local records reveal that both a woven rattan bridge and an iron suspension bridge successively spanned the stream until about 1776, when a timber cantilevered bridge was constructed to replace them. This suggests increasing use derived from growing commercial needs. Records indicate that the timber bridge was burned by soldiers from time to time. When the timber bridge was restored in 1882, four iron chains were strung from the abutments to stabilize the span. In 1942, the bridge was deliberately damaged in order to forestall Japanese troops who were entering from Burma and thus threatened to penetrate deeper into Yunnan and the temporary Nationalist capital in Sichuan. The bridge that is visible today is said to date from 1947–8 when it was rebuilt according to the original design. The level of decay seen in photographs over the past two decades suggests that diminished use arose from the availability of alternative modern routes across the Longchuan River. Recent repairs

of siding and the entryway using catalpa wood have increased safety for villagers who cross over the bridge with their cattle as they move from homesteads to and from fields.

Viewed structurally, Yezhujing is an extraordinary cantilevered bridge. Unlike most cantilevered supports that employ a beam to complete the distance between thrusting cantilevers, this bridge employs a series of four cantilevered beams that rise from both riverbanks before joining at the maximum height with a single horizontal beam connecting the two opposite cantilevers. The five long angle braces reinforcing the cantilevers may be recent additions to stabilize the structure. Within the corridor, which appeared quite new when visited in 2016, parallel sets of double posts have mortised into them arched crossbeams that support the roof. On each end is a modest entryway with impressive sets of brackets. The bridge is 30 meters (98 feet) in length with a net span of 27 meters (88 feet) and an overall width of 2.2 meters (7 feet). Across the full length of the corridor is a half-meter (1.6 foot)-wide raised wooden plank path to facilitate the passage of sure-footed animals.

III.6.6a, b The Yezhujing Bridge, spanning a wild river that runs through a canyon, has a dramatic arch resulting from the many cantilever systems required for such a long span. Source: ACO, 2016; TEM, 2016.

III.6.7 The Yezhujing Bridge, though seemingly isolated, still provides a safe crossing for local farmers. Here a woman leads two water buffalo to the distant fields. Source: TEM, 2016.

While there is very limited historical information about the Yongshun, Gao, and Tongji (Shunhe) bridges, each of the structures reveals the ingenious carpentry that matches practical needs with the physical attributes of the site where the bridges were constructed. Each bridge is a rather fragile structure utilizing only limited timbers that give shape to relatively narrow passageways for humans and animals. The Gao Bridge, for example, which spans a chasm and is said to date to 1466 during the Ming Dynasty, utilizes two rock outcrops as piers to support the timber beams that reach from the abutments to the natural stone piers. The framework of the 40-meter (131-foot)-long corridor is quite simple and uncomplicated with more than a dozen bents shaped by posts and crossbeams. These are linked with tie beams that run from bent to bent. The railing along the sides is uncharacteristically simple compared to other covered bridges in the region. In the past, the corridor was covered with roof tiles, but in order to reduce the weight galvanized iron sheets provide the roof cover. Today, the Gao Bridge is used infrequently because of the construction nearby of a highway bridge.

III.6.8 a, b The Gao Bridge spans a deep, rocky gorge, but the structure is a simple beam bridge with lightweight cover. Source: ACO, 2016; TEM, 2016.

The Yongshun Bridge, which clearly has been abandoned, was not just derelict but extremely unsafe to cross. As the photographs show, the bridge appears fragile and ready to collapse at any time. Said to have been first constructed during the Ming Dynasty and reconstructed many times over the centuries, it has a 20-meter (66-foot) span across a languid stream. Rough-hewn logs extend out from both banks that today are propped up with slanted timbers. Nothing remains of the original tile roof and many of the galvanized iron sheets are also missing.

Like several others in the Big Dipper configuration, the Tongji Bridge also crosses the Longchuan

III.6.10 Though long abandoned, the cantilever structure reinforced with two angle braces has not yet fallen into the river. Source: ACO, 2016.

III.6.9 The Yongshun Bridge exemplifies the angled cantilever structure typical of Yunnan but without the polygonal arch found in many other bridges. Source: ACO, 2016.

River. Said also to have been constructed along a trade route during the Ming Dynasty, the bridge was last stabilized in 1946 using sturdy catalpa logs. Over the past half century, it also has fallen into disrepair. Piled stone abutments with an adobe portico above, constructed with large timbers, provide support for the tilted cantilever arms beneath which are propped up with angle braces. A long log connects the cantilevers to complete the 27.5-meter (90-foot) span. Although earlier photographs revealed vertical boards as siding, none of the siding was in place in 2016.

III.6.11 Though it is still possible to walk through the Yongshun Bridge, doing so is "daring the Devil," especially since there is a modern bridge next to it. Source: ACO, 2016.

III.6.12a, b The Tongji Bridge in Tengchong County, though well-constructed, appears neglected today and has been reinforced with steel cables. Source: ACO, 2016; TEM, 2016.

Dali Bai Autonomous Prefecture, Yunlong County

While tea is the heralded commodity transported beyond Yunnan on the Tea-Horse Road network, salt also enjoyed a privileged and lucrative position in long-distance trade. Yunnan's ethnic minorities have a storied history of salt production from saltworks at many scales, including three large towns and many villages. One of the most famous and largest production centers was in Nuodeng, a compact Bai ethnic minority village spread along a steep slope that is cradled within

a U-shaped bend of the Bi River in the Dali Bai Autonomous Prefecture. When viewed from one of the surrounding mountains, peninsular Nuodeng and its winding riverine location appear like a Taiji symbol, a round shape divided into a dark and a light segment by an S-shaped line representing, respectively, *yin* and *yang*. Some 170 kilometers (106 miles) west of Dali Old Town and 7 kilometers (4 miles) from the Yunlong County seat, Nuodeng's salt production has a history that dates back to the Tang Dynasty. Extracted from deep wells and then processed by boiling the brine

III.6.13 The Tongji Bridge is approached through imposing adobe brick entries with massive timbers on both ends, probably there to provide weight on the cantilever system. Source: ACO, 2016.

in large wood-fired cauldrons, followed by the use of evaporation pans, the resulting crystallized salt was molded into cylindrical shapes. In this form, salt was bundled and transported widely, together with locally produced salt-cured ham made from the hind legs of pigs. Two other important salt-producing towns were Heijing and Shiyang, both in Chuxiong Yi Autonomous Prefecture in central Yunnan about 100 kilometers (62 miles) northwest of Kunming. While the Bai and Yi ethnic minorities played crucial roles in the historical production of salt, other minorities worked smaller saltworks

throughout Yunnan and in Sichuan. While none of these sites included covered bridges, there were covered bridges along some of the subsidiary routes.

No county in Yunnan Province has more covered bridges than Yunlong, which is the westernmost county in Dali Autonomous Bai Prefecture. The Bi River, a tributary of the Lancang (upper reaches of the Mekong River), is the north–south axis that binds the county. Together with its tributaries, the Bi is crossed by suspension bridges, rattan bridges, and multiple covered bridges. The most dramatic of the covered bridges are completely constructed of timber while some wooden arcades are set atop masonry bases. In 2013, the State Council inscribed the "Grouping of Old Bridges Along the Bi River" as a national-level cultural and historic site.

Because the terrain of Yunlong County is so mountainous, there are few roads and virtually all follow a river valley. While many Bai villages are located along these roads and rivers, there are also numerous villages settled by Yi minorities high up on the mountainsides, some accessible by road but many only via footpaths. In former times and even continuing into the present, goods were moved on horses, donkeys, and mules up and down steep trails that linked more remote upland settlements with the valley bottoms. While bridges of many types and sizes specifically facilitated stream crossings for the local population, some were critical crossings mainly for the caravans carrying both salt and tea to distant locations.

Tongjing Bridge

The Tongjing Bridge is the first covered bridge seen traveling north from Yunlong County Town, a classic scene of a covered bridge nestled in a village with mountains in the background. This grand bridge, some 40 meters (131 feet) long with a 29-meter (95-foot) span, is essential to Dapoluo Village because it joins the western and eastern parts separated by the river. Said to have been first constructed in 1776 and restored in 1935, the bridge still carries a constant flow of pedestrians as well as animals led by their owners.

The bridge is supported by a substantial assemblage of multiple cantilevers in a four-log line. This underlying structure is reinforced with a hefty arch/queenpost-like structure anchored in the abutments. Regarding the horizontal middle section, the roof is supported by either four or six vertical double posts, the inner of which protrudes below and pierces a deck crossbeam. Here, there are also massive log diagonals from the lower abutment supporting a massive square horizontal beam two-thirds of the way up, matched with another such horizontal directly above it, but no indication of them being tied together. In spite of close-up pictures, it cannot be determined how this structure supports anything. The deck crossbeams are supported from the verticals but are independent of this queenpost arrangement. There is evidence of either an earlier bridge supported by multiple angle braces placed into holes in the stone or an earlier bracing system for this bridge.

III.6.14 As seen from a distance, the Tongjing Bridge connects parts of a large village flanking a river and therefore carries both people and animals throughout the day. Source: TEM, 2016.

III.6.15a–d The approach to the bridge is uphill along a recently landscaped park. The entry is constructed of adobe brick with a single-tiered roof structure. Bai minority villagers still carry goods, as they have for hundreds of years, in large baskets on their backs. In other cases, donkey caravans transport greater quantities of goods over longer distances. Source: TEM, 2016.

a

b

III.6.16a, b Travelers from the west approach Tongjing Bridge on adobe brick steps, then cross between a sturdy polygonal arch structure. Source: TEM, 2016.

a

III.6.17a, b The Tongjing Bridge is an excellent example of a complex angled cantilever structure supported on several stone embankments. The diagonals of the polygonal arch can also be seen projecting up into the structure. Source: TEM, 2016.

Yongzhen Bridge

The Yongzhen Covered Bridge spans the narrow Dada River, a tributary of the Bi River, in Changchunpo Village, Changxin Township. With an overall length of 26 meters (85 feet) and a clear span of 16 meters (52 feet), it is shorter and more modest than the nearby Tongjing Covered Bridge. Resting on stone columns, the triple cantilevered structure has five log lines that are strengthened with three angle braces. As a result, the bridge rises rather precipitously for animals and people crossing it. Locals refer to it as a "rainbow bridge." Only a short horizontal section in the middle is level before a steep descent begins. The entryway on both ends is heavily ornamented and leads to a steep corridor with a wooden walkway for animals in the center. Both exterior sides of the bridge are covered by a skirt of vertical boards that help keep the interior dry.

According to the official plaque near the entrance, the original bridge was constructed in 1741 and subsequently renovated in 1875 and 1987. Not only was it a crossing along the Tea-Horse Road, the bridge was a link between Yunlong and county towns in Jianchuan and Eryuan.

Today, heavily laden donkeys still bring goods down from the hillside through the bridge, and at the edge of town workers transfer the goods to trucks.

III.6.18 The Yongzhen Bridge, similar to but more modest than the nearby Tongjing Bridge, continues to be an essential crossing for both villagers and pack animals. Source: TEM, 2016.

III.6.19 The Yongzhen Bridge shows evidence of its significance, with handsome entries featuring much ornamentation, an unusual feature among Yunnan's bridges. Source: TEM, 2016.

III.6.20 Yongzhen's interior has a steep walking path with crosspieces in the center for the many animals that use the bridge. Source: TEM, 2016.

III.6.21 Supported on five tall stone posts, Yongzhen Bridge's cantilever system also includes a polygonal arch system, whose diagonals are seen reaching into the bridge above. Source: TEM, 2016.

Wuli Bridge

The Wuli Bridge stands further up the road in the open countryside at a site spanning a small brook that leads to a path up the hillside. Only 16 meters (52 feet) long and with no siding, it is a modest bridge whose arch/queenpost-like structure with two slender posts reinforcing the lower crossbeam is easy to see. The underlying framework is quite simple, with only two short cantilevers supported by angle braces and a horizontal beam, the longer one supported by three angle braces. The cantilevers are recessed into the abutments, and consequently the deck is flat throughout, without any angle. Diagonal beams are embedded in the ground and support a horizontal beam. Two slender wooden verticals support the deck crossbeams by piercing the upper and lower horizontals and being pegged.

III.6.22 The modest Wuli Bridge once carried both goods and people on a rural trail. While the trail today is overgrown and impassable, it is easy to imagine its use in the past. Source: ACO, 2016.

III.6.23 Though not far from a modern road, the long retired Wuli Bridge appears to sit in the midst of a hilly wilderness. Source: TEM, 2016.

III.6.24a–d The Wuli Bridge combines a simple cantilever system with a polygonal arch embedded on the ground near the abutments. The bridge's polygonal arch, working independently of the cantilevers, helps support the deck, which once carried heavy animal caravans. The timber structure is easy to see since the bridge lacks siding. Source: TEM, 2016.

Caifeng Bridge

Located in Shundang Village, Baishi Township, some 74 kilometers (50 miles) from Yunlong County Town, Caifeng ("Colored Phoenix") Covered Bridge is well integrated into its surroundings. After going down a steep path from the village, visitors enter the bridge from the side, passing a door that leads into a temple. Said to have been first constructed between 1628 and 1644, the bridge was not renovated until the end of the nineteenth century. On the eastern end of the bridge, dated 1782, there is a stone tablet inscribed with regulations governing the passage of tea-horse caravans.

The Caifeng Bridge was swept away by flooding in 1993 and was rebuilt using all of the original material that could be salvaged.

Because of the bridge's length, at 39 meters (128 feet) and with a 27-meter (88-foot) span, there are four diagonal reinforcements to assist in supporting the "arch." There is a set of three cantilevers, each with five protruding logs, that thrust the bridge upward from the abutments. The upper ends of each cantilevered set are connected by a horizontal wooden beam approximately 9 meters (30 feet) long, some 11 meters (36 feet) above the water below. Four transverse crossbeams

a

beneath the deck are pegged into vertical members that offer support to the long wooden members connecting the two packets of cantilevers. The vertical members are attached to the oversized "queenpost" structure within the arcade. Vertical wooden skirts on both sides of the bridge protect the interior as well as the structure beneath.

III.6.25a, b Recently renovated, the Caifeng Bridge remains an important crossing for local residents. The narrow footpaths leading to the crossing are much as they were in the past. Near the approach to the bridge is a small shrine to a local deity. Source: ACO, 2016; TEM, 2016.

III.6.26a, b The Caifeng Bridge is approached on one end by steep steps that descend from the road to the bridge and to an obscure temple on the left. Once in the bridge, humans and animals are aware of the upward climb that is necessary to navigate it. Source: ACO, 2016.

III.6.27a–c The Caifeng Bridge, like others in Yunnan, has a dual support system of cantilevers beneath and a polygonal arch supporting the deck system, which also is assisted by lateral braces beneath the deck. Source: ACO, 2016.

Wenfeng Bridge, Dali Bai Autonomous Prefecture, Jianchuan County

Mapingguan, a relatively remote mountain village, indeed not more than a hamlet, is entered through a covered bridge built over a masonry arch. Translating as "Horse Pasture Pass," the area around Mapingguan traditionally provided good pasturage for pack mules and a resting place for muleteers who had survived the 1,500-meter (4,920-foot) difference in elevation via a steep route from the markets in the verdant Shaxi Valley. Located at the entry to the settlement, the Wenfeng Covered Bridge spans a narrow V-shaped gully. Beyond Mapingguan, further west, in the past were small-scale salt well production areas, especially in the valley around Misha, which contributed cargo for the caravan trade. Mapingguan, moreover,

controlled access to one of four checkpoints where the imperial government collected tax on the salt trade.

Less than 3 meters (10 feet) wide, 12 meters (39 feet) long, and dating to the late eighteenth or early nineteenth century, this covered bridge provided limited shelter for the processions of porters that passed its way. Its form is simple, an arcade-like wooden structure resting atop a single stone arch with stone and brick infill above it. The bridge was restored in 2008 and again in 2016, with the recent effort involving a rebuilding of the timber corridor that was once again capped with a tiled roof. This latest restoration was in anticipation of increased visitors because of the construction of a road up from the Shaxi Valley.

III.6.28 The Wenfeng Bridge is a very busy crossing at an intermittent stream in Mapingguan, an important trading post on top of a mountain. It was only in 2016 that a serviceable road was constructed from the valley floor to Mapingguan. Until then, the town was only accessible via a footpath. Source: ACO, 2016.

III.6.29 A large arched culvert covered with rubble stone collected from the stream forms the base of the Wenfeng Bridge. Source: TEM, 2016.

III.6.30a, b The narrow wooden corridor, rebuilt in 2016 shortly before our arrival, is much longer than the modest stone arch crossing the gully. The newness of the milled wood and baked roof tiles is obvious. Source: TEM, 2016.

Sichuan Covered Bridges

Throughout western China in the past, as elsewhere in hilly regions of the world, timbers that fell naturally or were intentionally felled and then placed across streams became, in effect, "bridges". With little thought given to design or aesthetics, spans of this type, mere logs, served as necessary workaday links along the mountain byways. Log crossings, of course, have severe limitations, not only because of rotting due to contact with soil and infestation by wood-eating insects, as well as sag, but also because fallen timbers are not necessarily long enough to span a needed gap. The circumstances that may lead eventually to the building of a bridge, let alone decisions made to impart a pleasing aesthetic to the structure, are often lost in the murkiness of history. Yet, as the discovery of hidden bridges of great beauty attests, even people living in remote areas sometimes quietly experimented with materials to create successful masterpieces of carpentry that combine functionality with beauty.

The vastness and topographical diversity of Sichuan has long captivated both Chinese and Western explorers and travelers. Indeed, the name Sichuan, which means "four rivers," boldly suggests the prominence of waterways in both the deep gorges and extensive alluvial plains that accompanied eons of erosion and deposition. The actions of humans to bridge Sichuan's major and minor rivers bequeathed ingenious structures of great complexity and exquisite beauty as well as unpretentious ordinariness. Given the nature of Sichuan's streams, materials traditionally were adjusted depending on the necessary span. Timber beams met the demands of narrow rivulets while stone arches could multiply according to need. And, as old photographs reveal, finished covered bridges are often imaginative, even quite fanciful. Isabella Bird (1899) referred to "roofed bridges" and "covered bridges" in Sichuan as "picturesque," including those she encountered in the Man-tze "barbarian" mountainous region. These groups, of course, are today identified as "ethnic minorities", such as the Qiang and Tibetans.

III.7.1 Located to the north of Chengdu, with many streams criss-crossing the plain, the covered bridge at Minzhu was frequently photographed a century ago. This covered bridge has both *pailou*-type entryways and a multitiered central tower. Bird remarked on the green roof tiles and the crimson interior. She described it as "a beautiful modern bridge." Source: Bird, 1899: Vol. 1, facing p. 52.

III.7.2 A rustic timber log bridge clearly serves as both a crossing and social space for villagers. Bird describes it as "after the manner of Switzerland." Source: Bird, 1899: Vol. I, p. 236.

III.7.3 This bridge was located in a village in the mountainous Weizhou area of Wenchuan County in northern Sichuan, an area populated by Tibetan and Qiang minorities. It was here that Isabella Bird, publishing under her married name Bishop, photographed many aspects of the cultural landscape. Source: Bishop [Bird], 1900: Vol. II, p. 107.

Unlike in the fertile, intensely cultivated lowlands of western Sichuan, where human effort in controlling water and enriching soil allows three crops a year, two of rice and a third of vegetables, which support some of China's densest populations, life in the surrounding mountains has always been arduous. Mountain villagers, whether the minority Han or ethnic minorities, struggle in order to wrest a livelihood from the forested slopes along which they live and from the rushing streams that pour down the hillsides. In areas of rugged terrain, life for villagers was rarely bound to the immediate environs of their dwellings but rather coursed along steep and windy paths down which men and women sought the bounty of the forests—logs, wild food plants, medicinal roots, bark, herbs, and wild animals—for their own use as well as for collecting and transporting to sometimes distant markets. Mountain paths frequently encounter ravines, sometimes filled with rapidly flowing streams that must be crossed in order to convey raw materials carried on shoulder poles or in baskets on peasants' backs. It is this geographical context within which the Jiemei Bridges took shape.

Jiemei ("Sisters") Bridges

Even a decade ago, one had to search hard to locate one of Sichuan's, even China's, most extraordinary surviving covered bridges, a pair of sister bridges that as far as we have been able to determine were never visited by Westerners in the past. A decade ago, while there was an occasional billboard portraying the existence of the Jiemei ("Sisters") Bridges along some of the mountain highways 180 kilometers (112 miles) northwest of Chengdu and west of the city of Mianyang in Sichuan Province, the bridges themselves could only be reached via an obscure and tiny dirt footpath that eventually opened up to what was undoubtedly a pair of actively used mountain bridges of inimitable beauty. By late 2016, the bridges had become a unique artifact in a comprehensive plan that has transformed a section of the Chaping River into a water rafting destination.

Overhanging a narrow gap about 10 meters (33 feet) above the bed of the Chaping River in Xiaoba Township, Anzhou District, the Jiemei ("Sisters") Bridges are twinned covered spans that share a common midstream pier, actually an angled stone outcrop that juts upward between them. Throughout much of the year, the stream languishes beneath as the water flows downhill. In spring, however, waters frequently rise abruptly as they disgorge meltwater from the uplands. When accompanied by continuous heavy spring rains, periodic inundations are known to sweep away fallen trees and other detritus with great destructive force. The striations etched into the rock walls that line the stream suggest the magnitude of continuing scouring over the years by flowing water.

While some type of bridge structure—some records even indicate a set of stone bridges as early as the twelfth century at this location—it was not until 1873 that local villagers combined their labor and financial capital to fashion the bridges seen today. All building materials were sourced locally. The longer bridge, referred to as the "elder sister," and the shorter as the "younger sister," are similar in structure and appearance, differing mainly in details. Each end is entered from a mountain path by a series of stone steps leading to a covered bridge constructed using the same carpentry techniques employed in building common homes and temples. Mortise-and-tenon joinery, without metal nails, is used to lock the 24 columns to an uncounted number of beams, roof timbers, and flanking balustrades made up of simple rails and posts, to give shape to a corridor. Approximately 3 meters (10 feet) wide, the flooring is simply rough-cut planks while the gallery structure overall is capped with baked roof tiles.

In April 2005, some 60 engineers, architects, historians, and local boosters came together to proclaim the importance of preserving the Jiemei Bridges, which had been declared a provincial-level architectural landmark. Local boosters were attempting to find a project that would engage visitors to stay longer than what was common as some came to visit and photograph their beloved pair of covered bridges. There were fears after the great Wenchuan Earthquake in May 2008 that the bridges were lost. It was not until March 2009 that news reports confirmed that neither of the bridges had fallen. In 2013, on the other hand, a major flood eroded much of the central abutment but the bridges themselves were not swept away.

Finally, in 2016, a viable project emerged that engages the beauty of the river with its waterfalls

and rapids and the quiet villages along a 6-kilometer (4-mile) section of the river. It is a small part of the much larger Thousand Buddha National Forest Park that stimulated the construction of a modern access highway which has benefited the remote villages here. By the summer of 2017, in excess of 1,000 visitors were spending more than a day enjoying the water features and overnighting in villagers' homes as a component of rural tourism, which officially, as of December 2017, is translated into English as "agritainment." Connected by a riverside path, areas were delineated for swimming, white water rafting, or simply floating or paddling in rather still water. While traditionally the Jiemei

Bridges provided a critical cross-water link along a mountainous byway used only by villagers, the covered bridges today offer not only a pleasantly cool place to rest but also a location to enjoy a picturesque landscape picture.

III.7.4 Looking upstream, the Jiemei twinned bridges, each supported by a massive set of logs, rest on a midstream outcrop. Source: ACO, 2006.

III.7.5 The view alongside the pair of bridges reveals the rather precarious leveling. Source: ACO, 2006.

III.7.6 For a utilitarian bridge in the mountains, this entry is quite dramatic because of its double-tiered roof with uplifted corners. The name board is a recent addition. Source: ACO, 2006.

III.7.7 The interior framework is simple and light with small dimension timbers. Source: ACO, 2006.

III.7.8 Adjacent to the twinned Jiemei bridges is a
shrine for the bridge god. Source: JDK, 2006.

III.7.9 Until recent times as tourism began to alter use of the site, the paired Jiemei bridges traditionally served to provide access between the hills beyond and nearby villagers. Villagers collected marketable herbs and other natural goods as well as grasses to feed their animals. Source: JDK, 2006.

Hongjun(Red Army) Bridge

While the color red is traditionally an auspicious color, it was rare for a covered bridge in the past to be painted crimson. Unlike barns and some covered bridges in North America, most timber bridges in China were left to weather to a natural hue. Red Army Bridges (Hongjun Qiao) are a twentieth-century phenomenon that arose as the armed forces of China's Communist Party emerged between 1928 and 1937. In the latter half of the 1940s, the Red Army was renamed the People's Liberation Army or PLA. Red Army Bridges today are found in many provinces, with the bulk of them acquiring that name during Mao Zedong's epic Long March between October 1934 and October 1935.

Mao's Long March route involved passage, often in multiple branches along networks of baffling mountain footpaths and obscure traces, through some of China's most difficult terrain from Jiangxi Province in south-central China through portions of Guangdong, Hunan, Guangxi, Guizhou, and Yunnan provinces. This arduous fragmented journey then led to the longest portion of the route along the rugged ridges of western Sichuan Province in southwestern China. Breaking beyond the bounds of the encircling mountains, the troops then crossed less mountainous routes through Gansu Province, finally terminating their trek in Yan'an in the tawny loessial plateau of Shaanxi Province. Mao claimed that the route was 25,000 *li* or 12,500 kilometers (7,767 miles) long, an improbably difficult trek to have completed in one twelve-month and three-day period, a rousing epic narrative that subsequently materialized as one of the founding myths of the People's Republic of China.

Pursued as they were by Nationalists forces, Mao's troops crossed torrential rivers and deep chasms that were often separated by craggy peaks with sheer cliffs, necessitating sometimes the creation of impromptu bridges. Trees could be dropped as makeshift footbridges or small craft tied together to form a pontoon bridge. Some streams could be crossed by fording shallow waters or sometimes a ferry could be used. In some cases, small bamboo or iron suspension bridges provided the only route from one hillside to another, each gaining notoriety in the epic Long March narrative.

No bridge along the route has acquired more fame than the Luding Bridge, a Qing Dynasty (1644–1911) iron chain suspension bridge, which was slung across the north–south flowing Dadu River in Sichuan Province that is constrained by steep precipices along both banks. Although not a covered bridge, mentioning it is necessary to provide some general information that contrasts it with the Qinglingkou Hongjun Covered Bridge. Built in the early eighteenth century, the original Luding Bridge was suspended using thirteen heavy iron chains, nine of which supported a wooden planking deck, while two chains on either side were to be grasped by those crossing the bridge. Since a principal function also was to facilitate the movement of tribute from Lhasa in Tibet to the imperial capital Beijing, the side chains also thwarted carts and animals from falling into the river below. On both ends of the bridge, the iron chains were anchored into massive stone buttresses, each of which had a building-like structure atop it. The Kangxi emperor visited the bridge in the eighteenth century, leaving behind an inscription, hence its fame also as an "imperial bridge." In 1776, the river rose more than 1 meter (3 feet) over the bridge, with significant damage to the iron chains. The last great battle of the Taiping Rebellion in the mid-nineteenth century occurred here with the loss of some 40,000 troops, said to have turned the river crimson for days.

Grace Service, an American, wrote in 1908, "… when one notes the open spaces, the irregularly laid planking of the flooring, the infrequent palings connecting the side chains, and the general airiness of the whole construction hanging so jauntily over wild and swirling water, one cannot help but feel that the bridge is sketchily built. Travelers from India, Tibet, Nepal and other parts of High Asia have safely crossed the raging Tung by this tenuous cobweb of man's ingenuity. It holds the charm and glamour of mystery, hidden away in this obscure Chinese valley"(Service, 1989, p. xxx). In July 1917, a storm turned the Luding Bridge bottoms up yet repairs quickly made it serviceable again.

However significant its pre-twentieth century prominence, the eminence of the Luding Bridge surged as a critical element during Mao's historic Long March when, in late May 1935, a squad of 22 soldiers stormed the suspension bridge in what the Communist canon points as a critical assault along the Long March journey. Subsequently, over a seven-day period, perhaps 12,000 peasant soldiers and their leaders were able to cross the raging river and continue to move north to victory. Had the assault failed, Red Army forces might have been wiped out and the revolution aborted. Often-repeated legend proclaims that the Luding Bridge, which had been stripped of some of its wooden planking to become a mere skeleton, swayed precariously high above the raging Dadu

River as the Red Army forces rushed across it while enemy forces on the other side set it afire and lobbed volleys towards them. Huang Zhen, militia leader and subsequent diplomat, immortalized this perilous effort in a contemporaneous sketch, one of only twenty-four drawings surviving that documents the Long March. His view is of a taut span extending from bank to bank high above the water. Later historical images draw attention to the fragmented state of the bridge and the battles that combatants encountered as they surged across, gripping the iron chains as they moved. Today, visitors encounter a reconstructed bridge that offers little that is daunting to those who cross it.

III.7.10 The battle crossing the Luding Bridge in May 1935 has become a tale of heroism known by all Chinese. Source: Unknown.

While the Luding Bridge has gained fame as the site of a heroic battle between the Red Army forces and the pursuing forces of Chiang Kai-shek, other Red Army Bridges served more mundane, but important, purposes. Along the route, armies sometimes billeted in villages and small towns where, according to local and official lore, property and weapons were confiscated by the Red Army from landlords and warlords, social change was fostered, and poor peasants were recruited. In some of these towns and villages, old bridges were informally renamed a "Red Army Bridge" to mark their new revolutionary role.

An imposing stone arched bridge in Qinglinkou, a village some 50 kilometers (31 miles) from Jiangyou City in the northwestern portion of Sichuan, is one such renamed bridge that also was painted red. Qinglinkou, which straddles a mountain stream, not only was an important market town for villagers living in the surrounding mountains but lay on the difficult interprovincial trade route between Chengdu to the south and Xi'an to the north. Towns such as Qinglinkou, here on the lower slopes of the mountains, held periodic markets that provided a place for those living off the mountains to market goods they had collected as well as purchase the limited needs they had. Paths typically connected towns with one another so that peasants could carry goods on shoulder poles or in wheelbarrows to market. Limited level ground meant that shops and stalls lined narrow stone-paved lanes with bridgeheads.Indeed, the bridge itself, as well as the courtyards of temples, served as locations for stalls and places to rest and talk. On non-fair days, towns were usually rather quiet places, while on fair days steady streams of pedestrians flowed into town. Throughout market towns of this type, numerous teahouses and wine shops served as sites for socializing.

Constructed during the middle of the Qing Dynasty and known originally as the Heyi ("Combined Benefit") Bridge, the span served as the link between the two halves of the town on both banks of the stream below. Little is known about the construction of the bridge and it is left to its current form to ascertain the facts. The bridge itself is comprised of a solidly built base of three symmetrical stone arches, a larger one in the center flanked by a pair of smaller arches. While most of the time the stream flowing beneath is languid, it can become a rushing torrent during early spring as it is fed by snow melting in the mountains, and in summer by torrential cloudbursts. Mounted via a series of broad stone steps from the main commercial lane in Qinglinkou, the bridge then leads to a second perpendicular lane in front of buildings that run along the stream to the town's main temple. The massive wooden building atop the bridge structure was constructed using mortise-and-tenon joinery, with each column set atop a square stone base. Rising above the roofline is a small garret, which at one time served as a shrine with a deity. Today, it is empty.

All of the wooden members are seen painted red, an obvious commemoration of the bridge's twentieth-century Communist reincarnation as a Red Army icon. In April 1935, the Fourth

Regiment of the Red Army established a "soviet" base in Qinglinkou, involving itself in a peasant struggle against landlords and propaganda relating to social change. While the Red Army camped in nearby shops, some of which today have placards stating their use, the army used the bridge as an "auditorium" for popularizing various movements. As foci of these efforts, slogans to inspire action and to warn against certain tendencies were emblazoned on walls and carved on old stone stelae and stone gravestones. Many of those carved in stone have been collected on the bridge, where one can read today both the 1930s slogans as well as the Qing Dynasty texts beneath. Among the bold slogans in red calligraphy are "The Red Army Is the Savior of the Poor," "Free Marriage," "Support Land Reform," "Participate in the Red Army's Division of Fields," and "Resolutely Oppose Imperialism and Fight the Japanese." Red stars and red flags, carved from stone, sit atop the balustrades. Villagers recall that the renaming of the Heiyi Bridge as the Hongjun Bridge occurred only after the founding of the People's Republic of China in 1949. With its storied covered bridge as a central feature, complemented by both a large assemblage of old shops and residences and striking scenery, Qinglinkou has become one of Sichuan's "old towns" favored by tourists.

III.7.11 Here the Hongjun Bridge is viewed from a balcony on an upper story of a streamside residence. The bridge is comprised of a solidly built base of three symmetrical stone arches, a larger one in the center flanked by a pair of smaller arches. Source: ACO, 2006.

b

III.7.12a, b Each of the two lofty *pailou*-style approaches to the Hongjun Bridge is different but both are painted red. Source: ACO, 2006.

III.7.13a, b Whether looking out from one of the portals towards the shuttered shops or downriver through the central bay of the bridge, the flavor of Sichuan's vernacular architecture is clear. Source: ACO, 2006.

b

a

III.7.14 Paved with heavy stones, each of the red columns is set upon blocks of granite. The loft above the central bay, where there once was an altar, was used to store the deities' sedan chairs used during processionals, but, of course, no longer serving those purposes. Source: JDK, 2006.

b

III.7.15a This blind person visits the bridge daily to chat with visitors. Here he is standing beside a carved stone instructional board left over from when the Red Army group was billeted in Qinglinkou. The text reads "The Red Army Is the Savior of Poor People." Source: JDK, 2006.

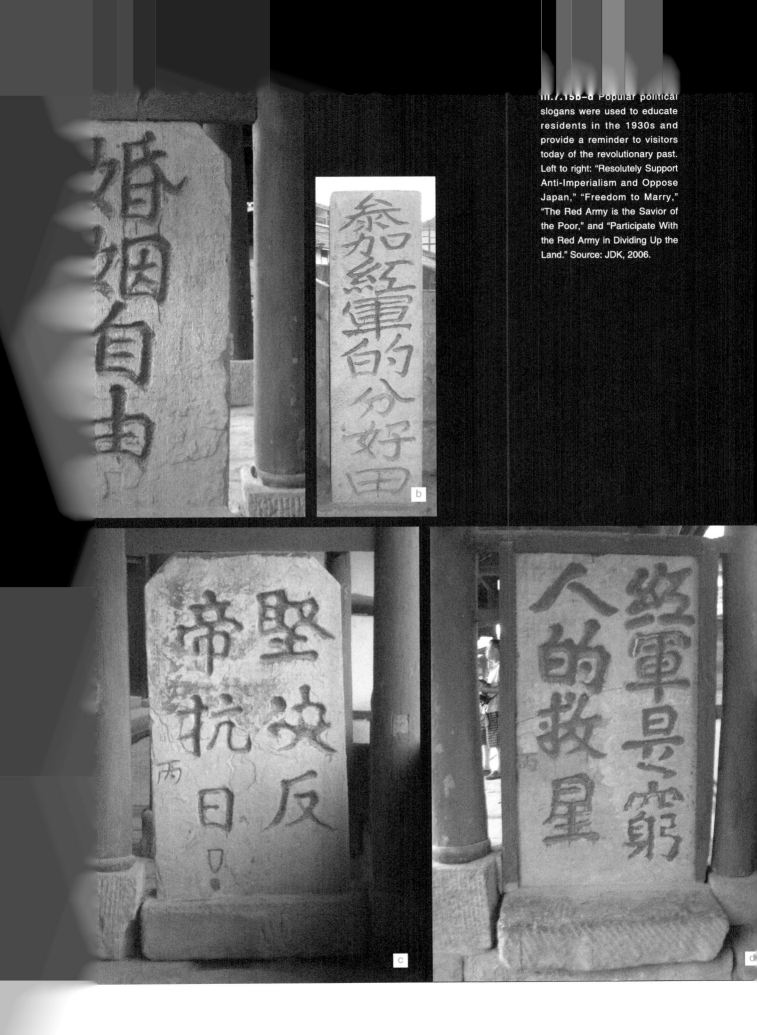

III.7.15b–d Popular political slogans were used to educate residents in the 1930s and provide a reminder to visitors today of the revolutionary past. Left to right: "Resolutely Support Anti-Imperialism and Oppose Japan," "Freedom to Marry," "The Red Army is the Savior of the Poor," and "Participate With the Red Army in Dividing Up the Land." Source: JDK, 2006.

Gansu Covered Bridges

The arid and semi-arid areas of western China are for the most part an extensive domain of treeless plateaus that stretch from Mongolia to Tibet and encompass the provinces of Gansu and Qinghai. They experience long, cold winters and short, warm summers. Nonetheless, it is in Qinghai that meltwater from the mountains collects as the headwaters of great rivers like the Yangzi (Yangtze) and Huang (Yellow). Streams here are often ephemeral even as their broad and dry riverbeds are evidence that flash floods resulting from periodic torrential rainfall sculpted them. Though much of the region is barren and sparsely populated,

an extensive network of trade routes traditionally crossed them. Throughout the late nineteenth and early twentieth centuries, explorers, scientists, missionaries, and consular officials, among many others, wrote of their experiences traversing Gansu, Qinghai, and Tibet, noting the overall desolation of the landscapes, the precariousness of travel, and the limitations of infrastructure. Some have left us photographic records of fragile covered and uncovered bridges constructed of timber, all the more remarkable because the adjacent areas are almost always treeless.

III.8.1 A bullock cart carrying timber for constructing bridges crosses the grasslands of western Suiyuan in today's Inner Mongolian Autonomous Region. Photograph by Rev. Claude L. Pickens, who surveyed Muslims in western China, c. 1933. Source: © President and Fellows of Harvard College, Arnold Arboretum Archives.

III.8.2 Labeled as "Leaving Shunhwa," which is today's Xunhua in Qinghai Province, a region heavily populated with the ethnic Muslim minority group called Salar. This short cantilevered bridge spanning a narrow but deep gorge has braces beneath and a type of interior truss for stability. Photograph by Carter Holton, c. 1933. Source: © President and Fellows of Harvard College, Arnold Arboretum Archives.

III.8.3 This timber cantilevered bridge, with yet to be used logs strewn on the adjacent treeless hillside, may or may not have been covered once completed. Photograph by William Purdom near Minzhou, Gansu, c. 1911. Source: © 2003, President and Fellows of Harvard College, Arnold Arboretum Archives.

Baling Bridge

While there are other relatively simple workaday yet functional covered bridges depicted in old publications and photographic archives, it is unusual to find a photograph of a complex and ornate covered bridge in this vast region today. However, there are several beautiful covered bridges found in what strikes even knowledgeable observers as unlikely locations. Nearly four hours by car to the southeast of Lanzhou in the semi-arid province of Gansu is Weiyuan, a nondescript out of the way town. Here, crossing the Qingyuan River, a tributary of the Wei that flows into the Huang (Yellow) River, is one of China's truly magnificent bridges, the Baling Bridge. As Peter Coyne has declared, this soaring bridge epitomizes the art of bridge craftsmanship due to the skill of the "carpenters of the rainbow" who created it (1992: 32–6).

As mentioned many times in this book, the expression "rainbow bridge" or *caihongqiao* is unfortunately used loosely throughout China to describe a broad range of bridge types, from long flat ones to short humped ones. Yet, in the Chinese mind, as in the minds of others in the world, the concept of a true "rainbow bridge" is a fantastic iridescent structure that rises precipitously as a symmetrically concentric arc. Elsewhere in this book is described the well-known uncovered timber-arched rainbow bridge that is a focus of Zhang Zeduan's late eleventh-century *Qingming shanghetu* painting, and which once soared from its abutments along the banks of the Bian River at Kaifeng, Henan Province. The large number of existing rainbow bridges in Zhejiang, Fujian, and Jiangxi provinces, also described elsewhere, reveal the continuity and endurance of techniques and approaches employed by carpenters to overcome steep and turbulent mountain streams with functional structures of notable beauty. All such rainbow bridges are remarkable and many express truly sophisticated methods of timber frame construction.

Yet, the Baling "Rainbow" Bridge stands unique since it not only spans a relatively flat streambed but its gracefully rising arc and articulated timber structure combine technical ingenuity with a refined aesthetic sensibility. Level bridges had crossed the Qingyuan River at this location just outside the South Gate of the walled city of Weiyuan from 1368 until the early part of the twentieth century. In 1919, as a result of some inspired civic boosterism, a decision was made to build a new wooden bridge on this site that was to be modeled after a well-known bridge in the provincial capital, Lanzhou.

Called the Wo ("Holding") Bridge, the Lanzhou bridge, which inspired the Baling Bridge, in time became better known by the homophonous name "Reclining Bridge" because of its steep incline, an appellation also sometimes applied to the Baling Bridge. Said to have provided a link on the Silk Road as it crossed the Agan River, the Wo Bridge was likely constructed during the Tang Dynasty (618–906) and restored towards the end, in 904. In 1952, because of the widening of a road near the bridge, there was discussion of dismantling what was considered a matchless bridge and reassembling it at a different location. Sadly, because of the discovery of severe rotting of the timbers, substantial overall structural damage, and insufficient resources to restore the bridge adequately, a decision was made to demolish Lanzhou's rainbow bridge. Written records show that the demolished bridge had a span of 22.5 meters (74 feet) and an overall length of 27 meters (89 feet). The enclosed portion of the covered bridge was 4.85 meters (16 feet) tall and 4.6 meters (15 feet) wide. A scaled wooden model was crafted and placed in the Lanzhou Museum as, one might suggest, a minor gesture to keep the memory of the bridge alive.

III.8.4 The Wo Bridge over a dry creek in Lanzhou, Gansu. Photograph by Harrison Forman, 1937. Source: American Geographical Society Library, University of Wisconsin-Milwaukee Libraries.

Although the source of funds for and details concerning the construction of the Baling Bridge are not clear, the magnitude of its construction suggests that the distinctive bridge was to stand as a civic icon. Spanning 29.4 meters (96 feet), one-third greater than its Lanzhou antecedent, it has an overall length of 44.5 meters (146 feet) and a width of 6.2 meters (20 feet). Sweeping to a height of 15.4 meters (51 feet) above the stream, the roof of the symmetrical gallery reaches even above the surrounding treetops.

In an area deficient in timber, the bridge stands out in terms of the abundance of large logs used in its underlying cantilevered structure and the attentive carpentry finishes employed in the construction of the surmounting open-sided structure on top of it. Four layers of bundled logs, each layer longer than the one beneath it, were embedded as cantilevers in each of the facing stone abutments. Projecting outward at an upward symmetrical angle, a total of ten sets of bundled logs reach a high point without touching, leaving a gaping breach that was spanned with a set of bundled horizontal beams to compose a sweeping curve that soars nearly 30 meters (98 feet). Crossbeams mortised to uprights tie the understructure to the deck, providing increased stability for the bridge. At both ends, additional stone and masonry work not only created a stepped entryway with walls but also afforded needed downward pressure on the abutments below to stabilize the embedded cantilevers. The heavy, yet elegant, open-sided wooden arcade, with its bracket sets and upturned tile roof, and its mortise-and-tenon joinery, while appearing to be somewhat fragile is actually quite heavy and exerted considerable downward forces that offset the load on the cantilevered beams. Sixty-four columns lift the roof structure and divide the gallery into thirteen structural *jian* or bays. The covered corridor that sweeps upward along a gentle curve from the brick and tile entryways was given shape beneath by segmental chords that mask whatever

jaggedness is inherent in the structure and serve also to protect the underlying structure from the elements.

III.8.5 Unlike other soaring covered bridges that span a deep ravine, the Baling Bridge crosses a shallow stream in a generally flat area. Source: ACO, 2006.

III.8.6 Viewed from beneath, the sequence of cantilevered logs is quite clear. Source: ACO, 2016.

III.8.7 A substantial brick-faced entry capped with elaborate upturned eaves is found on both ends of the bridge. The gates restrict access except under approved circumstances. Source: ACO, 2006.

III.8.8a, b Ornamental details of the entry portico, above the upswept eaves and below the bracket sets. Source: JDK, 2006.

III.8.9a, b The rise and fall of the steps in the interior steps are steep from the entry portico on both ends of the bridge. Visitors must grasp the handrail and there are no benches to sit on. Source: JDK, 2006.

III.8.10 A commemorative calligraphic plaque by Sun Fo, the son of Sun Yat-sen, states "Long Rainbow of the Wei River." Source: JDK, 2006.

III.8.11 A view from the apex landing of the Baling Bridge reveals the sluggish stream and broad river valley. Source: JDK, 2006.

Hebei Covered Bridges

Throughout rural and urban China there is an incredible array of Buddhist and Daoist free-standing temples and extensive walled temple complexes, many of great age. Some are in a stunning state of preservation, with well-maintained halls, pagodas, and quarters for monks and devotees. Sadly, a far greater number, while picturesque, with awe-inspiring old buildings and ancient trees, are quiet sites visited by tourists who all too often have little appreciation of the cultural context that once brought them to life. Throughout the mountains of China there are secluded Daoist and Buddhist temples built for monks and nuns who favored quiet mountains and deep forests for their meditative practices, thus wanting to retreat as hermits from the clamor of secular life in hard to access locations. Over time, some of these small hermitages developed into great monastic complexes, especially among the peaks held sacred by Buddhists and Daoists who believed that the variegated landscapes possessed a spiritual force or essence. In some cases, lay practitioners, knowing of these intrinsically special remote redoubts, came to make arduous pilgrimages to them by climbing countless steps or following steep paths and ledges in order to pay homage to images of Buddhas, Bodhisattvas, and innumerable deities and immortals. While some temples, such as the Jinci Temple in Taiyuan, incorporate noteworthy bridges in the spatial layout of their precincts, many more temples traditionally had nearby bridges associated with them or, as we see thoughout this book, many covered bridges once had, and many

still have, within them an altar for offerings and supplications.

Jingxing (Qiaoloudian) Bridge

Traditionally and idiomatically referred to as a "pavilion in the air," a rare religious structure perched on a bridge, with both existing *only* in relation to the other, is found in an aerie in the Cangyan Mountains quartz sandstone formation some 70 kilometers (43 miles) southwest of Shijiazhuang, Hebei. Here, the Jingxing Bridge and the Qiaolou Hall built atop it are fully integrated into the landscape and represent a magical tour de force by stone masons and carpenters. This craggy mountainous area is part of the better-known Taihang Mountain range, which straddles the rugged border between Hebei and Shanxi provinces. With peaks that soar some 1,000 meters (3,281 feet) above the plains below, deep ravines, and rock surfaces with often grotesque shapes characterize the precipitous landscape. Swiftly moving mountain streams, moreover, toss boulders from high areas to those below, creating great danger. Anyone contemplating living on its slopes is challenged to find sufficient level land to construct a building.

Qiaolou Hall ("Bridge-Building Hall") is the main structure of Fuqing Temple, whose extent spreads along the mountain pathways where countless grottos and small structures serve as individual votive locations for a broad pantheon. In fact, the Qiaolou Hall and associated bridge are but the middle level of the temple complex, with religious structures both at the base of the steps as well as at higher locations. At least some of the buildings are said to have been built at the end of the Sui Dynasty (589–617) or the beginning of the Tang Dynasty (618–907). This traditional dating, however, has been contested with opinions that suggest the construction took place sometime later, between the eighth and twelfth centuries. While accurate dating is important, the lack of precision does not detract from the fact that this extraordinary bridge-hall structure has been standing, not precariously but firmly, for more than a thousand years.

Qiaolou Hall, which is situated on a stone arch bridge that spans a precipitous chasm between opposing cliffs, appears to be suspended some 70 meters (230 feet) above the ground below. The bridge-hall is reached only after climbing a winding staircase, here called a "heavenly ladder," with some 360 stone steps. In the first instance, the structure is a bridge that allows passage from one mountain stone pathway to another which could only be accessed by a bridge. Secondly, the bridge serves as the level foundation for a two-story religious building. Together, the bridge and building form an indivisible structural unit.

Reminiscent of the extraordinary stone Zhaozhou Bridge, which is also in Hebei Province, the underlying bridge structure beneath the hall is in the form of a single arched span with a pair of open spandrels in the roughly triangular space between the exterior curve of the arch. Open spandrels of this type lighten the load carried by the arch. Overall, the bridge has a length of 15 meters (49 feet), a width of 9 meters (30 feet), and stands at least 70 meters (230 feet) above level ground. The half-moon shaped arch itself has a diameter of 10.7 meters (35 feet) and a structural height of 3.3 meters (11 feet). Overall, the scale and structure of the bridge are reminiscent of ones found elsewhere in Hebei.

Common wooden components were utilized in the construction of the two-story temple hall. Eaves columns create a roofed gallery around the structure, which itself is five bays wide and three bays deep. The double-tiered roof is covered with yellow roof tiles. Inside are numerous statues of deities still worshipped by countless breathless pilgrims who make the arduous journey upwards into the mountains to reach this majestic site. While the two-story hall has been renovated several times because of deterioration of its wooden components, there are no records of repair of what might seem to be a potentially unstable bridge structure, but which, nevertheless, has remained securely lodged between a pair of facing precipices.

Film producer Ang Lee utilized the awe-inspiring Cangyan mountainscape, including the immediate environs of the inimitable Jingxing Bridge, for some of the fighting scenes in his 2000 movie *Crouching Tiger, Hidden Dragon*.

III.9.1 With a modern service bridge behind it, the two-story Fuqing Temple appears to be clutched between the opposing cliff faces. Source: ACO, 2006.

III.9.2 Viewed from an upper vantage point, the cleft between the layers of quartz sandstone provided a challenge to those who contemplated constructing both the bridge and the pavilion-like hall atop it. Source: ACO, 2006.

III.9.3 Occupying the full width and breadth of the bridge as well as some 70 meters (230 feet) above the base, the Qiaolou Hall was constructed with building materials—wood, tile, stone, and paint—all carried up the steep steps. Source: ACO, 2006.

III.9.4 Surrounded by painted walls and eighteen *luohan*, the principal Buddha is Shakyamuni (Gautama Siddartha) and two other Buddhas. Source: ACO, 2006.

III.9.5a–c A cliffside trail leads to this brick furnace where devotees can purchase or make golden ingots by folding paper. Called "golden paper," the flammable ingots are then burned in the furnace as "spirit money" that wafts away to the ancestors. Sources: ACO, 2006; JDK, 2006; JDK, 2006.

Jiangsu Covered Bridges

Unlike the mountainous provinces of China in which dramatic covered bridges are common, Jiangsu is essentially flat and the broadest portion of a region the Chinese refer to as *shuixiang* or "water country." Extensive plains devoted to agriculture cover more than two-thirds of its area, with nearly 20 percent water, principally canals, lakes, and rivers. While bridges were common in the past, helping to stitch the region together, most were humpbacked stone structures that rose precipitously from the banks of watercourses so as not to impede boat traffic while permitting foot traffic. Movement of people and goods in the past was principally by shallow draft boats that navigated the maze-like hydrography while passing under the high arches of the bridges.

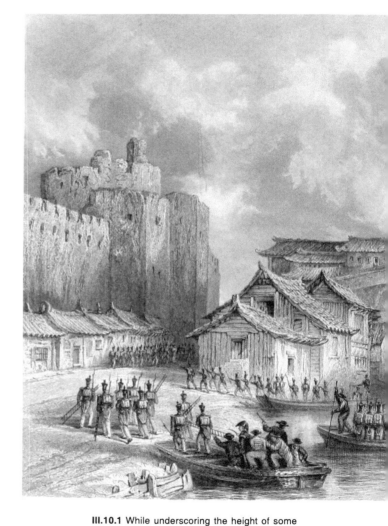

III.10.1 While underscoring the height of some humpbacked stone bridges in Jiangsu, this drawing also reveals something rarely seen on such bridges, a series of structures. Whether they are shops or residences or a combination of both is not known. On the left are British soldiers disembarking in 1842 during the last battle of the First Opium War at Zhenjiang, a walled city on the south side of the Yangzi River, opposite Yangzhou. Drawn by Thomas Allom from a sketch by Capt. James Stoddart, RN. Engraved by J. M. Starling. Source: Allom and Wright, 1843: Vol. 4, p. 38.

The region abounds in covered passageways, either across water bodies as bridges or adjacent to them as corridors, but none like the mid-nineteenth century etching. The covered structures seen today are almost all in private gardens, especially the classical gardens of Suzhou, Yangzhou, and other watertowns. Within these walled gardens, generally called scholar or literati gardens, the designs seek to recreate secluded landscapes in miniature with both representative topographical and cultural features.

Wuting ("Five Pavilions") Bridge

Unlike most of the rather understated literati garden bridges found in Suzhou and other cities in the Jiangnan region, a geographic area that refers to lands generally south of the lower reaches of the Yangzi, including its delta, the Wuting ("Five Pavilions") Bridge in Yangzhou is a showy, stylish, and novel composition that is unrivaled in China. From some angles the bridge looks like a waterside building but from others it clearly serves as a bridge to allow both foot and boat traffic. Built in Yangzhou in 1757 across a narrow inlet in Slender West Lake, a natural waterway feeding mountain runoff into the Grand Canal, to the back of the Lianxing Temple, the Five Pavilions Bridge is formally called the Lianhua ("Lotus Flower") Bridge because of its resemblance to the open spreading petals of the flower.

Yangzhou, once one of the great cosmopolitan cities of late imperial China, is neither appreciated nor visited today in the way it once was. Indeed, it was in Yangzhou that Marco Polo claimed to serve as governor for three years in the latter part of the thirteenth century. Located on the left bank of the Grand Canal a few miles north of the Yangzi River, the city prospered during the Qing Dynasty (1644–1911) because of its primacy in the national monopoly salt trade. During the eighteenth century, especially, a time known for conspicuous consumption, extravagant displays of wealth, and creative construction, wealthy merchants, unconventional artists, and literary scholars brought about a transformation of the walled city's cultural landscapes. Here, stimulated by several inspection visits by the Qianlong Emperor, a radical transformation of the city's landscapes emerged which displayed new tastes and innovative structures. Special attention was paid to building gardens of different sizes, including manipulating water bodies, piling up rocks, clustering vegetation, and inserting structures on and around them in order to heighten desired aesthetic effects. It was in this context that the space known as Slender West Lake, within which the rather eccentric Wuting ("Five Pavilions") Bridge was built, took shape as a component of a crafted landscape picture.

The base of the stone bridge has an overall length of 55.3 meters (181 feet) and rises about 8 meters (26 feet) above the water. Set upon twelve piers of varying sizes, the bridge incorporates thirteen hemispheric arches as well as a pair of arch fragments set beneath the stairs that rise to five square, open-sided pavilions atop its base. Adjacent to the four single-eaved structures that comprise the bridge, the main central pavilion has a double-eaved roof that rises above it. Supported by slender scarlet pillars, each of the roofs of the symmetrical cluster of pavilions is covered with imperial yellow tiles. While threaded through the center of the pavilions is a linking corridor connecting the stairs, the presence of low benches along the sides encourages visitors to tarry and not simply transit the structure. Taken together, this bridge serves less as a means of passage than as a scenic spot to enjoy the surrounding mix of hills, vegetation, water, and boat traffic.

During the first quarter of the nineteenth century, the gardens of Yangzhou became increasingly neglected and dilapidated as the gracious city generally entered a period of decline. Along Slender West Lake the scene was described as a "yardful of broken pottery" (Finnane, 1985: 306). Overall, the city was subsequently devastated

during the depredations associated with the Taiping Uprising in the mid-nineteenth century, as it had been earlier when the Manchus defeated the Ming imperial armies. Indeed, all of the roofed structures above the stone base of the Wuting Bridge were burned, as were other buildings throughout the city. During the waning years of the Qing Dynasty, and again in 1933 and between 1951 and 1953, attempts were made to restore the bridge structure to its earlier magnificence.

As a result of these impacts over a century and a half, Yangzhou as a city has been eclipsed by those elsewhere in the Jiangnan region that rose to meet new commercial needs or were able

to substantially restore the faded landscapes of their glorious past. Though less familiar than Hangzhou or Suzhou, Yangzhou once was known as a charming place in which great wealth accumulated and high culture flourished. Today, while transportation to Yangzhou is somewhat inconvenient, the well-planned city is worth a visit to see its restored waterways, gardens, and associated bridges, as well as to search for opportunities to savor its literati cultural past. Flower festivals have an impressive history in Yangzhou, and it is in such places as Slender West Lake that one can enjoy the cultivated lakeside scenery of another time, including its bridges,

and today's periodic flower festivals while being sculled across the water in painted barques.

Interestingly, an expansive Yangzhou-style garden has been planned for construction in the United States National Arboretum in Washington, DC. While most of the architectural and landscape features in the proposed garden will be recreations of those seen in Yangzhou, none of the publicly available drawings reveal a covered bridge. A proposed Five-Pavilion Terrace may mimic the Wuting ("Five Pavilions") Bridge in Yangzhou, but it is doubtful it will sit astride the lake that is being excavated.

III.10.2 The pavilions atop the stone arches affirm that the Lianhua Bridge is a covered bridge. Source: ACO, 2006.

Ill.10.3 With its arch over water and a signboard with the words "Lotus Blossom Bridge," the structure is indeed a bridge. Source: JDK, 2006.

III.10.4 The view across flowering lotus in front of the steps that lead to the Lianhua Bridge highlights that the "cover" is a lavish and extensive pavilion. Source: ACO, 2006.

III.10.5 As with the majority of China's pavilion bridges and covered bridges, this structure includes benches to sit on. The horizontal board boldly proclaims Lianhua Qiao "Lotus Flower Bridge." Source: ACO, 2006.

III.10.6 The multitiered uplifted eaves above each of the five pavilions are similar to those found on other covered bridges and other buildings throughout China. Source: ACO, 2006.

Guangdong Covered Bridges

China's elegant pavilion bridges, whether having timber or masonry components above the deck, are a special type of covered bridge found nowhere else in the world in such large numbers. While graceful pavilion bridges in China may appear rather simple and singular in form, some are quite complex in their composition, as can be seen clearly in Yangzhou's Wuting ("Five Pavilions") Bridge discussed above.

Guangji Bridge

An exceptional example that goes beyond the polar opposite notions of simplicity and complexity is the unique Guangji Bridge in Chao'an County, Chaozhou City, Guangdong Province. Sometimes the structure is simply called the Chaozhou Bridge. The bridge spans the Han River some 50 kilometers (31 miles) upstream from the important port city of Shantou, where it provides a critical east–west link between Guangdong and Fujian provinces. Little known outside China, the Guangji Bridge, also called the Xiangzi Bridge, has historically been celebrated in China as one of the country's "four famous ancient bridges," each renowned because of technological innovation. The three other bridges—Hebei's Zhaozhou Bridge, Fujian's Luoyang Bridge, and Beijing's Lugou Bridge—are discussed in *Chinese Bridges* (Knapp, 2008b).

What distinguishes the historically significant Guangji Bridge is that it originally comprised a sequence of 24 pavilions each atop a stone pier connected by granite beams. Divided into eastern and western sections, these interconnected pavilion bridges were interrupted midstream by a series of 18 boats that formed a floating or pontoon bridge, which could be opened or closed in response to boat traffic on the river. This form of 24 pavilions and 18 boats reached its apogee around 1435 during the Ming Dynasty (1368–1644) and continued until 1958. Some three centuries before the Ming Dynasty, during the Song (960–1279), the predecessor crossing was an incomparable pontoon bridge formed from 86 shallow-draft boats lashed together to support a continuous transverse deck for pedestrian and other traffic to cross. Over the centuries, piers and pavilions were constructed that little by little led to the combined pavilion bridge/pontoon bridge completed during the Ming Dynasty.

III.11.1 This historic drawing of the Xiangzi Bridge at Chaozhou clearly outlines the interlinked series of pavilions from both shores as well as the movable pontoon bridge that connects them. Source: Unknown.

III.11.2 The Ming Dynasty period Guangji Bridge was celebrated in this 2009 postage stamp triptych. Source: RGK Collection.

As heralded as was the Ming Dynasty Guangji Bridge, the bridge underwent cycles of rebuilding and deterioration as prosperity and natural disasters impacted the Chao-Shan region. Over time, market stalls of various sizes came to occupy spaces in the once elegant pavilions above the piers. While fine shops as arcades on top of historic bridges can be seen today in Italy, England, France, and Germany, those along the Guangji Bridge were never high class, merely improvised structures. The sad state of the bridge, especially in the absence of pavilions, was revealed by the pioneering Scottish photographer John Thomson in 1869. He declared that "the bridge over the river is, perhaps, one of the most remarkable in China," expressing that "Like old London Bridge, with its shops and places of business, the bridge at Chao-chow-fu affords space for one of its city markets." While a few pavilions were evident in the distance in his photographs, it is clear that many crude structures had been constructed in their place above the granite piers. The overhanging extensions propped up by timber poles served as latrines, Thomson hinted, in that "from a purely sanitary point of view, the house projecting as it does over the water offers many advantages" (1873–4: 19).

III.11.3a–c By the middle of the nineteenth century, as these three photographs clearly show, the Guangji Bridge had deteriorated significantly, with the pavilions transformed into shacks. Photograph by Jim Thomson, c. 1869. Source: Wikimedia commons https://commons.wikimedia.org/wiki/File:CHAO-CHOW-FU_BRIDGE.jpg

a

III.11.4 Arrayed between the two sets of pavilions, the boats formed a pontoon bridge that could be swung open to let river traffic pass, c.1888–1906. Source: John Preston Maxwell Papers, Cadbury Research Library, University of Birmingham and Historical Photographs of China, University of Bristol.

Through the turmoil of the late nineteenth and early twentieth centuries, the Guangji Bridge continued to deteriorate even as photographic images portrayed its perennial role as a route across the Han River. By the end of the nineteenth century, as a photograph by a missionary illustrates, the orderly placement of the pontoon boats had become a crushing assemblage and the classical pavilions were gone. Over the following years, even the beams between the piers weakened and were not always replaced with stronger ones. Finally, in 1958, all of the deteriorated components of the once grand Ming Dynasty bridge were swept away and a modern bridge, used principally by pedestrians and human-plied vehicles, was constructed atop the old stone piers. About the same time, the old walls and gates around Chaozhou were also razed.

III.11.5 After 1949, the dilapidated upper portion of the Guangji Bridge was torn down. A passageway was laid on top of the original piers. Source: http://www.yododo.com/photo/011F70 05CC672CDBFF8080811F6C2A3C. Accessed August 10, 2016.

III.11.6 In 1976, further improvements opened the bridge to truck and bus traffic. Source: http://www.yododo.com/photo/011F7005CC892CDEF F8080811F6C2A3C. Accessed August 10, 2016.

Unlike so many instances where imposing structures from the past were clearedaway in the haste to modernize, and past structures merely lingered in memory, thoughts began to emerge among some in Chaozhou as the twentieth century came to an end about restoring the bridge as an historical showpiece. The State Council's declaration in January 1988 that even in memory the utterly transformed bridge was worthy of protection at the national level further awakened interest in its restoration. As tourism in Chaozhou increased, especially from Southeast Asia where

nineteenth-century emigrants from the Chao-Shan area had established themselves, much of the area near the bridgehead was slated for reconstruction. This included a rebuilt city wall and gates as well as streets with false fronts on shops to recollect old-time Chaozhou as a tourist attraction. In this area, distinctive products such as Chaozhou cuisine, *kongfu* tea, ceramics, and carved wood were highlighted. Reconstruction of the reimagined Guangji Bridge was completed in 2007 with 24 new-style pavilions and 18 semi-stationary boats assembled together that are opened to passing river traffic twice a day. Lit up in the evening in iridescent colors, each of the reconstructed historical structures has brought the riverside area back to life.

III.11.7 Reconstructed and reimagined in 2007, the Guangji Bridge has 24 new-style pavilions atop newly placed piers that are connected via walkways. As in the past, there is an opening with 18 semi-stationary boats that form a pontoon bridge, which are swung aside twice a day to allow river traffic to pass. Source: ACO, 2008.

III.11.9 With the reconstruction of the historical crossing, a replacement row of connected boats forms a pontoon bridge. Photograph by Luis Evers. Source: Wikimedia https://commons.wikimedia.org/wiki/File:Guangji_Bridge,_China1.jpg.

III.11.8 As dusk begins to settle in, the pavilions are lit up in iridescent colors, highlighting the roof structures. Together with the nearby promenade, the riverside area comes to life for both locals and visitors. Source: ACO, 2008.

REFERENCES

Allom, Thomas and G. N. Wright (1843), *China, in a Series of Views, Displaying the Scenery, Architecture, and Social Habits of That Ancient Empire*, Vol. 4, London: Fisher, Son, & Co.

Barnes, Irene H. (1896), *Behind the Great Wall: The Story of the C.E.Z.M.S. Work and Workers in China*, London: Marshall Bros.

Bird, Isabella L. (1899), *The Yangtze Valley and Beyond: An Account of Journeys in China, Chiefly in the Province of Sze Chuan and Among the Man-Tze of the Somo Territory*, Vol. 1, London: John Murray.

Bishop [Bird], Isabella L. (1900), *The Yangtze Valley and Beyond: An Account of Journeys in China, Chiefly in the Province of Sze Chuan and Among the Man-Tze of the Somo Territory*, Vol. 1, New York: G. P. Putnam's.

Canfield, Suzette H. (1971), "Bridge Construction and Repair in the Ming and Ch'ing," *Papers on China*, East Asian Research Center, Harvard University, 24: 19–40.

Chen Zhenguo 陈镇国 (2013), *Fujian mugong langqiao* 福建木拱廊桥 [Fujian's Timber Arch Covered Bridges], Fuzhou: Fujian meishu chubanshe 福建美术出版社.

Chengdu wenwu kaogu yanjiusuo 成都文物考古研究所 (2008), "Chengdu shi qingyang qu Jinsha cun Handai langqiao yizhi faxian jianbao" 成都市青羊区金沙村汉代廊桥遗址发掘简报 [Preliminary Report on the Excavation of a Han Dynasty Covered Bridge at Jiansha Village, Qingyang District, Chengdu], *Chengdu kaogu faxian* 成都考古发现 [Chengdu Archaeological Discoveries], pp. 249–70.

Cheng Fei 程霏 (2013), *Min-Zhe diqu guanmu gong langqiao yingzao jiyi* 闽浙地区贯木拱廊桥营造技艺 [The Building Artistry of the Woven Arch Bridges of Fujian and Zhejiang], Hefei: Anhui kexue jishu chubanshe 安徽科学技术出版社.

Coggins, Chris et al. (2012), "Village Fengshui Forests of Southern China: Culture, History, and Conservation Status," *ASIANetwork Exchange*, 19(2): 52–67.

Coyne, Peter (1992), "Carpenters of the Rainbow," *Archaeology*, 45(2): 32–6.

Cushman, Jennifer Wayne (1993), *Fields from the Sea: Chinese Junk Trade With Siam During the Late Eighteenth and Early Nineteenth Centuries*, Ithaca: Cornell University Press.

Dai Zhijian 戴志坚 (2005), *Zhongguo langqiao* 中国廊桥 [China's Covered Bridges], Fuzhou: Fujian renmin chubanshe 福建人民出版社.

Du Halde, Jean-Baptiste (1735/1739), *Description Geographique, Historique, Chronologique, et Physique de l'Empire de la Chine et de la Tartarie Chinoise* [A Geographical, Historical, Chronological, Political, and Physical Description of the Empire of China and of Chinese Tartary], Paris: P. G. le Mercier.

Finnane, Antonia (1985), "Prosperity and Decline Under the Qing: Yangzhou and Its Hinterland, 1644–1810," Ph.D. dissertation, The Australian National University.

Left Anlan Bridge, crossing the Nanpan River in Luliang County, Yunnan. Source: RGK Collection.

Fletcher, Robert and J. P. Snow (1934), "A History of the Development of Wooden Bridges," *Transactions of the American Society of Civil Engineers*, No. 99.

Fortune, Robert (1852), *Journey to the Tea Countries of China; Including Sung-Lo and the Bohea Hills; With a Short Notice of the East India Company's Tea Plantations in the Himalaya Mountains*, London: John Murray.

Freeman, Michael and Selena Ahmed (2015), *Tea Horse Road: China's Ancient Trade Road to Tibet*, Bangkok: River Books.

Fuchs, Jeff (2008), *The Ancient Tea Horse Road: Travels With the Last of the Himalayan Muleteers*, Toronto: Viking.

Fugl-Meyer, Helge (1937), *Chinese Bridges*, Shanghai: Kelly and Walsh.

Gardella, Robert (1994), *Harvesting Mountains: Fujian and China Tea Trade, 1757–1937*, Berkeley: University of California Press.

Gill, William John and Henry Yule (1880), *The River of Golden Sand: The Narrative of a Journey Through China and Eastern Tibet to Burmah*, 2 vols., London: John Murray.

Gong Difa 龚迪发 (2013), *Fujian mugong qiao diaocha baogao* 福建木拱桥调查报告 [Research Report on the Timber Arch Bridges of Fujian], Beijing: Kexue chubanshe 科学出版社.

Johnston, Reginald Fleming (1908), *From Peking to Mandalay: A Journey From North China to Burma Through Tibetan Ssuch'uan and Yunnan*, London: John Murray.

Jones, Peter Blundell and Derong Kong (2006), "The Case for an Oral Architecture: Carpentry and Communal Assembly Among the Dong of Southwest China," *Architectural Research Quarterly*, 20(2): 145–58. https://doi.org/10.1017/S1359135516000257.

Jones, Peter Blundell and Xuemei Li (2008), "What Can a Bridge Be? The Wind and Rain Bridges of the Dong," *The Journal of Architecture*, 13(5): 565–84.

Kendall, Elizabeth (1913), *A Wayfarer in China: Impressions of a Trip Across West China and Mongolia*, Boston and New York: Houghton Mifflin Company.

Knapp, Ronald G. (1984), "Chinese Bridges," *Orientations*, 15(6): 36–47.

_____ (1988), "Bridge on the River Xiao," *Archaeology*, 41(1): 48–54.

_____ (1993), *Chinese Bridges*, Hong Kong: Oxford University Press.

_____ (2005), *Chinese Houses: The Architectural Heritage of a Nation*, Rutland, VT: Tuttle Publishing. Published in Chinese as *Tushuo Zhongguo Minju* 图说中国民居, trans. Ren Yunan 任羽楠, Beijing: Sanlian shudian 三联书店, 2018.

_____ (2008a), "Bridges in the Lower Yangzi Watertowns: Jiangsu, Shanghai, and Zhejiang," in Ronald G. Knapp, *Chinese Bridges: Living Architecture From China's Past*, Rutland, VT: Tuttle Publishing, pp. 160–79.

_____ (2008b), *Chinese Bridges: Living Architecture From China's Past*, Rutland, VT: Tuttle Publishing.

_____ (2008c), "Rainbows and Centipedes: 20th Century Discoveries of China's 'Lost Bridges'," *Orientations*, 39(4): 30–9.

Knapp, Ronald G. and Kai-Yin Lo, eds. (2005), *House Home Family: Living and Being Chinese*, Honolulu: University of Hawaii Press. Published in Chinese as *Jia: Zhongguo ren de jujia wenhua* 家：中国人的居家文化, Beijing: Xinxing chubanshe 新星出版社, 2011.

Kieschnick, John (2003), *The Impact of Buddhism on Chinese Material Culture*, Princeton: Princeton University Press.

Lau, D. K. (1984), *Mencius*, New York: Penguin Books.

Li Yuxiang 李玉祥 and Zhang Lianggao 张良皋 (1994), *Lao fangzi: Tujia diaojiaolou* 老房子：土家吊脚楼 [Old Dwellings: Tujia Stilt Dwellings], Nanjing: Jiangsu meishu chubanshe 江苏美术出版社.

Liang Sicheng (1982), *Liang Sicheng wenji* 梁思成文集 [Collected Works of Liang Sicheng], Beijing: Zhongguo jianzhu gongye chubanshe 中国建筑工业出版社.

Liu Dunzhen 刘敦桢 (1979), "Zhongguo zhi langqiao" 中国之廊桥 [China's Covered Bridges], in *Kejishishi wenji*, Vol. 2 科技史文集, 第二辑, Shanghai: Kexue jishu chubanshe 科学技术出版社, 9–13. See also "中国之廊桥," in 刘敦桢文集（三）, Beijing: Zhongguo jianzhu gongye chubanshe 中国建筑工业出版社.

Liu Hongbo 刘洪波 (2016), *Dong zu fengyuqiao jianzhu yu wenhua* 侗族风雨桥建筑与文化 [Architecture and Culture of Dong Wind and Rain Bridges], Changsha: Hunan daxue chubanshe 湖南大学出版社.

Liu Jie 刘杰 (2017), *Zhongguo mugong langqiao jianzhu yishu* 中国木拱廊桥建筑艺术 [The Architectural Artistry of China's Timber Arch Covered Bridges], Shanghai: Shanghai renmin meishu chubanshe 上海人民美术出版社.

Liu Jie 刘杰 and Chen Changdong 陈昌东, eds. (2016), *Xiangtu Fu'an* 乡土福安 [Bucolic Fu'an], Beijing: Zhonghua shuju 中华书局.

Liu Jie 刘杰 and Hu Gang 胡刚, eds. (2011), Xiangtu Qingyuan 乡土庆元 [Bucolic Qingyuan], Hangzhou: Zhejiang guji chubanshe 浙江古籍出版社.

Liu Jie 刘杰 and Lin Weihong 林蔚虹, eds. (2007), *Xiangtu Shouning* 乡土寿宁 [Bucolic Shouning], Beijing: Zhonghua shuju 中华书局.

Liu Jie 刘杰 and Shen Weiping 沈为平 (2005), *Taishun langqiao* 泰顺廊桥 [Lounge Bridges in Taishun], Shanghai: Shanghai renmin meishu chubanshe 上海人民美术出版社.

_____ (2007), "Zhongguo hongqiao zai yanjiu: shilun bianmu gongqiao he bianmu gongliang qiao de mingming ji qi yuanyuan" 中国虹桥再研究试论编木拱桥和编木拱梁桥的命名及其渊源 [Further Research on Chinese Rainbow Bridges: Exploration on the Naming and Origin of Woven Timber Arch Bridges and Woven Timber Arch-Beam Bridges], *Chengshi yu sheji xuebao* 城市与设计学报 [Cities and Design]. 1: 193–210.

Liu Yan 刘妍 (2017), "Gewebebogenbrücken: Geschichten struktureller Gedanken" [Woven Arch Bridges: Histories of Structural Thinking], Ph.D. dissertation, Technische Universität München. http://mediatum.ub.tum.de?id=1299210.

Luban jing (1993), facsimile reproduced in Klaas Ruitenbeek, *Building & Carpentry in Late Imperial China: A Study of the Fifteenth Century Carpenter's Manual Lu Ban jing*, Vol. 3, Pt. 2, Leiden: E. J. Brill.

Luo Zhewen 罗哲文, Liu Wenyuan, 刘文渊, and Liu Chunying 刘春英, eds. (2001), *Zhongguo ming qiao* 中国名桥 [Famous Bridges of China], Tianjin: Baihua wenyi chubanshe 百花文艺出版社.

Maclay, Rev. R. S. (1872), "Birthplace of Chu-Hi," *Chinese Recorder and Missionary Journal*, 4(12): 309–12.

Mao Yisheng 茅以升 (1978), *Bridges in China: Old and New*, Beijing: Foreign Languages Press.

_____(1986), *Zhongguo guqiao jishu shi* 中国古桥技术史 [Technological History of China's Bridges], Beijing: Beijing chubanshe 北京出版社.

Mao Yisheng 茅以升, chief ed. (1986), *Zhongguo gu qiao jishu shi* 中国古桥技术史 [A Technological History of Ancient Chinese Bridges], Beijing: Beijing chubanshe 北京出版社.

Mennie, Donald (1926), *The Grandeur of the Gorges*, Shanghai: A. S. Watson & Co.

Miller, Terry E. and Ronald G. Knapp (2014), *America's Covered Bridges: Practical Crossings, Nostalgic Icons*, Rutland, VT: Tuttle Publishing.

Needham, Joseph (1971), *Science and Civilization in China: Physics and Physical Technology*, Vol. 4, Pt. III, Cambridge: Cambridge University Press.

Ningde shi wenhua yu chubanju 宁德市文化与出版局, eds. (2006), *Ningde shi hongliangshi mujiegou lang wuqiao kaogu diaocha yu yanjiu* 宁德市虹梁式木结构廊屋桥考古调查与研究 [Archaeological Survey and Analysis of the Rainbow Type Wooden Covered Bridges in Ningde City], Beijing: Kexue chubanshe 科学出版社.

Pan Hongxuan 潘洪萱 (1982), *Gudai qiaoliang shihua* 古代桥梁史话 [Historical Comments on China's Old Bridges], Beijing: Zhonghua shuju 中华书局.

Peters, Richard (1815), "A Statistical Account of the Schuylkill Permanent Bridge, Communicated to the Philadelphia Society of Agriculture, 1806." Reprinted in *Memoirs of the Philadelphia Society for Promoting Agriculture*, Philadelphia: Johnson & Warner, Vol. 1, pp. 1–88.

Que Weimin (2005), Application for 2005 UNESCO Asia-Pacific Heritage Awards.

Rawski, Evelyn S. (1972), *Agricultural Change and the Peasant Economy of South China*, Cambridge, Mass: Harvard University Press.

Ruan, Xing (2006), *Allegorical Architecture: Living Myth and Architectonics in Southern China*, Honolulu: University of Hawaii Press.

Ruitenbeek, Klaas (1993), *Building & Carpentry in Late Imperial China: A Study of the Fifteenth Century Carpenter's Manual Lu Ban jing*, Leiden: E. J. Brill.

Service, John S., ed. (1989), *Golden Inches: The China Memoir of Grace Service*, Berkeley: University of California Press.

Shi Kaizhong 石开忠 and Wan Zhixian 宛志贤 (2010), *Drum Towers and Roofed Bridges*, Guiyang: Guizhou Ethnic Publishing House.

Sun Jiasi 孙家驷, ed. (2011), *Chongqing qiaoliang zhi* [Records of Chongqing Bridges] 重庆桥梁志, Chongqing: Chongqing daxue chubanshe 重庆大学出版社.

Svensson, Marina (2018), "Heritage 2.0: Maintaining Affective Engagements With the Local Heritage in Taishun," in Christina Maags and Marina Svensson, *Chinese Heritage in the Making: Experiences, Negotiations and Contestations*, Amsterdam: Amsterdam University Press, pp. 269–92.

Tang Huancheng 唐寰澄 (2011 [1957]), *Zhongguo gudai qiaoliang* 中国古代桥梁 [China's Old Bridges], Beijing: Zhongguo jianzhu gongye chubanshe 中国建筑工业出版社.

Thomson, John (1873–4), *Illustrations of China and Its People. A Series of Two Hundred Photographs, with Letterpress Descriptive of the Places and People Represented*, 2 vols., London: Sampson Low, Marston, Low, and Searle.

Wang Jiakai 王家凯 (2015), Yunnan guqiao qianshi jinsheng 云南古桥前世今生 [Yunnan's Old Bridges Past and Present], Kunming: Yunnan renmin chubanshe 云南人民出版社.

Weiss, Fritz and Hedwig (2009), *Ba-Shu lao zhaopian: Deguo Weisi fu fu de Zhongguo xi nan ji xing* 蜀老照片：德国魏司夫妇的中国西南纪行 [Old Photographs in Ba and Shu: Travels of Hedwig and Fritz Weiss in Southwest China], Chengdu:

Sichuan daxue chubanshe 四川大学出版社 .

Wilson, Ernest Henry and Charles S. Sargent (1914), *A Naturalist in Western China, With Vasculum, Camera, and Gun: Being Some Account of Eleven Years' Travel, Exploration, and Observation in the More Remote Parts of the Flowery Kingdom*, New York: Doubleday.

Wu Zhengguang 吴正光 , Lou Qing 娄清 , and Yang Xin 杨信 , eds. (2004), *Guizhou de qiao* 贵州的桥 [Guizhou Bridges], Guiyang: Guizhou keji chubanshe 贵州科技出版社 .

Xue Yiquan 薛一泉 (2005), *Jiedu langqiao* 解读廊桥 [Reading Covered Bridges], Beijing: Zhongguo minzu sheying yishu chubanshe 中国民族摄影艺术出版社 .

Xue Yiquan 薛一泉 , Ji Haibo 季海波 , and Chen Weihong 陈伟红 , eds. (2014), *Mugong qiao chuantong ying zao jiyi* 木拱桥传统营造技艺 [Traditional Construction Artistry of Timber Arch Bridges], Hangzhou: Zhejiang sheying chubanshe 浙江摄影出版社 .

Ye Shusheng 叶树生 and Chen Weihong 陈伟红 eds. (2011), *Qingyuan langqiao* 庆元廊桥 [Covered Bridges of Qingyuan], Hangzhou: Xiling yinshe chubanshe 西泠印社出版社 .

Yule, Henry, trans. and ed. (1875), *The Book of Ser Marco Polo, the Venetian, Concerning the Kingdoms and Marvels of the East*, London: John Murray.

Yule, Henry and Henri Cordier, trans. and eds. (1903), *The Travels of Marco Polo: The Complete Yule-Cordier edition*, 2 vols., London: John Murray.

Zhang Chongli 张崇礼 and Zhang Qin 张沁 (2012), Dali gu qiaoliang 大理古桥梁 [Old Bridges of Dali], Kunming: Yunnan minzu chubanshe 云南民族出版社 .

Zhang Jianwei 张剑葳 (2007), "Zhongguo chuantong jianzhu zhong de yansheng wenhua" 中国传统建筑中的厌胜文化 [The Yansheng Culture of Chinese Traditional Architecture], *Ershiyi shiji* 二十一世纪 [Twenty-first century], Chinese University of Hong Kong 香港中文大学 , 6: 89–96.

Zhang Jun 张俊 and Chen Yunfeng 陈云峰 (2008), *Yunnan guqiao jianzhu* 云南古桥建筑 [The Architecture of Yunnan's Old Bridges], Kunming: Yunnan meishu chubanshe 云南美术出版社 .

Zhong gong Qingyuan xianwei xuanchuanbu 中共庆元县委宣传部 , ed. (2007), *Zhongguo langqiao zhi du: Qingyuan* 中国廊桥之都：庆元 [China's Covered Bridge Capital: Qingyuan], Hangzhou: Xiling yinshe chubanshe 西泠印社出版社 .

Zhou Fenfang 周芬芳 , Lu Zeqi 陆则起 , and Su Xudong 苏旭东 (2011), *Zhongguo mugong qiao chuantong yingzao jiyi* 中国木拱桥传统营造技艺 [Traditional Construction Artistry of China's Wooden Arch Bridges], Hangzhou: Zhejiang renmin chubanshe 浙江人民出版社 .

Zhu Yongchun 朱永春 and Liu Jie 刘杰 (2011), "Handai gedao yu langqiao kaoshu" 汉代阁道与廊桥考述 [Examination of the Han Dynasty Court Road and Covered Bridge], Jianzhu xuebao 建筑学报 , pp. 90–4.

Zhuang Guotu 庄国土 (1998), "The Impact of the International Tea Trade on the Social Economy of Northwest Fujian in the Eighteenth Century," in Leonard Blussé and Femme Gaastra, eds., *On the Eighteenth Century as a Category of Asian History: Van Leur in Retrospect*, Ashgate: Aldershot, pp. 193–216.

Zwerger, Klaus (2006), *Vanishing Tradition: Architecture and Carpentry of the Dong Minority of China*. Hong Kong: Orchid.

——— (2015), *Wood and Wood Joints: Building Traditions of Europe, Japan and China*. 3rd edition. Basel: Birkhäuser.

ACKNOWLEDGMENTS

This book breaks new ground in addressing a subject that has never been viewed comparatively in any language, Chinese included, and could not have been researched and written without the assistance of other individuals and organizations.

Since 2005 we have been fortunate in having ongoing interactions with Chinese scholars, officials, and local citizens who have been playing critical roles in the preservation of China's unique woven arch timber bridges. They have taught us much about these extraordinary structures as we attended conferences held in five counties in Fujian and Zhejiang provinces where these bridges are found. We are especially appreciative of assistance from Dai Zhijian, Gong Difa, Li Yuxiang, and Zhao Chen.

Since our interest has been in covered bridges more generally beyond Fujian and Zhejiang, we traveled widely throughout China to document little known covered bridge-building traditions. Those we interacted with are too numerous to mention by name, but we are nonetheless grateful for their assistance. We particularly appreciate the accommodations provided by Brian Linden, Jim Spear, and Chris Barclay, whose efforts to promote sustainable tourism facilities in China are exemplary. In Yunnan, Yang Wendou masterfully responded to our request for a complex itinerary that brought to light covered bridge traditions that were little known outside that region, which are featured in this book. Yang Wendou's knowledge of the Bai language and culture opened our eyes to a China we had not previously known.

Frank Yih, a highly regarded Chinese-American who has put the Rotarian's motto "Service above Self" to great use in China, has been an inspiration and a champion of our research. Knapp met him in 2005 at a time he was supporting Liu Jie's first conference in Taishun County, Zhejiang. Beyond the fact that Frank Yih's HuaQiao (China Bridge) Foundation seemed to be especially appropriate in supporting efforts to study covered bridges in China, his personal philanthropic efforts focusing on education, public health, and welfare initiatives in underdeveloped areas of China are praiseworthy. We are very grateful that Frank Yih stepped forward to sponsor the publication of this book, first in English and later in a Chinese translation.

It is wonderful that Shanghai Jiao Tong University Press took on this project. The cooperation of Li Dan, Director of the International Cooperation Department and editor Li Sufei has been smooth. We also earlier consulted with Dong Yuexin and Zhu Yi. We worked very closely with the designer Zhu Linjun on a daily basis in real time but twelve hours apart. There were many design challenges with a manuscript of this complexity with over 680 illustrations that had to be placed within the textual narrative. Zhu Linjun, a fine book designer with a well-developed aesthetic sense and openness to consultation, navigated these well. We are fortunate that she joined the team in bringing forth this comprehensive book that underscores the fact that China's covered bridge tradition is no less important than those in Europe and North America.

Over the past decade, this book has undergone a number of significant conceptual changes. As the manuscript was finalized, no one played a greater role than Noor Azlina Yunus whose copyediting skills have significantly improved the readability of the text. Azlina has an exceptional understanding of all of the phases that must be considered in bringing forth a beautiful book. Her recommendations have been essential. Azlina's efforts were central in several of

Knapp's earlier books published by Tuttle/Periplus. Her work with Miller and Knapp on *America's Covered Bridges* convinced us that *China's Covered Bridges* would benefit from her knowledge of writing and publishing. With no other editor has it been possible in real-time via email to make decisions 24/7.

Image Sources The source of each of the more than 680 images in the book is indicated as part of the caption for that image.

Historical Images Some digital archives have been especially supportive in responding to our requests for permission to use historical images of China's covered bridges:

American Geographical Society Library, University of Wisconsin-Milwaukee Libraries, USA

Arnold Arboretum Archives © President and Fellows of Harvard College, USA

Cadbury Research Library, Special Collections, University of Birmingham (DA26) and Historical Photographs of China, University of Bristol, UK

Edward Bowra Collection, University of Bristol, Royal Society for Asian Affairs, London, UK

Harvard-Yenching Library © President and Fellows of Harvard College, USA

Historical Photographs of China, University of Bristol, UK

National Society for the Preservation of Covered Bridges, Richard Sanders Allen Collection, USA

Peter Lockhart Smith and Historical Photographs of China, University of Bristol, UK

Sidney D. Gamble photographs, David M. Rubenstein Rare Book & Manuscript Library, Duke University, USA

Current Media We are especially grateful for the following Chinese media outlets for their online images:

backchina.co baidu.com chinadaily.com 163.com fjsen.comglobaltimes.cnkknews.cc people. com qjzsjq.com qznns.com sina.com sohu.com thepaper.cn weibo.com yododo.com 66wz.com

INDEX

Note: (a) Numbers in **bold** refer to illustrations.

(b) Location is given as an abbreviation after the name of a bridge:

AH	Anhui	HUN	Hunan
BJ	BeijingMunicipality	JS	Jiangsu
CQ	Chongqing Municipality	JX	Jiangxi
GD	Guangdong	QH	Qinghai
GS	Gansu	SC	Sichuan
GX	Guangxi	TW	Taiwan
GZ	Guizhou	YN	Yunnan
HEB	Hebei	ZJ	Zhejiang
HUB	Hubei		